RAWHIDE TEXAS

RAWHIDE TEXAS

BY WAYNE GARD

NORMAN · UNIVERSITY OF OKLAHOMA PRESS

By Wayne Gard

Rawhide Texas (Norman, 1965)
The Great Buffalo Hunt (New York, 1959)
Fabulous Quarter Horse: Steel Dust (New York, 1958)
The Chisholm Trail (Norman, 1954)
Frontier Justice (Norman, 1949)
Sam Bass (Boston, 1936)
Book Reviewing (New York, 1927)

Library of Congress Catalog Card Number 65–14801

Copyright 1965 by the University of Oklahoma Press, Publishing Division of the University. Composed and printed at Norman, Oklahoma, U.S.A., by the University of Oklahoma Press. First edition.

T EXANS COULD BE DIVIDED between those who try to live down the legend that has grown up about the state and those who try to perpetuate and expand it. Typical of the latter are those who hobble down Broadway in cowboy boots and the politician who tried to ride a horse into the lobby of a metropolitan hotel at the time of a Democratic National Convention.

The legend of Texas and Texans has been in the making for more than a century and owes much to dime novels and movie scenarios. It was well established when Alexander E. Sweet put some of it into words in 1882. The typical Texan of the myth-makers, he said, "is a large Jabberwock, a hairy gorilla, who is supposed to reside on a horse. He is half alligator, half human. He eats raw buffalo and sleeps out on a prairie. He is expected to carry four or five revolvers in his belt, with an assortment of cutlery in his boot. It is believed that a failure to invite him to drink is more dangerous than to kick a can of dynamite. The only time the typical Texan is supposed to be peaceable is after he has killed all his friends and can find no fresh material to practice on."

Yet, however exaggerated this legend may have become, there is a core of truth in its insistence that the average Texan is unusually breezy, independent, and self-reliant. His tendency to brag is shown in many speeches and writings, while election returns indicate his refusal to wear a brass collar. Although Texas is where the South and the West meet, the Texan tends, in most respects, to be more Western than Southern.

What makes the Texan tick as he does? One can read scores of military and political histories without finding more than a hint of

v

the answer. More revealing is the social history of the people of Texas—the story of their long and often heroic conquest of the discouraging conditions that most of them faced in the period of settlement as the frontier was pushed westward.

The pioneer settler had to grapple with summer drouths and winter blizzards, with epidemics of diseases he little understood, with scalping Comanches and predatory beasts, with fires that swept his fields and pastures, with swarms of grasshoppers that darkened the sky and devoured his crops. He had to be as tough as the rawhide he braided into quirt or lariat. Only the sturdy survived.

Along with those who plowed the virgin sod and seeded the ranges with cattle and sheep were others who deserve credit. They included the saddlebags preacher who swam his horse across swollen streams to keep his appointments, the frontier doctor who often rode fifty miles to deliver a baby or set a broken bone, the schoolmarm who might lose her life in an Indian raid, and the editor who might be shot in the back by someone about whom he had told the painful truth.

This book is neither a formal social history nor an argument for a thesis. It is merely a series of informal sketches of various aspects of pioneer life in Texas. They depict some of the more heroic and colorful activities of a bygone era, and together they may throw a bit of light on the emerging Texas character. They are the outcome of an observation of Texas life for thirty-two adult years, much travel about the state, and a great deal of digging into the state's past.

Although most of the hardy frontiersmen had passed from the scene before this book was undertaken, I have known personally a number who grew up in the pioneer period and helped to make history. Among those with whom I talked were Captain June Peak of the Texas Rangers, who had hunted buffalo, chased Sam Bass and his brigands, and served as marshal of frontier Dallas; Charlie Terrell, who had killed buffalo and wild pigeons and was treated with a madstone after a dog bit him; Marvin Hunter, a pioneer editor, whose bout with home remedies is recounted in these pages; J. B. Cranfill, who had risked his life in a fight with a rival editor; Will Williams, who remembered swarms of grasshoppers that covered the fields;

Mrs. William Casey, who had gone through the horrors of the Galveston hurricane of 1900; and several men who had ridden up the Chisholm Trail with herds of Longhorn cattle. Much other information was gleaned from manuscript letters and diaries, early newspaper accounts, and published memoirs.

Scores of persons, including librarians and archivists, helped in gathering factual material for this book. Among those especially helpful were Fred R. Cotten, past president of the Texas State Historical Association; C. Boone McClure, executive secretary of the Panhandle Plains Historical Society; Miss Llerena Friend, librarian of the Texas Collection of the University of Texas Library; Chester V. Kielman, archivist of the University of Texas Library; Dorman H. Winfrey, director and librarian of the Texas State Library; James M. Day, archivist of the Texas State Library; and Decherd Turner, librarian of the Bridwell Library of Southern Methodist University.

Joe B. Frantz, chairman of the department of history of the University of Texas, Walter B. Moore, editor of the *Texas Almanac,* and John W. Wagner of the Texas Mid-Continental Oil and Gas Association each read a chapter of the manuscript in earlier form. Mrs. Marguerite B. Creighton, librarian of Highland Park High School, Dallas, read the whole manuscript; and my wife, Hazel D. Gard, read both manuscript and proofs. All opinions and errors are my own.

WAYNE GARD

Dallas, Texas
March 20, 1965

RAWHIDE TEXAS

WHAT TEXAN HASN'T REPEATED THE OLD SAYING that only a newcomer or a fool will predict Texas weather? On the wind-swept plains, changes come with such dramatic suddenness that they give rise to many bits of folklore. A West Texan recalled that, after he had left some postholes out overnight, the next morning they were standing four feet in the air, frozen solid. Elsewhere two frogs that poked their heads out of the water as a norther approached were frozen in the ice. Fish that flopped out of the water to see the strange clouds landed on ice.

Camping buffalo hunters, struck by a norther, said they had to break the ice from the top of their boiling coffee before they could pour it from the pot. A farmer reported that a gale hit so quickly at night that it froze the flame in his lantern as stiff as an icicle. It was so cold, he added, that the courthouse clock was rubbing its hands together.

Then there was the Collin County farmer who was plowing with two mules. When a sunstroke killed one, he went to the barn to bring out a replacement. But before he could get back to the plow, a blue norther came up and froze the other mule to death.

Those who experience the sudden changes don't find such folk tales as exaggerated as others may. "When I saw the tumbleweeds jump away from the north fence like a jackrabbit leaving a nest of yellowjackets," said the late Frank Bryan of Groesbeck, "I knew that a norther had hit. By morning it was so cold that I had to run backward to spit."

Of course, the typical Texan wouldn't swap Lone Star weather for that of any other part of the country. He delights in the spring

3

showers that bring out the redbud and dogwood blossoms and the lacy fronds of the mesquite. He enjoys the cool summer breezes from the Gulf of Mexico, especially when there is a watermelon to slice in the back yard. He relishes the frosty autumn mornings when he can go out after deer or ducks. Yet none of that keeps him from joking about the sudden changes, especially the swift slap of a cold north wind.

A howling norther greeted the first white man to set foot in Texas. In November, 1528, when Pánfilo de Narváez and his men approached the Texas coast in horsehide boats they had built in Florida, a norther blew them out into the Gulf so far that it took them three days to get back to land. Even after they landed, recorded Cabeza de Vaca, the shivering Spaniards might have frozen to death had not friendly Indians taken them to their villages where they had campfires burning.

Frontiersmen dreaded the dry norther almost as much as the wet one that brought sleet or snow. Many referred to the dry kind as a "blue norther" because of the low clouds of dark blue that lay across the horizon at its approach.

Dr. John Washington Lockhart, who spent sixty years on the lower Brazos River, recalled that when a blue norther would come up, "for three days it would almost freeze the life out of every living thing. A black cloud could be seen approaching from the north, and often its pace would be swift. Its appearance would be angry. It had an inky blackness, its outer edges sometimes taking on a greenish cast. There rolled along in front of it a blue mist of smoke."

Some have claimed that they could detect the approach of a norther by an odor like that of burning hay or charcoal. Others have said that they could learn of its coming by watching the actions of birds and animals, which seemed to sense the danger. Usually the norther strikes after a period in which the air has been still and sultry.

Two of the founders of Texas, Moses Austin and his son, Stephen F. Austin, lost their lives as a result of sudden northers. Another Texas statesman, John H. Reagan, feared a similar fate. In October, 1840, traveling alone on horseback, he went to sleep under the stars

4

on the prairie near Wills Point. When he awoke, a fierce norther was blowing. By daybreak the ground was covered with ice.

Riding on to the Kaufman prairie, he could see King's Fort, ten or twelve miles to the southwest. By the time he reached Cottonwood Creek, about four miles from the fort, he was too stiff to guide his horse; but his steed kept to the trail. At the gate, Reagan was too frozen to speak. Friends filled a large tub with spring water and put him in it, clothes and all. When he had thawed enough to talk, they laid him in a bed by the fire.

"If I had not been thawed out as I was," he recalled, "I certainly would have lost my life. The skin on my face, neck, arms, and legs came to look as though it had been scalded. There were no medicines in camp, though the men had some bear oil with which they greased the parts that were burst; and I had for many days a burning fever."

Soldiers on the prairies or plains always dreaded a norther. When General Zachary Taylor had his troops encamped near Corpus Christi late in 1845, one observer wrote: "Furious northers were shivering the frail tent poles and rending the rotten canvas. The torrents drenched and the fierce blasts shook the miserable couches of the living. Their last groans mingled in fearful contempt with the howlings of the pitiless storm."

Two decades later Elizabeth Custer, wife of Lieutenant Colonel George A. Custer, had her first experience with a Texas norther. This one came up in the night and was preceded by a period in which the air was heavy and suffocating. "The wild blast swept down on us with a fury indescribable," she wrote. "Our tent shook, rattled, and flapped as if with the rage of some human creature. It was hard to tell whether one was at sea or on land."

Texas stockmen have been hit by many a blizzard. No one can foresee when an arctic gale will sweep down across the plains, covering the ranges with ice and snow. Sheep usually fare a little better than cattle since they have thick fleeces, will eat weeds that cattle spurn, and will satisfy their thirst by eating snow. Cattle unable to find shelter turn their rumps against the wind and wait for help.

When drifts are piled high over the trails, the feed brought by ranchmen often comes too late.

Hungry and numb, the cattle drift with the wind. Without food or water, they become thin and gaunt. Glistening icicles hang from their muzzles, from their ears, and even their eyes. Some find protection in timber or canyons, but others freeze stiff on the open prairie. Many drift against a fence and pile up against the barbed wire and icy posts and die together.

Even on the usually mild Gulf Coast, sudden blizzards sometimes bring sheets of ice and disaster to livestock. In one winter almost the whole coastal plain was strewn with the carcasses of fine cattle that had tried in vain to escape from a frigid blast.

Many an old-timer has recalled the blizzards of frontier days. The late Judge O. W. Williams of Fort Stockton long remembered the deep snow of December, 1878, which he had encountered while on a surveying expedition in Hale County. "Our horses, staked out for the night, were gaunt and shivering," he said. "Our mules, tied to the wagon, had eaten the wagon box, part of the sideboards, and as much of our tent ropes as they could reach."

With no houses in the whole county, the party sought refuge at the head of Blanco Canyon, twenty miles away. On their dreary ride, they caught sight of a small bunch of buffalo and decided to try to kill some fresh meat. As their horses were too nearly starved for a chase, Williams and another man crawled through the deep snow on their hands and knees until close enough to shoot two buffalo.

In the era of the open range, a severe blizzard might cause cattle to drift hundreds of miles. In the winter of 1880 the Texas Panhandle was covered with thousands of Longhorns that had drifted south from the Arkansas River and even the Platte country. Sheltered pastures along the Canadian and the Red River were grazed clean by cattle that had been driven long distances by storms.

To protect their ranges from such drifters from the north, Texas cattlemen built in 1881–82 a drift fence clear across the Panhandle. This fence, which extended 175 miles or more from the Indian Territory to New Mexico, cost a fortune to build but failed to hold. When a frigid blast hit on January 7, 1886, thousands of cattle drifted into the fence and froze to death. But, in other places, cattle from the Indian Territory, Kansas, and Colorado toppled it over or crossed above it on frozen drifts.

Uncounted thousands of cattle froze to death in the Panhandle that winter. John Hollicot, manager of the LX Ranch, said he skinned 250 cattle to the mile for thirty miles along the drift fence. Some ranchmen lost 65 to 75 per cent of their herds. In Hansford County, L. S. Carter found a settler's wagon with the team lying dead in the harness. Inside the wagon were the frozen bodies of a man and his wife and their three children.

Texas was lashed by one of its coldest blizzards early in 1899. February 11 had been a balmy day, with many people out in their shirt sleeves. But that night a blizzard swept in from the northwest, sending the mercury down. By morning it was down to twenty-three degrees below zero at Tulia, in Swisher County. In a line camp near Eden, Arch Benge and two other men huddled in a dugout. They had a fire going, Benge recalled, "but we nearly froze for eight or nine days. We'd killed a beef on the eleventh and hung it up. After the blizzard hit, it froze stiff. We had to go out and chop off beef-steaks with an ax." At that time the stagecoach did not have to ford the Concho River near San Angelo but crossed on the ice.

After the turn of the century, winter still brought occasional blizzards that froze some cattle. At the XIT Ranch, William E. (Ed) Farwell went through one storm that caused seventeen cows and one horse to drift off a bluff west of Channing. He found the bodies in a single pile in the canyon below. In another Panhandle storm, cattle kept drifting into a fence corner, trampling the snow and falling over the fence. More than fifty carcasses were piled up there, blanketed with snow.

Persons caught out in a blizzard would build a fire if they could, only to be burned on one side while freezing on the other. This was almost true even in the frontier log cabins. Lyman B. Russell, who as a boy lived in a cabin near Helena, Texas, in 1853, recalled that "when a blue norther struck, we children would stand around the fire in the stack chimney that my father had built of brick and turn around like spareribs hung in front of the fire to roast in hog-killing time. One of those cold spells was a shin-burner and a back-freezer."

Out on the buffalo range, a hunter hit by a sudden blizzard might rip open a freshly killed buffalo bull, tear out the entrails, and crawl into the cavity for warmth. But unless he was careful, the next morning might find him locked inside the frozen carcass, dependent on his companions for release.

In the towns, some of the adults relied on peppered food for warmth, and more on strong drink. Corn whisky and apple toddy were favorite preventives of frostbite. In Houston in 1838, when the village had only three stoves, men used to light fires in front of the saloon on cold evenings. There, with President Sam Houston sometimes joining them, they would enjoy hot drinks and merry speeches.

By the time the danger of blizzards is past, the Texas tornado season starts. The plains country is a favorite playground for the powerful twisters that strike most frequently from March through June. Their most common time of day is between four and six in the afternoon. The trade-mark of the tornado is its pendant, usually funnel-shaped, cloud.

When this funnel dips to the ground with a terrific roar, the destruction starts. The twister reduces buildings to rubble, crushes automobiles, and lifts houses from foundations and trains from tracks. Sometimes it shears trees from a bluff as with a giant sickle. Often the loss of lives is heavy; the tornado that hit Goliad in 1902 and the one that swept through Waco in 1953 each killed 114 persons.

A twister that can drive a pine board through a steel girder, that can blow straw through plate glass without breaking either, that can lift a railway locomotive and set it back on its track, headed in the opposite direction, can do almost anything. And often it does. In one farm home a twister sucked all the oil from a kerosene lamp without breaking either the lamp or its glass chimney. Elsewhere another embedded a bean in an egg without cracking the shell.

A tornado that made a mile-wide swath near Gainesville in 1854 bent enormous trees down to the ground and killed seven people. It moved a heavy ox wagon several hundred yards, blew two women three-quarters of a mile, and put a horse and a sheep in

8

trees, ten feet above the ground. A twister that struck the Brazos River at the mouth of Cedar Creek in 1868 blew water out of the river and left big catfish stranded far from the bank.

Texas tornadoes have done so many strange things and have inspired so many folk tales that it is hard to winnow fact from fiction. At Sherman a twister drove a plank into a tree trunk so firmly that a man could hang from it. Near Lorraine a farmer was putting on a sock when the wind struck and wrecked his house. It dumped the man into a horse trough, but he kept hold of the sock. The Dallas tornado of 1957 lifted an automobile over a two-story house and set it down on the other side without a scratch.

Many stories of freakish results of tornadoes were gathered by Professor Howard C. Key of North Texas State University. He told of a Texas tornado that turned iron washpots inside out and of another that pulled up a mile-long wire fence and left it in a neat roll. Near Desdemona, he reported, a tornado struck a farm home during supper. It destroyed the whole house except the dining room. The family resumed the meal by the light of a kerosene lamp that had kept on burning while the destruction was taking place.

Tornadoes have plucked feathers from chickens and have even lifted babies from their cribs and deposited them in shallow puddles. William Porter said that in a twister at Cisco in 1893 he was swept into the air and slammed into something that felt like a wire fence. Then he began hearing "Nearer My God to Thee." He had banged into his new player piano, and the wind of the funnel had started it playing the roll that happened to be in place.

Near Frankston, wrote Professor Key, a tornado swept across the prairie toward a country school that had four teachers and seventy-eight pupils. The teachers herded the children into the shelter of a nearby ravine, getting them down the six-foot embankment just in time to escape flying trees, boards, and debris.

Too late, one of the teachers remembered that two fourth-grade girls, Maxine and Patsy, had gone to the outdoor toilet before the storm struck. Later she learned that the pair had emerged and had started running along the road toward home. In the ravine all the children remained safe, although each of the teachers was hurt, one suffering a broken leg.

Key was told that when a twister hit a farm home near Clyde the family rushed into the storm cellar. A few minutes later they saw a panful of fresh eggs take off, one at a time, from a shelf. Each egg passed through a hole in the cellar door; but when the empty pan followed, it hit against the opening and stopped the suction.

Late summer often brings drouth to Texas. Some people escape to the Colorado Rockies, but most merely resign themselves to torrid, cloudless days and sultry nights. Yet, to the old-timer, no dry spell seems as severe as those he went through as a youth. Recent drouth conditions have led many oldsters to recall the cracked earth and black blizzards they knew long ago. "Back there things were so bad," said Richard R. Smith, "that you could run a whole herd of cattle through the entire length and breadth of the Colorado River."

One grizzled cowman claimed that he had seen the Brazos River so nearly dry that a person in low shoes could walk across it without wetting his feet. "That's nothing," countered another, "I came up the Trinity when we couldn't see the banks for the clouds of dust raised by the steamboat's paddles." Pat Mordecai of Whitesboro said he saw a lizard carrying a canteen of water.

Drouths in the old days made even worse hardships for farmers and stockmen than they did later. Few of the pioneer nesters and ranchmen had wells. Still fewer had windmills and tanks. When the streams and water holes dried up, crops, grass, and many animals withered and died.

One of the most tragic drouths in the Southwest was that of 1859–60. Yet this one hit Texas less severely than it did Kansas, where thirty thousand settlers left the territory to find food and many of those who remained subsisted largely on acorns and on relief food sent from the East.

Texas suffered another severe drouth in 1864. Streams went dry and grass withered. Thousands of cattle perished from thirst. In some localities, losses were estimated as high as 75 per cent. The hardest-hit stockmen tried to salvage their cattle by offering them at one to two dollars a head. Even at such prices, there were few buyers.

10

In 1881, rain failed again. Many of the small streams dried up, and some cattle died. Then, two years later, a worse drouth struck the southwestern plains.

This dry spell of 1883 hit the Texas cow country a staggering blow. The sky was cloudless; it held only the blazing sun that parched and cracked the earth. Stockmen said the sun was "hot enough to raise blisters on a boot heel." Dust hovered over the plains and settled on the brown, shrunken grass. Fires, from the embers of careless campers or the sparks of train engines, raced over many of the pastures, leaving only charred, blackened turf. With even the stubble gone, the cattle browsed on chaparral, munched prickly pear, and chewed the blooms of Spanish dagger.

Even worse than the lack of grass was the scarcity of water. Creeks that had served large herds held only powdery dust. Settlers on the upper Brazos and the Colorado never had seen those rivers so low. In some streams the trickle still flowing was so salty that cattle refused to drink it. Water holes that had lasted through other hot summers were dry. Some cattle, wading into the mud to suck up the ooze and green scum, sank into the mire and suffocated.

The half-wild Longhorns, although toughened to hardship and scant fare, were crazed by thirst. Rolling their tongues in agony, they bawled for water. Day by day their moaning grew weaker. Their ribs showed, and their eyes became more sunken. Some of the herds lost many head, first the cows with young calves, then the calves and yearling steers. The smaller ranchmen suffered first and most severely. Those who could do so moved their piteously lowing cattle to better pastures and water but found their stock restless and hard to control. This disastrous situation led many cowmen to cut the new barbed-wire fences of their neighbors to let their thirsty herds reach water.

One of the worst of all Texas drouths, and the earliest recalled by many pioneers, was that of 1886. By May the lack of rain had begun to blight the grass, grain, and garden crops. Before that month ended, the town of Cisco ran entirely out of water. Each day the railroad brought a car with two big tanks of water from Albany.

11

Cisco people bought it by the barrel or by the bucket. By the middle of July, cattle were dying by the thousands, and many of the settlers were pulling out.

As gaunt, half-starved horses pulled the covered wagons back east, many farmhouses and even whole communities were deserted. On one abandoned cabin in Blanco County, someone had chalked on a board nailed across the door:

> 250 miles to nearest post office.
> 100 miles to wood.
> 20 miles to water.
> 6 inches to hell.
> God bless our home.
> Gone to live with the wife's folks.

Many of those who stuck to their farms and ranches had a rough time. Walter P. Stewart was living on a ranch near Graham when the 1886 drouth hit. "Thermometer up to 108," he wrote in his diary on May 9. "Hottest, driest weather I have ever seen at this time of year." On May 12 he wrote: "No rain since April 14. Oats and wheat ruined." On May 31; "Cameron and Stewart creeks getting dry."

Stewart recorded a temperature of 115 on June 16. "Our south pasture burned. A lot of grass we could ill afford to lose. Was set by a camper's fire." In mid-July he wrote: "This is the driest, most unfavorable year the country has ever known. Crops are an entire failure. No grass of this season's growth. Little water. We are contemplating moving our stock east, as they cannot live here much longer. Livestock increasingly restless, uncontrollable in their pitiful lowing and to the point of dangerous desperation."

To save their herd of a thousand cattle, Stewart and his brothers decided to drive the stock east to grass and water. On July 17, with the mercury at 115, they rigged up water barrels and chuck boxes. Two days later they started off. "The herd is restless, thirsty, and scenting water in the two holes in Cameron Creek." The next day the cattle stampeded for water. On the twenty-first the men watered their horses at an enclosed pond but had to hold off the cattle. On the following day the cattle were restless and troublesome, having been without water for two days. But rain on the home ranch enabled the men to turn the cattle back in time to save them.

Tragedy brought by the drouth of 1886 didn't keep some from joking about the situation. "The weather has been so dry here for the last three weeks," noted the *Taylor County News*, "that the wells are empty and the fish in the creeks are carrying toadstools for parasols. Water is getting so scarce that Baptists and Campbellites are beginning to favor sprinkling. Potato bugs are crossing the creek as the Israelites crossed the Red Sea. A prominent prohibitionist has ordered a case of beer from Decatur—he wants lather to shave himself."

At Anson a prankster who appeared on the street carrying a long slicker was arrested by the sheriff for disturbing the peace. He was released only after he had bought cigars for the crowd. One editor wrote: "The drouth in Texas is so intense that potatoes are cooked in the ground. All the people have to do is dig them. The workmen carry salt in their pockets and don't have to go home for dinner." A report from Dalhart said that, with all the vegetation blown away, birds were building nests with pieces of barbed wire.

As conditions became worse, help came from many sources. From Chicago the Union Stock Yards mailed the governor a check for $1,850 for drouth relief. St. Louis merchants sent ten carloads of provisions. The Dallas *News* and the Fort Worth *Gazette* sponsored a relief fund. Ballinger people, although themselves pinched, sent thirteen wagon loads of food to those in the stricken village of Comfort. Congressmen sent big packages of garden seeds for planting the next spring.

Drouths like that of 1886 gave rise to much folklore about Texas dryness and dust storms. Some said that Texas crows had to fly backward to keep the sand out of their eyes. Ranchmen around San Angelo complained less about losing their cattle and sheep than about the lack of creek water to mix with their corn whisky and tarantula juice. They had to use sissy soda water that came in bottles.

Every dry spell loosened the topsoil and allowed the wind to blow more away. A Wilson County farmer, in Floresville on an

13

errand, said he had to rush back home. The wind, he explained, had just blown all his good peanut soil over on the land of a neighbor. "Now the wind has changed and is blowing it back. I must hurry home and plow it in or it will be blown over on the land of my neighbor on the other side."

Yet drouths and dust storms never discouraged pioneer Texas farmers and ranchmen for long. With rawhide tenacity, most of them believed there was bound to be a rain the next year. After one of the blackest dust storms, one farmer looked out of his cabin to see what was left. "Looks as if the wind blew about all the dirt away," he said to his wife. "But we haven't lost everything. We still have the mortgage!"

Drouths like that of 1886 were an invitation to those who claimed they could draw rain from the skies. Farmers and ranchmen who had spoofed at Indian dances and incantations for rain became so desperate that they were willing to try anything. They listened eagerly to anyone who said he could bring rain.

In Texas most of the early attempts to make rain involved the use of explosives. Veterans of the Civil War recalled that artillery bombardments often were followed by rain. So they used cannons to try to shake rain loose from the clouds. A group of South Texans joined in such a rain-making effort in the spring of 1891.

That was a time of severe drouth. Thousands of cattle were dying from hunger and thirst. Some ranchmen in Duval County heard that army men were firing explosives into the clouds at Midland and El Paso. So they hauled an old cannon from the King Ranch and prepared for action. With some army help, they set up their equipment on the Collins Ranch, three miles from San Diego. They filled small cloth bags with powder and soaked them in nitroglycerin. A meteorologist, John Ellis of Oberlin College, went aloft in a captive balloon to check the clouds.

After days of waiting, dark clouds filled the sky. The rainmakers were ready. They sent up balloons filled with sulphuric acid gas, then exploded them with the cannon. One blast came so close that it blew down the soldiers' tents. Nothing happened at first, but

14

by nightfall rain began to soak the parched grass. Whether the firing had anything to do with it, no one knew.

In August of that year, rainmakers were at work elsewhere in Texas. On the South Plains, self-titled General Robert St. George Dryenforth was sure he could bring water from the clouds. Dryenforth, who had been commissioner of patents, left a lucrative Washington law practice to test his rain-making theories.

After persuading Congress to appropriate nine thousand dollars for this work, Dryenforth started bombarding clouds near Washington. He succeeded only in stampeding cattle and arousing the farmers. "Your bomb," wrote one, "is worse than thunder. Please move your dynamite away."

On the *Llano Estacado,* after Dryenforth's initial bombardment, rain came the next day. "One more shower like that," said a local politician, "and you could be elected governor of Texas." On August 16, 17, and 18, the General kept on blasting at the clouds. Finally rain began to fall. It continued for two and one-half hours.

This was a big rain for that part of Texas, near the New Mexico line. Congratulations and invitations poured in. Dryenforth wrote an exultant article for the *North American Review*. But an Abilene preacher, whose flock had been praying for rain for six weeks, demanded that the Lord be given some of the credit. And Weather Bureau officials pointed out that, on the same day, heavier rains had fallen on many sections of Texas not affected by the General's cannonade.

Nearly two decades later, Texas saw another effort to draw rain by the use of dynamite. In the spring of 1910, three years after he had bought the 200,000-acre Curry Comb Ranch in West Texas, C. W. Post, the breakfast-food king, became interested in making rain. To his ranch managers he wrote: "Perfect a suitable kite to carry two pounds of dynamite. Make fifteen or twenty of them, each with a five-minute fuse."

The kites were ready in June. But just as they were about to be launched, rain began to pour and continued for several days. The next year Post decided to try again, this time not with kites but

15

with explosions on the ground, along the edge of the Caprock. The 171 charges of dynamite threw dirt and rocks into the air—but brought no rain. Several later trials were made, that year and the next, but without making any certain change in the weather.

During the drouth cycle of 1915–18, which brought heavy losses to ranchmen and farmers in the Southwest, the Rock Island Railroad hired a rainmaker from Australia to bring relief to the communities it served. This cloud chaser was provided with a box-car, from which there soon arose vapors of various colors and vile smells. After several weeks in which no rain fell, the rainmaker was dismissed. As soon as he departed, torrents began to fall and almost washed away the railroad's embankment.

Another flurry of rain-making efforts came in the early 1950's. They stemmed from the success of Vincent Schaefer of the General Electric Company in a laboratory experiment in 1946. He had seeded a cloud of cool moisture to convert it into ice particles. But doing this on a large scale over the Texas plains proved much more difficult.

Faith in this new technique quickly spread over the mesquite and cactus country. The returned war pilot in search of a quick fortune tied an old plane together with baling wire and began drop-ping dry ice on the clouds. The man who had played out as an oil wildcatter swapped his doodlebug for a rain-making machine and started blowing silver iodide gas up into the sky. Local farmers' organizations and several cities, including Dallas, gave fat contracts to the new rainmakers. But, when the promised increase in rain failed to appear, the contracts were dropped. One observer re-marked that it would have been cheaper, and more entertaining, to import a band of Navahos and have them do a rain dance.

On the Texas Gulf Coast the late summer drouth often ends in a burst of fury, since September is the month for hurricanes. Tropi-cal storms brewed far away in the Caribbean sometimes lash inland with terrifying force. They overturn fishing boats, wreck the less sturdy buildings, and destroy citrus groves. Yet sea walls and stronger construction have helped to moderate repetitions of the devastation that took place on and about Galveston Island in September, 1900.

16

Then wind and waves battered most of the city of Galveston to splinters and took at least six thousand lives.

On Friday evening, September 7, the sky over the island became dark and foreboding. Strong wind and towering waves drove bathers and picnickers from the beaches. Bathhouses and a streetcar trestle were toppled by the wind. Yet, although hurricane warnings had been relayed from Washington, few persons gave much thought to the storm. They assumed that this one would be no worse than others they had experienced.

On Saturday morning most Galveston people went about their activities as usual, thinking that the storm would subside soon. Instead, the gale became stronger and the waves higher. Then rain began to fall in torrents. Soon some of the frailer houses near the beaches were crumpled and set adrift. The water pushed into the lower streets and lapped at the doors of other houses.

Only after tasting the water and finding it salty did some realize that the Gulf was rising to sweep over the island. Many waded through water as high as their shoulders to reach higher ground and safer buildings. Some lost their footing and perished in the swirling waters.

As the wind and waves lashed more viciously and the water rose higher, windows were smashed and some of the stronger houses in which people had taken refuge were crushed and began to float off. Those of the city's 37,000 residents who were caught downtown were a bit better off in having sturdier buildings in which to find shelter. Nearly one thousand gathered in the five-story Tremont Hotel, hurrying up to the mezzanine when the flood swirled across the ground floor.

At 5:15 P.M. the Weather Bureau's wind gauge, which had registered eighty-four miles an hour, blew away. Soon afterward the wind reached a velocity which the weathermen estimated at 110 to 120 miles an hour. At six o'clock the Angelus began to ring out from St. Mary's Cathedral. Then suddenly the towers swayed and the two-ton bell crashed to the floor. About that time the storm reached its peak, after which the wind and waves began to subside; yet few of the survivors were able to leave their places of safety until Sunday morning.

17

That morning those who were able went out through puddles and slime, looking for food, searching for missing members of their families, and gathering the dead. They were horrified at the wreckage and at the death toll. A number of residents lost all members of their families. Bodies were strewn over the island, some with the clothing whipped off by the wind and some mutilated by falling debris. The heavy task of burial in the sea took days. Some of the bodies, improperly weighted, washed back to the shore and had to be buried again.

Armed guards patrolled the streets, ready to shoot anyone found pilfering. One man was said to have been caught cutting fingers from bodies to take the rings. Quickly the soldiers pulled a sugar sack over his head and shot him.

Among those who went through the storm in Galveston were Morris Sheppard, later a United States senator, and young King Vidor, who became a motion-picture director. Heroes of the catastrophe included the two weathermen, Isaac and Joseph Cline, who were brothers. The two, who later saw long service in New Orleans and Dallas respectively, warned persons who lived on low ground to flee to safer places. They also sent reports to Washington until the wires gave way.

One of the many who had harrowing experiences was an attractive young schoolteacher with reddish-gold hair, Daisy Thorne. She lived with her mother in the three-story Lucas Terrace apartment house of sixty-four rooms. After having to forego her usual evening dip in the surf on Friday, she took pictures of the mounting waves on Saturday morning. Before the storm abated, it had destroyed the whole apartment house except for Daisy's room, in which twenty-two persons were huddled. A few days after the storm, Daisy was married, with mud caked several inches deep in the church aisle.

One who would hear the roar of the hurricane for more than sixty years was Mrs. William Casey, who was twenty-two years old and was expecting a baby any day. With her husband, who was a printer, and her mother, she lived in a frame cottage only about five blocks from the Gulf.

Like most of their neighbors, the Caseys hadn't noticed the

Weather Bureau's warnings that a storm was headed toward the island. On Friday evening they walked down to the beach. There they saw waves dashing over Murdoch's bathhouse, but they supposed the water would subside soon.

About two o'clock Saturday morning the Caseys were awakened by the roar of the wind from across the channel. They became more alarmed in the hours that followed, as rain and waves deluged the city and the wind blew in windows and toppled chimneys. Mr. Casey brought into the house some fryer chickens he had in a coop in the back yard. He put them in the bathtub and threw in some feed.

By four in the afternoon, with much of the city under five feet of water, glass was crashing from the windows of the Casey home. The Caseys could see the shutters and chimneys blowing on all sides. Swirling water began coming in through the kitchen door. Then part of the roof blew off. With a sinking feeling, they remembered that none of them could swim. The condition of Mrs. Casey added to the difficulty of getting her to a place of safety.

In a two-story house next door lived the Caseys' landlord. He was Archie Hutchings, former captain of a coastal vessel, who had a wife and a son and a daughter. As a young man, he had seen the devastating effects of the storm of 1888. So when he built his home, he drove ship's spars into the ground around the sides to hold it in place. Moreover, he could swim.

Captain Hutchings proved to be a good neighbor. About five o'clock, with the storm almost at its height, he swam to the Casey home and brought its three occupants, one at a time, across the rushing waters to safety. From the second floor of the Hutchings home, the Caseys saw their house blow over on its side. The two families obtained a little light by using strips of cloth dipped in grease. They wondered what they would do if the Casey baby arrived in the night.

Deep in the night they heard a terrible screaming. The men went to the door, but the wind knocked them down flat. In the morning they discovered that the screams had come from a couple who had sought refuge in an above-ground cistern. When it floated off and was pounded against a telephone pole, they were battered and bruised.

19

On Sunday the Caseys found their little black and tan dog safe in their attic, a stray kitten with him. Their house furnishings were ruined and their chickens gone. Mr. Casey went out through the debris-covered streets to look for food for his hungry and ailing womenfolk. But he was refused, since at first only women and children applicants were being served.

After a few days, the Caseys obtained passage on one of the out-going refugee trains. They were headed for Dallas, where Mrs. Casey had been reared. They arrived there on the eighteenth, ten days after the storm. They were just in time. The Casey baby, a son, came that day.

More than six decades later, in September, 1961, a storm of even greater force, Hurricane Carla, struck the Texas coast, with its center below Galveston. It crushed buildings and mowed down large trees, interlacing others. Galveston's sea wall held, but the new cities and towns along the coast made the devastation even greater than in 1900. Many families lost all their property. Much of the damage came from tornadoes and floods which accompanied the hurricane winds.

Fortunately, the evacuation of nearly half a million people from their homes on or near the coast, in response to warnings, made the loss of life relatively small. The hurricane brought new examples of heroism, as in the case of a woman telephone operator in Brazoria who stuck to her post into the night until the lines went down.

INJUNS! even when spoken in a whisper, could be a hair-raising word on the Texas frontier. No one knew this better than Mrs. Sarah Hibbins, who had come to the southwestern wilderness when it still was a part of Mexico. At that time, settlements of colonists from the states were small and far apart. Always, especially when the moon was full, there was danger of raids by savages who were looking for horses—and scalps.

Sarah Hibbins had come a long way from Illinois. She had been reared on a farm in Jackson County, in the southern part of that state, bordering on the Mississippi River. She was Sarah Creath then. A comely blonde, she was admired widely for her looks, her graceful manners, and her generous nature.

In a day when couples married young, Sarah was wooed and won by a sturdy and ambitious farm youth, John McSherry. Like many other young men in the 1820's, McSherry had the Texas fever. In Texas, Stephen F. Austin and other colonizers were offering big tracts of free land. The soil was fertile, and settlers were coming in. True, there were wild beasts and redskin raiders, but some thought the gain would be worth the risk. John McSherry was set on going to Texas, and Sarah was willing to go with him.

Soon after their wedding, the young couple boarded a Mississippi steamer for New Orleans. There they took a coastal ship for Texas. They obtained land from the grant of Green DeWitt, along the Guadalupe River in the southern part of the state. This was fine country, partly wooded with oak and mesquite, but wild and lonely.

In 1828 young McSherry picked a site on the west side of the Guadalupe and built his log cabin. The new home was near a creek and had a clear spring about two hundred yards from the door. The view was pleasing; but the nearest neighbors were Andrew Lockhart and his wife, ten miles up the Guadalupe.

John McSherry cleared patches of land and planted corn and other crops. In the winter he hunted wild turkeys and deer and chopped firewood to keep the cabin warm for the baby boy who came early in 1829. Sarah was busy, too. She learned to cook wild game and to make clothes for the baby, whom they named John. But sometimes she worried over all the stories she heard about Comanche attacks.

The stories weren't mere idle tales. On a pleasant day later in 1829, John McSherry went out to the spring about noon to bring back a bucket of water. As he came up the bank with the filled bucket, a band of Indians sprang from the bushes, letting out wild yells. In a moment, McSherry lay lifeless on the grass, with his scalp gone.

Sarah, who heard the yells and saw what happened, quickly barred the cabin door and picked up her husband's rifle to defend herself and her baby. The Indians, finding that they could not break in, soon left. But the frantic young widow, fearing they might be hiding nearby, dared not go out to the body of her husband.

Fortunately, an Irish settler, John McCrabb, rode up to the McSherry cabin that evening. He had not known of the Indian raid but merely had hoped to spend the night at the McSherrys'. When he learned of the tragedy, he put the young mother and her baby on his horse and started off afoot with them toward the Lockharts'. By the light of the stars, they followed the faint trail to the neighbors' cabin, which they reached before daybreak. There warm hearts and kind hands did all they could for the shocked woman and her baby.

The young widow, with her baby, stayed at the home of the hospitable Lockharts until she was courted and wed by another pioneer settler, John Hibbins, whose cabin was on the east side of the Guadalupe. Again happiness seemed her lot. Hibbins was prospering, and more settlers were coming in. Both parents were pleased when a new baby arrived in their home.

Yet the danger from Indians continued. There were so many raids that the settlers demanded better protection. Stephen F. Austin had formed a small group of Rangers, in which each landowner was required to serve a month or provide a substitute; but their efforts were not enough. Late in 1835, as Texans were preparing to revolt against Mexican tyranny, the colonists made plans to raise a battalion of 150 Rangers to keep the Indians in check. Each Ranger would receive $1.25 a day but would provide his own horse, saddle, and blanket.

Meanwhile, Sarah Hibbins had left Texas, in the summer of 1835, to visit relatives in her childhood home in Illinois. She took along both her young baby and her older child, John McSherry. When she returned to Texas by steamer the next winter, her brother, George Creath, came along. From New Orleans they went by water to Columbus, a short distance up the Brazos River. There, early in February, 1836, her husband met them with an oxcart; and they began the tedious ride back to their frontier home.

Their route took them to Beason's Crossing on the Colorado River and thence to the Navidad. From there they followed the Bahia road and made their last camp on Rock Creek. They were only about fifteen miles from the Hibbins cabin. Another day's travel would bring them home.

The camp on Rock Creek was as peaceful as anyone could want. But its quiet changed suddenly as a band of thirteen savage Comanches leaped from hiding and attacked the whites, who were caught by surprise. The warriors quickly killed the two men, plundered the wagon, and took Mrs. Hibbins and her two children with them as captives. They bound her on one of their mules and tied the seven-year-old John on another.

Widowed by redskin savagery for the second time in less than seven years, Mrs. Hibbins was almost overcome with grief and fear. She knew the Indians were taking her and the children northward, away from the white settlements. Would she ever escape? Many frontier women had not. Although some had been ransomed, others had been killed or made slaves.

Soon the fate of her baby was decided. The frightened infant cried so much that one of the braves became irked at hearing the wailing. He grabbed the baby, bashed his head against the nearest tree, and tossed the body aside to await the wolves or the buzzards.

After several days, the Comanches crossed the Colorado River and made camp on Shoal Creek, near the site on which the capital city of Austin was to rise. That night a cold north wind led them to seek the shelter of a cedar thicket and to wrap themselves in buffalo robes. This time they didn't bother to tie their two prisoners or to put out guards. They were too far from the settlements to worry about either the escape of the mother and child or an attempt to rescue them.

But courageous Sarah Hibbins had not given up. She knew that it was now or never. Another day's journey would take the Comanches beyond the reach of pursuers. She knew, too, that if she tried to escape, she would have to abandon to the savages the only child she had left. The decision was hard, but she did not hesitate.

As soon as she thought all the Indians were asleep, she took a long look at the boy she might never see again, tucked a robe about him, and stole away from the camp. To keep from leaving a trail, she headed for the creek and waded downstream in the cold water. For what seemed like two hours she waded on, undeterred by rocks, snags, or chill. She thought she had gone about five miles.

Then her blood seemed to freeze as she heard young John calling, "Mamma! Mamma!" The creek had circled the camp, where her son had wakened and missed her. Again she had to decide quickly. Should she go back and give the boy the comfort of his mother's presence? Or should she go on and try to find settlers or others who might try to rescue him?

Determined Mrs. Hibbins closed her ears to her son's cries and waded on down the creek. She knew there would be settlements on the Colorado. Through brush and vines she walked all night, ever fearful of pursuit. Morning brought no rest. She hastened on down the river. Her clothes were in shreds, and some of her scratches were bleeding, but she must try to find help for her John.

Nearly all day Sarah Hibbins hurried on. She paused only to call as loudly as she could, in hope to finding someone who could

24

help her. Once some men in the river bottom heard her faintly. But they thought the call came from Indians and did not answer.

Finally, in the late afternoon, the distraught woman saw cows grazing near the river. As they were milk cows, she thought there must be a pioneer home nearby. Therefore, she waited to follow them home. Before long the cows headed slowly off; and the tired, hungry woman followed. When she heard a rooster crow, she knew she was near a farm home. The cows led her to the home of Jacob Harrell, where she sank exhausted into the nearest chair.

As soon as Mrs. Hibbins found breath enough to tell her story, Harrell took her to the nearby cabin of Reuben Hornsby, where she was given food and clothing. She learned that, in spite of all her walking, she was only about ten miles from the Indian camp from which she had escaped.

Fortunately, Captain John L. Tumlinson and some of his Texas Rangers arrived at the Hornsby cabin only a few minutes after Mrs. Hibbins. Tumlinson was a hardy frontiersman who had come from North Carolina and had settled at Columbus, farther down the Colorado. In the preceding month he had been chosen to head the first organized company of Texas Rangers and had recruited sixty men. The job of the Rangers was to protect the settlements against Indian raids and to hold the frontier while regular Texas troops fought the Mexicans in the revolution about to start.

Captain Tumlinson and his men were assigned to a post on the headwaters of Brushy Creek, about thirty miles northwest of the site of Austin. At this time in February, Tumlinson and some of his young Rangers were on their way to their new post, where they had been told to build a blockhouse. They had planned to camp that night near the Hornsby cabin.

After hearing Mrs. Hibbins' story, the Rangers ate a hasty meal and set out. They took Reuben Hornsby along as a guide. In the night they found what appeared to be the trail of the Comanches; but, fearing to lose it in the darkness, they stopped to wait for daylight. At dawn they followed the trail without difficulty. About ten o'clock that morning, the Rangers caught up with the Comanche party. The warriors were preparing to break camp, on Walnut Creek, about ten miles northwest of the place from which Mrs. Hibbins had escaped.

Tumlinson decided to attack at once, from two sides. He led one group, while Lieutenant Joseph Rogers led the other. The Rangers rode into the camp with their guns popping. Taken by surprise, the Indians rushed for the shelter of a cedar brake. They left everything in the camp except the weapons they could grab hastily. One of Tumlinson's men, Noah Smithwick, lost control of his horse, which carried him into the fleeing savages. A Comanche dodged behind a tree and fired at Smithwick with a musket but missed him.

Unable to check his horse, Smithwick jumped off and ran after his assailant on foot, knowing the latter's gun was empty. The Ranger fired and saw the Indian fall. Leaving the warrior for dead, Smithwick ran on, reloading his gun. After a limb had knocked off his hat, Smithwick was mistaken by one of his comrades for a Comanche. This Ranger was about to shoot him when another knocked his gun aside.

But the Indian whom Smithwick had shot was not dead. Lying on the ground, he reloaded his gun and fired at Tumlinson. He missed the Captain but killed his horse. Then another Ranger, Conrad Rohrer, ran up and snatched the gun from the wounded Comanche and used it to give him a blow on the head, crushing his skull. The other Indians escaped through the cedar brake. Two Rangers were wounded, though not seriously.

Where was little John McSherry? The Indians had wrapped him in a buffalo robe and tied him to a mule, ready to take up their homeward journey. One of the Rangers, supposing him to be a Comanche, shot at him twice; but both times his gun missed fire. He was about to pull his trigger a third time when another Ranger, recognizing the boy, knocked the muzzle up and destroyed the aim.

Experiences as harrowing as those of Sarah Hibbins were the lot of more than a few pioneer Texas women. Only a few weeks after the capture and escape of Mrs. Hibbins, a party of settlers was traveling eastward across southern Texas. There were eleven men, two of them with their wives and three young children. They had spent nearly a year in the poorly planned colony of Dr. John Charles Beales on Las Moras Creek, near the Río Grande. Unable to grow crops on the barren soil and fearing Indian attacks, they were returning to the coast.

In the party were Mr. and Mrs. John Horn and their two sons, John, aged five, and Joseph, three and one-half. The Horns had come from England late in 1834, but were disappointed in missing the promised land of plenty.

Two days after crossing the Nueces River, the party made camp beside a small lake on the afternoon of April 4, 1836. There, after turning out the oxen to graze, some of the men began cooking venison for dinner while others fished in the lake or repaired their guns. John Horn was stringing some alligator teeth for his sons. Mrs. Horn had just bathed the baby daughter of the other woman, Mrs. Harris, who was gathering wild fruit.

Suddenly, as Mrs. Horn went to one of the wagons to find a dress for the baby, a band of nearly naked Comanches rode into the camp on mules. Frightened, Mrs. Horn ran to her husband, who told her there was no danger. But as he spoke, an arrow pierced one of the men, killing him almost instantly. The Comanches, who numbered more than forty, quickly dispatched most of the white men, killing Horn by striking him on the back of the head with a double-barreled gun.

The Indians jerked the Horn boys from their mother and, after looting the wagons, started off on their mules, with the women riding behind two of the warriors. After about two miles, the Comanches reached their camp, where they received shouts of welcome from several hundred of their tribesmen. The prisoners, almost suffocated from the stench of stale horse meat, were allowed no food or drink. The boys were stripped naked, and the hands and ankles of the women were tied. They had no defense against the swarms of mosquitoes and other insects.

In the morning, as the Harris baby began to cry from cold and hunger, Mrs. Harris asked the Indians for food for the little girl. "Yes, she shall have something to eat," said a tall warrior. At that, he picked up the baby, swung her by her arms, tossed her as high as he could, and let her fall to the ground. By the time he had done this three times, the baby had no more need of food.

The women, who had assumed that all the men in their party were killed, were surprised to see Harris and a young German brought before them. But they gained no satisfaction from seeing them, for both men were tortured, killed, and scalped before their eyes.

Finally, as some of the Comanches went out to catch mustangs for eating, the two women and the boys were given a little water and some horse meat. Then the Indians resumed their wanderings across the prairies, often through scratchy brush. The prisoners, taken along on horseback, often had to go two days at a time without food while their captors had plenty. The boys were forced to go naked, exposed to sunburn, scratches, and insect bites. The younger Horn boy, Joseph, had his shoulder bruised by a fall; but, even though maggots crawled about in the sore, his mother was not allowed to treat it.

Cruelty to the four prisoners continued for days. One of the Comanche women often took Mrs. Harris by the throat and choked her until she turned black in the face. When young Joseph fell from a mule into a stream, a savage stabbed him with a lance just below the eye and pushed him back into the water. He forced the boy to walk the rest of the day. That evening he lashed the mother with a whip and cut off her hair. The next day some of the Indians amused themselves for an hour by tossing the boys into a stream and rescuing them only after they were nearly drowned. Both were unconscious when they were brought back to the camp.

Later the Indians settled in semipermanent lodges and adopted the boys into the tribe. They separated the two women, giving Mrs. Harris menial tasks and putting Mrs. Horn to work cleaning and dressing buffalo hides. In June, 1837, they sold Mrs. Harris to some Mexican traders. In the following September, they took Mrs. Horn across the high plains to San Miguel, New Mexico. There they traded her for a horse, four bridles, two mirrors, two knives, and some tobacco, powder, and balls. By that time, Mrs. Harris had gone to Missouri with a wagon train of Santa Fe traders.

While Mrs. Horn stayed in San Miguel and Taos, some of the Americans and Mexicans tried to find and recover her sons. They reported that John, still naked, had been told to hold a horse through a cold night and had been chilled to death. Little Joseph, they said, could be taken only by force. Discouraged and in poor health, Mrs. Horn left Santa Fe with a caravan on August 22, 1838. She arrived at Independence, Missouri, on the last day of September. Later she wrote the story of her captivity, which was published in a small book.

Only a month and a half after the capture of the Horn and Harris women and their children, another band of Indians—several hundred Comanches and Caddoes—roamed across eastern Texas. In the wooded upper valley of the Navasota River the Indians spied Fort Parker, a private outpost which several families of pioneer settlers had built two years earlier for protection against attack.

This structure, close to a fine spring, consisted of a stockade, which covered nearly an acre, with two cabins or blockhouses at diagonal corners. The walls of the stockade had been built of split cedar timbers set firmly in the ground, touching each other and reaching fifteen feet above the surface. Transverse timbers were fastened along the top, and portholes were made at frequent intervals. The blockhouses had two stories, the upper story jutting out over the lower.

Eight or nine families—thirty-four persons in all—lived in the fort and tended their crops in nearby fields. Several other families lived in log cabins a mile or two away.

On the morning of May 19, 1836, three of the men left the fort early to work in their fields about a mile away. Soon after they had gone, the band of marauding Indians arrived at the fort. They showed a white flag as a sign of friendship. When Benjamin Parker went out to talk with them, they asked the location of a water hole and demanded beef, saying they were hungry. Parker returned to the fort to report what they had said, but when he went out again to the Indians, they surrounded and killed him. Then the whole force, with blood-curdling yells, attacked the fort.

The inhabitants of the fort had become careless and were not prepared for such an attack. Some of them escaped; but when the battle ended, the Indians had killed five of the Parker men and had captured five women and children. The captives were Mrs. Elizabeth

29

Kellogg, Mrs. Rachel Plummer and her two-year-old son James, Cynthia Ann Parker, aged nine, and her younger brother, John, aged six. The Parker children were among the four of Silas and Sallie Parker, who had moved from Illinois to Texas in 1833. The father was killed in the battle while trying to save his niece, Mrs. Plummer; but the mother and the two younger children escaped.

About six months later a band of Delawares bought Mrs. Kellogg and took her to Nacogdoches, where they delivered her to General Sam Houston for $150, the amount they had paid. Mrs. Plummer was taken west to the mountains, where, with little clothing, she suffered much from the cold. While she was looking after the horses and dressing buffalo skins, her feet were frostbitten. In October she gave birth to a second son.

One cold morning, when the baby was about six months old, a warrior took him by the throat and strangled him until he appeared to be dead. Then he threw him into the air repeatedly, letting him fall on the frozen ground. A few minutes later, when the Indians discovered that the baby still breathed, they again tore him from his mother's arms. After tying a rawhide rope around his neck, they dragged him through a thicket of prickly-pear cactus, tearing his flesh. Then one of the mounted Indians tied the other end of the rope to his saddle and dragged the baby's body in a circle until it was torn to pieces.

Mrs. Plummer remained a captive for eighteen months. Finally she was ransomed by a Santa Fe trader, William Donahue. She went with him and his wife to Independence, Missouri, and early in 1838 returned to Texas, where she died a year later. Her son James, after six years of captivity, was ransomed late in 1842 and taken to Fort Gibson. His grandfather went after him and brought him home to Texas early the next year.

The two captured Parker children were placed in separate bands. Gradually their early memories faded as they were trained in Indian ways. When John reached manhood, he went with a raiding party into Mexico after horses. The Comanches also captured several Mexicans, among them a beautiful girl whom John married.

Later he was abandoned by the Indians and, with his wife, started a stock ranch in northern Mexico.

For five years Cynthia Ann never saw a white person. Then, when she was about fourteen, two traders with a Delaware guide found her living near the Canadian River with a family that had adopted her. One of the traders, Colonel Lem Williams, tried to ransom her, but his offers were refused. He was allowed to talk to Cynthia Ann as she sat by the foot of a tree; but she, perhaps told not to talk to him, made no reply.

Two years later another trading party found Cynthia Ann in a village on the Canadian. By that time she was married to a Comanche chief, Peta Nocona, and had two young sons. Exposure to the sun had made her almost as brown as the Comanches, and the memory of her early life had grown dim. She said that she was happily married and showed no desire to return to Texas.

In 1858, Cynthia Ann was seen at the battle of Antelope Hills, fought near the South Canadian by several hundred Comanches against a company of Texas Rangers and a band of friendly Indians. She and the other women escaped, their retreat covered by Comanche warriors.

Two and one-half years later, young Captain Lawrence Sullivan Ross of the Texas Rangers, better known as Sul Ross, was in command of a force in pursuit of marauding Comanches. He had forty Rangers, twenty army cavalrymen lent from Camp Cooper, and about seventy volunteer citizens serving without pay.

While traveling up the Pease River on December 18, 1860, Ross saw buffalo running and thought that Indian hunters must be near. After a bit of scouting, he found a Comanche camp beside a small stream. He quickly attacked the camp, taking the Indians by surprise. Chief Peta Nocona was among those killed. His two sons escaped, one of them to become Chief Quanah Parker; but his wife, Cynthia Ann, and a two-year-old daughter, Prairie Flower, were captured.

Cynthia Ann was dirty and scantily clothed, but Captain Ross discovered from her blue eyes that she was a white woman. Although she spoke no English, he suspected that she might be Cynthia Ann and sent for her aged uncle, Isaac Parker, who then lived on Grapevine Prairie. When Isaac Parker questioned her through a Mexican interpreter at Camp Cooper, he obtained no response. Then, as he was about to leave, he said, "The name of my niece was Cynthia Ann."

At that, the woman's face lighted and she patted her breast. "Cynthia Ann!" she said. "Me Cynthia Ann."

Cynthia Ann was recaptured too late to readjust happily to the life of the whites. Her mother tongue gradually came back, and she learned to spin and weave; but she longed for her missing sons and tried several times to escape. In 1861, the Texas Legislature granted her a league of land and a pension. In 1864, soon after the death of her daughter, she died at the home of her brother in Anderson County. In 1909, Congress voted $1,000 for a monument in her honor.

Indians raiding the cabins of frontier settlers were less likely to torture and scalp the women and children than to carry them off to hold for ransom, but there were many exceptions. In the late fall of 1860, about fifty-six Comanche warriors from north of the Red River made a bloody foray into the cross timbers and the prairies of Texas, killing palefaces and capturing horses. On November 26, they attacked three families near Jacksboro, killing most of the members. On the next morning, which was cold and rainy, they rode on south, along the line of Palo Pinto and Parker counties. From the farm of John Brown, fifteen miles northwest of Weatherford, they took eighteen horses. Soon afterward, meeting Brown on the road, they killed and scalped him, cut off his nose, and lanced him in every part of his body.

Then the band rode on a few miles south to the home of young Ezra and Martha Sherman and their children. Ezra was away from the house, where Martha and the children were eating their midday meal. As the mother was taken by surprise and had no weapon, she tried to talk the intruders into leaving; but they refused. "Vamoose, vamoose!" they said. "Indians no hurt."

As soon as the Comanches had the family out of the cabin, they began wrecking the place. They ripped open straw and feather beds and dumped the contents on the floor. Taking cups and saucers, the Indians drank from a barrel of molasses that the Shermans had provided for the winter. One picked up Mrs. Sherman's Bible and carried it off. The braves tried to set the cabin afire, but the rain kept it from burning.

Soon a more evil intent was apparent. Some of the warriors, saying that they wanted "squaw," tore the clothes from Mrs. Sherman and, despite her screams, threw her on the cold, wet ground. While her eldest child, a son, hid in a pile of brush and watched in horror, they began torturing her. They beat her with a heavy stick, shot arrows into her body, stabbed her, and cut open her shoulder blade. Then, while others held her down, with her legs apart, each warrior jerked off his breechcloth and had his way with her. Finally she lost consciousness and lost count.

Later Martha came to with a start as she felt a sharp knife tracing a circle about her skull. The arc was made unusually wide, to have most of her long hair on the scalp. But the skin refused to come loose, even when she was dragged by a pony. Only after a husky warrior placed one foot firmly on each of her shoulders and pulled with all his might was there any loosening. Then the scalp came off with a pop like that made by a cow pulling her foot out of the mud.

After shooting more arrows into her, the Indians left her for dead. Yet she lived in agony for three days, telling her story to neighbors before her suffering ended. Three weeks later, in the battle of Pease River, her Bible, with her name on the flyleaf, was recovered from the Comanches.

In view of the frequent raiding and scalping, many of the white settlers in Texas concluded that the only good Indian was a dead one. They attacked and scalped in retaliation, often making little effort to distinguish between friendly tribes and hostile ones. Parties of Texas settlers out after Indian raiders killed and scalped eleven Indians in Bee County in 1858, six in Milam County soon afterward, and four north of Blanco in 1870. Even Texas Rangers scalped their Indian victims on several occasions.

When fourteen young men from Cooke County, short of cash, went wolf hunting along the Red River near Red River Station to obtain hides to sell at fifty cents each, they ran into a camp of ruffians. Two men standing by the fire looked as if they were pulling taffy. On approaching the strangers and talking with them, the wolf hunters learned that the campers had just killed a pair of friendly Caddoes. What they were pulling were strips of skin from the Indians' backs. They intended to plait the tanned strips into horsewhips and sell them in the East.

Sam Houston had been a friend of the Indians, especially of the Cherokees, who had moved into eastern Texas in the winter of 1819–20. Early in 1836, on the eve of the Texas Revolution, the provisional government of Texas sent Houston and John Forbes to make a peace treaty with the Cherokees, one that would recognize their title to the lands they occupied. The treaty was signed on February 23 of that year; but although the Cherokees observed it and did not molest the Texans, the Texas Senate, formed later, never ratified the pact.

Mirabeau B. Lamar, who succeeded Houston as president of the Texas Republic, hated all Indians and decided to oust the Cherokees. On June 27, 1839, he ordered them removed from Texas and driven across the Red River. He sent troops under General Thomas J. Rusk to do the job. Chiefs Bowles and Big Mush tried to make peace. When they did not succeed, they asked for time to harvest their corn and other growing crops, but were refused. The Cherokees also were denied pay for their crops and improvements.

Young John H. Reagan, who was at the scene, described Chief Bowles as "bareheaded, bare-legged, and much tanned by the sun." Even at eighty, he was well muscled. He stood tall and straight, with dignified movements, and commanded respect.

The Texas troops attacked the Cherokees on July 15 on the Neches River, in Henderson County, burning their villages and their fields of corn. The next day they followed the fleeing Indians into Van Zandt County, where Chiefs Bowles and Big Mush were killed. Reagan described the death of Bowles: "Chief Bowles displayed great courage. In the second engagement, he remained on horseback, wearing a military hat, a silk vest, and a handsome sword presented to him by President Sam Houston. He was a magnificent

34

picture. But his horse was disabled; and as he dismounted, he was shot in the back and fell."

The wounded chief forced himself into a sitting position, facing his pursuers. As Captain Robert W. Smith rushed toward him, gun in hand, Reagan yelled, "Captain don't shoot him!" But Smith fired and the chief fell dead with a bullet in his head.

Sam Houston never forgave Lamar for driving out the peaceful Cherokees. On October 7, 1844, Houston, again president, spoke at a grand council of Indians near the falls of the Brazos River. "I made a peace with the Comanches," he said. "That peace was kept until a bad chief took my place. The chief made war on the Comanches and murdered them in San Antonio. He made war, too, on the Cherokees and drove them from the country. Now this has to be mended. War can do us no good."

In 1854 the Texas Legislature established an Indian reservation on the upper Brazos, and several hundred Indians of various tribes, including some Comanches, were kept there. But five years later, after frontier settlers had objected to having any Indians near them, officials decided to move the Indians north across the Red River. Major Robert S. Neighbors, in charge of the removal, wanted to let the Indians take their stock along, but this was not allowed. After delivering his charges, Neighbors wrote to his wife, "I have crossed all the Indians out of the heathen land of Texas." Back in Texas, Neighbors was assassinated on September 4, 1859, by a man who resented his befriending the Indians.

The removal left Texas free from settled Indians except for a few remnants here and there. Notable among those were small groups of the related Alabama and Coushatta tribes, who had come from east of the Mississippi River early in the 1800's. These friendly Indians lived mainly along the Neches River and the lower Trinity. In 1854 the state bought land to give them a small reservation in the wooded section of southeastern Texas called the Big Thicket.

Yet the removal did not end the danger of Indian raids for pioneer Texas families on the fringe of settlement. Roving warriors of the Plains tribes, mainly Comanches and Kiowas, continued to leave their homes north of the Red River for expeditions into Texas.

35

They hunted buffalo in the Panhandle, stole horses and cattle there and in other sections, attacked wagon trains, and raided and burned isolated homes. Many a lonely stone chimney bore mute testimony to such a blaze. The Indians killed and scalped scores of farmers and ranchmen and members of their families, sometimes carrying off women and children for ransom. Most of the raids were made at night, usually at full moon, but some attacks came by day.

Occasionally the Indians, not content with stealing horses and cattle, indulged in savage massacres. They wanted to frighten away the buffalo hunters and the settlers and to stop the building of railroads. On May 17, 1871, a band of about 150 Kiowas and Comaches, truants from the Fort Sill reservation, were raiding in northern Texas. They were led by four Kiowa chiefs—Satanta, Satank, Big Tree, and Eagle Heart. In the flats of Salt Creek, near the present town of Graham in southeastern Young County, the raiders swooped down on a wagon train.

This was a corn train of ten wagons drawn by four mule teams and one horse-and-mule team. It belonged to Captain Henry Warren, a government contractor, and was en route between Fort Griffin and Fort Richardson. The warriors destroyed the wagons, killing the wagonmaster and six teamsters. They left the victims stripped, scalped, and otherwise mutilated. They beheaded some and scooped out their brains. From others they slashed fingers, toes, and private parts and stuffed them into their mouths. They gashed bowels and placed live coals in the exposed abdomens. They tied one scalped man between two wagons and roasted him to a crisp. They drove away forty-one mules.

Only five teamsters escaped. One of them, Thomas Brazeal, although wounded in the foot, made his way twenty-two miles to Fort Richardson near Jacksboro. There he found General William T. Sherman, who was making an inspection tour of the frontier posts. Sherman ordered pursuit of the raiders.

Soon afterward, Chiefs Satanta, Satank, and Eagle Heart voluntarily visited the office of Laurie Tatum, agent for the Kiowas and Comanches, at Fort Sill. There Satanta said that he had led the raid and boasted of killing the teamsters and driving off the mules. Satanta

TORNADO CLOUD OVER DALLAS IN 1957

The trade-mark of the tornado is its pendant, usually funnel-shaped cloud. When this funnel dips to the ground with a terrific roar, the destruction starts.

Dallas NEWS *photograph by Bill Winfrey*

INDIANS PREPARING TO ATTACK SETTLERS
"Injuns!" even when spoken in a whisper could be a hair-raising word
on the Texas frontier.

HARPER'S WEEKLY, *May 2, 1868*

CREASING WILD HORSES
The most spectacular and least successful method of capturing wild horses
was by creasing . . . which called for an expert marksman.

Sketch by A. R. Ward, HARPER'S WEEKLY, *November 21, 1868*

Drying Buffalo Hides and Meat in the Panhandle, 1874
The grizzled buffalo hunters cleared the plains for the cowman. . . . In
the middle 1870's jerked buffalo hams sold at three cents a pound in
Dallas and hides brought $1.00 to $1.50.

Photograph by George Robertson

JAVELINAS IN THE BRUSH
"A ball of fur with a butcher-knife run through it . . . the meanest little
creature you can find."

Texas Parks and Wildlife Commission

MAKING SUGAR FROM CANE
Sirup-making days were neighborhood events.

HARPER'S WEEKLY, *April 4, 1874*

LIENDO PLANTATION
Bricks for the foundation and chimneys of the home, built in 1852–53,
were made from the red clay of the Brazos.

Dallas NEWS *photograph by Frank X. Tolbert*

SAN JOSÉ MISSION, SAN ANTONIO
The typical mission brought a pleasing Spanish architectural style to
Texas.

Texas Highway Department

made similar boasts to Sherman after the General arrived there a few days later. General Sherman ordered the arrest of all four chiefs. Young Eagle Heart escaped; but the others were manacled, placed in a wagon, and sent back to Texas for trial. On the way, Satank drew out a knife he had concealed and attacked one of his guards. He was killed by a soldier riding behind the wagon.

Satanta and Big Tree were tried in a civilian court at Jacksboro. They were convicted and condemned to die, but Governor Edmund J. Davis commuted their penalty to life imprisonment. The two chiefs were placed behind bars at Huntsville, but at the request of the federal commissioner of Indian affairs, they were released on parole on October 8, 1873. After renewed raids, Satanta was arrested and returned to the Texas prison, where he killed himself by jumping from a second-story window on October 11, 1878. Big Tree reformed, became a Baptist deacon, and lived until November 13, 1929.

The raids continued through the middle 1870's wiping out some families of new settlers and causing others to turn back to their old homes or find safer localities elsewhere in the West. The depredations were worst in the northern counties of Texas, since those were closest to the Indian reservations. Texas Rangers and army troops took the trails of some of the roving bands; but the Rangers, although valiant, were too few to be fully effective, and the troops moved too slowly and were untrained in Indian fighting. The soldiers came upon smoldering campfires but seldom saw any redskins.

After white buffalo hunters came down from western Kansas into the Texas Panhandle in the spring of 1874, the fury of the Indians rose to a high pitch. The slaughter of the buffalo, upon which they had depended for food, clothing, and shelter for generations, was so great that the extinction of the animals seemed near. The fact that the Indians had agreed to stay on the reservations and eat beef supplied by the government did not lessen their rage.

Urged on by a fanatic medicine man, bands of Comanches, Kiowas, and Cheyennes joined in the early summer of 1874 to try to wipe out the white buffalo hunters from the Texas Panhandle. At dawn on June 27, several hundred of them, in battle array and with

37

terrifying war whoops, attacked the little trading post of the hunters, known as Adobe Walls. This place, two miles north of the South Canadian River, had only a few crude buildings of sod and pickets surrounded by a stockade corral. At that time it was inhabited by twenty-eight men and one woman.

The Indian horsemen were armed with guns, bows, and lances. They pounded on the doors but were unable to break in. They killed and scalped two freighters who had been sleeping in their wagons outside, and later they mortally wounded a hunter who had run out into the stockade to look after the horses. The Indians fought most of the day but became wary of going within range of the hunters' Sharps rifles—guns which the redmen said would "shoot today and kill tomorrow." In the afternoon, when all the horses of the whites had been killed or driven off and several Indians were dead, the attackers retired.

While this attack ended most of the hunting in the Panhandle by whites for a year or more, it also strengthened the determination of the army to end such depredations. In late September of that year, a military force commanded by Colonel Ranald Mackenzie caught up with a large band of truant Comanches, led by Chief Quanah Parker, who were encamped in the deep Palo Duro Canyon.

At dawn on September 27, Mackenzie's soldiers scrambled down the cliffs of the canyon and attacked the big camp. Although casualties were few, the troopers burned the Indians' tipis and destroyed a large supply of food, including dried buffalo meat. They captured 1,424 horses and mules, of which 1,048 were shot to keep them from being recaptured. Afoot and discouraged, the Comanches plodded back to their reservation with nothing to show for their unlawful expedition.

With most of their tipis and horses gone and with buffalo becoming scarce in their area, the Comanches had less opportunity for raids into Texas. In the summer of 1875, a small band of them, half-starved, straggled in to Fort Sill and surrendered. They had to resign themselves to eating government beef. They still could be a nuisance as beggars and petty thieves, but their power as raiders of the settlements was broken.

SHOOTING DOVES AND QUAIL would have been snorted at as child's sport by the Texas frontiersman with his flintlock. Buffalo, panthers, and bears were more to his liking. Hunting them had an element of danger that spiced the adventure. True, he shot deer and wild turkeys, and sometimes even wild pigeons, to keep his dinner table loaded; but the stories he told his grandchildren more likely described his encounters with bruins in the deep woods.

Many early settlers found excitement in bear hunts in the fall after the crops were harvested. Next to the buffalo, as Noah Smithwick noted, the black bear was Texas' largest game animal. Smithwick, who had come to Texas in 1827, at nineteen, spent much of his time hunting bears on Hamilton Creek.

Smithwick trained a pack of hounds for trailing. They could chase the bears through cane brakes and thickets that horses could not penetrate. This pioneer also had a hunting pony so well trained that he could leave the mount anywhere and trust him to remain until wanted. Often, he recalled, "we had to rush in and dispatch a bear with knives when he was brought to bay, the dogs closing in on him so that it was impossible to shoot without endangering them."

Eli J. Shelton, who came to Texas in the same year as Smithwick but was only four then, grew up in the Honey Grove country and had many encounters with bears. Once, when he was just big enough to hold a rifle, he went after an oversize bruin that was bothering his father's cattle. After merely wounding the bear with his first shot, he gave chase with his dog. Noting that the beast was heading for a thicket, he crawled into a tree that had been blown down and waited to intercept him. As the bear passed, young Shelton

39

pulled the trigger and felled the animal, one of the largest that had been seen in the neighborhood.

On a later occasion, Shelton recalled, he and his wife's brother tracked a bear in the snow. They tried to keep their dogs in the rear, but the hounds took after the game ahead of the men. The bear made a big circle in the snow and finally neared the hunters again.

As the lumbering animal came within range, Shelton's brother-in-law shot at him but missed. Next Shelton fired, breaking the bear's thigh. As two of the dogs rushed up, Shelton advanced, gun in hand, toward the wounded bear. Then suddenly the bear sprang away from the hounds and attacked the hunter.

When Shelton thrust his rifle into the face of the bear, the latter grabbed it with his mouth. The hunter shoved the muzzle farther in, to keep the bear from biting him. But the bear took a firm hold on the gun. In trying to bite the barrel in two, he broke one of his teeth. Then he jerked the rifle out of his tormentor's hands.

By that time the dogs were closing in again and partly distracting the attention of the bear. Again he sprang from the dogs and tried to get at Shelton to claw and hug him with his huge paws, but the hunter dodged behind a tree.

The animal made repeated efforts to claw and bite, but finally Shelton pulled out his knife and plunged it into the bear's side. After a few more attempts, he was able to make a fatal thrust.

Later, during a Christmas frolic on the Sulphur River, the dogs chased a large bear that headed for a cane brake. As the bear passed, Shelton fired into the open mouth of the animal but only wounded him. Then Shelton pulled out his knife and stabbed him. The bear lunged at him, grabbing his arm and tearing the cuff off his coat sleeve. But the third stab of the knife proved fatal.

The late Frank Bryan of Groesbeck said that his father, who was born at Bryans Mill in Cass County before the Civil War, used to go bear hunting regularly in the fall. At that season the bears were rolling in fat before their winter hibernation.

Since bears ate pigs, the East Texas farmers didn't dare raise hogs in the unfenced woods country until after they had got rid of the bears. Bear carcasses also were useful to feed to the hogs. The fat was rendered into lard, which would not congeal even in cold weather. The bear hams were cured and smoked in the manner of hog hams.

The hounds were valuable, noted Bryan. "They always would close in if a bear were wounded enough to smell of fresh blood. That wild closing in for the kill usually would get a dog or two slapped or hugged to death. Thus it was necessary to kill the bear so as not to bring fresh blood. That was done by knocking it in the head with a stout hickory club about the size of a baseball bat."

The hounds, he explained, would bring a bear to bay by circling and hamstringing it, forcing it to sit down and slap at its pursuers. Then "a couple of Negro men, both armed with clubs, would approach from opposite directions. When the chance offered, one would knock the bear in the head. That way there was no fresh blood for the hounds to smell, and they would stay beyond reach of the slapping claws."

A few bears, he added, remained in the Hurricane Rake across northern Cass County until in the 1870's. "That's where the last bear hunting in East Texas was done. The Hurricane Rake was a landmark swath of twisted trees laid down by a cyclone in the 1830's."

Frederick Law Olmsted, who made a hunting trip into the Texas hill country in 1854, was told of an unusual bear hunt that had taken place just before his arrival. Armed only with a knife, a settler had gone after a bear on a rocky ledge. The bear gave the hunter a crushing hug, apparently trying to push him over the cliff, but the man succeeded in stabbing the bear seven times, killing him.

A few days later the same frontiersman wounded another bear and followed him into a pile of rocks. The bear disappeared into a hole through which his pursuer was unable to follow. The man closed the hole with a large slab and went back for help. Then he and a companion tried to smoke the bear out. When that failed, they enlarged the opening of the cave. Then, with his friend holding him by the heel, the hunter crawled in. After some groping, he found the carcass and attached a rope with which the two men pulled it out.

With one bear to his credit that day, the hunter went into the cave again, his double-barreled pistol in his hand and his knife in

41

his teeth. After making a narrow and difficult turn, he heard the breathing of another bear. In the darkness he aimed at the sound and fired both barrels, then retreated as fast as he could.

The two men closed the passage until they could make torches of beeswax to carry into the cave. Then the hunter went back in with a torch and found the bear he had shot. After it had been dragged out, he went in again. In a narrow cleft of the rocks he found a third bear dead, apparently smothered by smoke. With it out, the hunter squeezed in again and crawled on. In the light of his torch he saw a pair of eyes and shot between them. Then he saw another pair of eyes looking at him from another direction. He shot again, and soon his neighbors were carrying home five bears tied to poles—all the outcome of a single day's hunting.

In the winter of 1874–75, while hunting buffalo in the Texas Panhandle, John R. Cook and Buck Wood found two black bears in a persimmon grove. Cook shot one of them, breaking his back. Then Wood shot at the other, which had broken from cover and was running for the hills. A second shot by Cook killed the first bear, but Wood's first shot had gone wild. Both men chased the second bear, but Wood's horse was scared and would shy from the bear. Finally Wood dismounted and wounded the bear as his horse bolted for camp. Soon the bear was running in the same direction, with Wood pursuing on foot. As the bear circled and turned back toward the persimmon grove, Cook perched in the crotch of a small tree and waited.

By this time the wounded bear had slowed down, and his tongue was lolling. Cook prepared to try a shot from his perch, but Wood called to him not to shoot. Wood, who was gaining on the bear, then brought him down with a shot. Then the men discovered that Cook's horse also had bolted, leaving them afoot with the Canadian River between them and the camp. They stayed long enough to skin the bears and hang the hides and meat in trees before walking to the river and calling for someone to bring their horses across to them.

Sometimes capturing bears was almost as hazardous as hunting them. One such experience was that of Alligator Davis, a Texas

Ranger under the famous Jack Hays. Davis, who had won his nickname by dragging a six-foot alligator to shore from the Medina River barehanded, was on a scout with Hays. Thirty miles from the settlements, they saw two bear cubs. Davis wanted to capture one and take it back as a present to the wife of a merchant. After being clawed and bitten, he managed to tie the bear's legs and load the cub on his horse, back of the saddle.

The horse, disliking the idea of carrying a live bear cub, snorted and pranced; but Davis mounted and started off. Before long the bear took a bite out of the horse's rump. At that, the horse began bucking and sent Davis sailing into the air. The horse kept running until he joined a band of mustangs, from which he could not be recovered. Davis had to mount behind Hays and ride double the rest of the way back to San Antonio.

In November, 1885, some Panhandle cowpunchers roped a large black bear and took it to Mobeetie. They tied it to a post back of one of the saloons, intending to butcher it for Christmas. But one afternoon some inquisitive dogs came around, tormenting the bear. The animal broke its chains and took out through the Negro section of the town, going through paling fences as if they were straw. Half a dozen cowboys rode after the bear but could not catch it. Finally the bear ran into the business section of the frontier town, where the marshal downed it with a six-shooter.

Bear hunting had its share of tall tales. Bruin was the hero or villain of many stories when bears were common in Texas. One hunter, who had a stick of dynamite but was short of bullets, smeared his shoes with honey and left the dynamite similarly smeared, on the trail. A big bear soon followed and conveniently blew off his own head.

One pioneer Texas woman who wanted a new fur coat jerked a hibernating bear out of a hollow tree, sank her sharp teeth into his neck, and held on. As the bear tried frantically to escape, he tore himself out of his thick hide, which the woman quickly converted into a fine winter coat.

Another bear turned the tables on a hunter who kept trying to

43

shoot him without effect. The bear merely stood up and laughed. While the man was dozing earlier in front of his campfire, the bear had taken not only the bullets from his gun but the flint as well.

Out along the Pecos River, a cowboy was riding along the trail when his horse suddenly shied. Coming in the opposite direction were a mother bear and her two cubs. Wanting a cub, the cowhand jumped from his horse and, after a chase and the loss of his hat, captured one of the pair. But when he looked back at his horse, the mother bear was in the saddle, with the remaining cub on behind. The big bear had donned his hat and was riding off, quirting the horse with a rope.

Unlike the black bear, the passenger pigeon offered no sport to hunters; but its vast numbers made a lasting impression. Those who saw the great flocks of frontier days never forgot them. A flock might be more than a mile wide and several tiers deep. Flying at a mile a minute, it might take ten to fourteen hours to pass a given place. Such an air armada made the sky so dark that domestic fowls assumed that night had come and went to their roosts.

The passenger pigeon was a little larger and more brightly colored than the mourning dove or turtle dove. Its claim to note came mainly from its spectacular habit of assembling in flocks of almost unbelievable size. Near Louisville in 1813, John James Audubon saw one continuous flock which he believed held more than one billion birds. Another reliable ornithologist, Alexander Wilson, reported a flock which was 240 miles long and which appeared to have two billion birds.

About half of Texas was within the winter orbit of these whirring flocks that nested farther north. The birds ranged over the eastern part of the state, but lack of food kept them from the Great Plains. Millions of them sometimes roosted at the salt domes a few miles from Fort Houston, in what became Anderson County. They would alight on the trees and bushes with an almost deafening whir. Pioneer settlers and their wives and children would gather with rifles, scatter-guns, and poles for the slaughter. Some blinded the pigeons at night with lanterns or bonfires. The settlers filled barrels with salted meat and saved some of the down for use in pillows. They left many of the birds to rot.

The pigeons often visited the cross timbers of North Texas, where they could feast on acorns. They also liked seed grain. In the day when pioneer farmers sowed their wheat merely by scattering the grain on top of the ground by hand, a flock could eat a field clean of seed in a few minutes.

One of the flocks roosted near Jacksboro in the spring of 1876. "Wild pigeons are plenty in the woods west and north of town," George W. Robson wrote in the *Frontier Echo* of March 24. A week later he reported, "The wild pigeons are infesting this country in an untold quantity." That meant that the farmers feasted on pigeons— and that their hogs had a hard time finding enough mast until the next crop of acorns fell.

In the winter of 1881–82, wild pigeons occupied a large roost at the head of Frio Canyon in southern Real County and northern Uvalde County. A year later a large flock wintered near Lampasas. Occasionally they were abundant in Nueces Canyon in southeastern Edwards County and northwestern Uvalde County. Several birds were shot near Corpus Christi as late as 1889. The last wild pigeons reported in Texas were three shot by commercial hunters in 1896.

A first-hand account of passenger pigeons in the state was left by a veteran politician, the late Charles V. Terrell of Austin. Terrell, who grew up in Wise County, recalled in his memoirs that a post-oak timber on Sandy Creek afforded a temporary roost for a vast flock in the fall of 1870. In this woods, about ten miles northwest of Decatur, the acorn and berry crops had been unusually heavy.

At daybreak the pigeons would leave the roost and fly in separate large bunches in various directions to obtain food and water. At sundown all would return to the roost for the night. Residents of Decatur and surrounding sections took advantage of this opportunity to load their dinner tables with fresh game.

Terrell, who was only nine at the time, said that late one afternoon he and his brother John and two hired hands hitched two horses to a hack and drove to the roost. They had three double-barreled, muzzle-loading shotguns. It was a hazy evening, with low-hanging clouds. Soon, in the distance to the west, the hunters could see millions upon millions of the birds approaching. They were flying low, coming to the roost after an active day of foraging.

This impressive sight amazed the four youths. The pigeons were so thick, Terrell recalled, "that they darkened the sky like a Texas blue norther or an Oklahoma dust storm. There were so many birds and they were so heavy that they broke many of the limbs from the trees where they roosted and often broke down the trees themselves. When they left, the trees were so stripped of their branches that it looked as if a cyclone had passed."

As the pigeons approached, Terrell added, "the fluttering and flapping of their wings and the intense, continued chattering could be heard half a mile away. As darkness approached, they began to alight on the trees. With our lanterns we blinded them and then began to shoot. As I was not large enough to shoot, my job was to pick up the birds and put them in our sack."

Soon it became apparent that the shooting, with reloading, was too slow and too expensive. So the youths cut and stripped long poles and used them to knock the heads off the blinded birds. Quickly they filled their bag and started home. Since they had more pigeons than they needed, they gave some to neighbors.

The passenger pigeon, already on its way out at the time of Terrell's trip to a roost, had been noticed by many explorers and colonists. Its long tail, small neck and head, and attractive plumage gave it an air of elegance; and the speed of its flight led some to call it the blue meteor. There seemed no limit to the flocks in which it assembled for both nesting and migration. The birds in motion were an awesome spectacle, and the ground under a roost or a nesting place was left covered with inches of dung that made a marked addition to the fertility of the soil.

Commercial hunting, largely with nets, killed off the wild pigeons. By 1805 they were selling in New York and Boston at one cent each and whole shiploads were being sent abroad. Fifty years later the New York market was selling half a million pigeons a year. As a result, rewards of $2,250 offered in 1910 for a nest or nesting colony found no takers. The last captive bird died of old age in the Cincinnati Zoological Garden in 1914. Since then, only a few fading specimens mounted in museums have reminded visitors of the once abundant wild pigeons that stirred the imaginations of Texans and others on the frontier.

While East Texans knifed black bears and knocked passenger pigeons from their roosts, the more adventurous souls on the plains of West Texas were capturing wild horses and shooting buffalo for their meat and their hides.

The herds of mustangs in the grasslands were the progeny of horses the Spaniards had brought across the Atlantic. After wandering from ranches in Mexico or, more often, after escaping from Indians who had stolen them, they had gone wild and had multiplied. J. Frank Dobie estimated that at one time there were approximately one million mustangs in Texas and another million scattered elsewhere in the West.

Some of the early Texas settlers from states to the east went out into the plains to capture and break wild horses for cow ponies or for sale. The several methods they used were those already employed by Spanish, Mexican, and Indian mustangers.

The most spectacular method, but the one probably least often used, was creasing or nicking. Either running down the mustang he wanted or hiding beside a water hole or a salt lick, the hunter would send a bullet through the top of the animal's neck, at the root of the mane and close to the spinal column. This would stun the horse and cause him to drop to the ground long enough for the mustanger to tie the feet and put on a halter or a rope.

Creasing called for an expert marksman, and not even the best shot was successful often enough to make this method pay as well as others. In most cases, the bullet either missed and frightened away the horse or broke his neck. Frank Collinson, an early buffalo hunter, wrote that talk of going out to catch horses by creasing was "pure bunk. I have tried it many times and have broken their necks scores of times and never caught a horse that way and never knew anyone who did." Collinson also cited George Causey, one of the most successful buffalo hunters, who settled in the heart of the mustang range. When asked if he ever had creased a mustang, Causey answered, "No, but I have killed hundreds trying to. I generally break their necks."

Snaring, like creasing, would catch only one horse at a time. The hunter would place the noose of a rope on the ground near a salt lick or suspend it from branches on a mustang trail through a grove. But this method did not always work. It was difficult to hide the rope from the suspicious mustangs, and some of those caught would choke to death or get their necks broken.

Sometimes a pair of mustangers would waylay wild horses at a water hole. One would ride close to the drinking place while his partner concealed himself near the trail a mile or more away. After the mustangs had drunk their fill, the first man would come out and start chasing them at full speed. Because of the water they had just drunk, they would be unable to run as fast as usual. As they came to the place where the second rider was concealed, he would rush out after them, thus causing them to change their course. In the ensuing confusion, the men might be able to rope a choice mustang or two.

Another method, which called for two or more men, was walking the mustangs down. The men, on horseback, would take turns following a band of mustangs without trying to chase them. When the rider came close, the wary mustangs would dash off, often going around in a circle and thus wearing themselves down. At night, a partner either would relieve the rider or would bring him food and a fresh mount. After several days during which the wild horses were kept away from water and were unable to obtain enough grass or sleep, they became so nearly exhausted that they could be roped or driven into a pen.

On the Staked Plains of West Texas in the spring of 1878, a buffalo hunter, John R. Cook, watched an outfit of eight Mexicans, with a score of saddle horses capture thirty-five wild mares which they wanted for breeding, The leader, named Valdez, picked a band of mustangs and started two of his horsemen toward them, walking their mounts. When the riders came close, the mustangs would spurt off, sometimes going fifteen to twenty miles before starting to graze again. As they went around in a big circle, the other Mexicans were able to foresee their movements and to take water, meat, *tortillas,* and fresh horses to the pair following the wild band.

On the third day, which was cold, the older and weaker mustangs dropped out of the circle. On the fourth day the others were so tired that the Mexicans had to come close and drive them to keep them moving. Some of the horses would lie down, said Cook. "Then the stinging rawhide of the lariat would be snapped at them and strike unerringly where the vaquero intended it to. Up they would get and reel ahead." That night the men drove the mares into their camp, where the next morning they roped, crippled, and branded them. After a few days of rest, water, and grass, they were ready to be trailed to a ranch in New Mexico.

Many of the mustangs were captured by driving bands of them into a large pen or corral. Often the posts and poles of the fence were covered with brush to keep the wild horses from becoming suspicious. Outside the gate were wings which extended out in both directions, sometimes for half a mile, to help guide the mustangs into the pen. Although the pen had to be built where there were trees and bushes to be cut, it was placed, if possible, near a watering place of the roaming bands.

With a rider posted at the end of each wing, the other riders drove a band of mustangs toward the pen. Some of the horses would turn away from the pen, and others might have to be chased two or three days before they would go between the wings. When they entered the wings, the men stationed there would join in driving them toward the gate. Once they were inside, the gate would be closed and a blanket thrown over it. The captive horses would be brought under control by necking them with gentle mounts or by handicapping them by fastening a heavy wooden clog to a front leg or tying one end of a short rope to a front leg and the other end to a hind leg.

Much more numerous on the Texas plains, and attracting many more hunters, were the vast herds of buffalo. One pioneer described a herd that he said covered fifty square miles. Another told of seeing between two and three million "shaggies" at one time.

49

Unlike the mustangs, the buffalo rarely were wanted as captives; they were in demand for their meat and especially for their hides. In the middle 1870's, jerked buffalo hams sold at three cents a pound in Dallas and buffalo hides brought a dollar to a dollar and a half.

In those days, long wagon trains hauled the hides to Denison and Dallas from Fort Griffin, the chief headquarters of the Texas hunters. One of the trains might include as many as forty wagons, each drawn by six or eight mules. The dried hides were piled high and were held in place with ropes and poles. After the first railroad reached Fort Worth, in July, 1876, most of the hides were shipped from that city.

Out on the unsettled plains of western Texas, an estimated 1,500 hunters were killing buffalo for their hides in the winter of 1876–77. From Fort Griffin they worked in small groups, peeling and drying the hides as the animals were killed. An expert rifleman could keep several skinners busy. But all had to keep a sharp eye out for hostile Comanches, who resented the slaughter.

At Fort Griffin, on the Clear Fork of the Brazos River, about four acres of ground were piled with hides waiting for wagon trains to haul them to Fort Worth. In the latter town a reporter noted one morning in May, 1877, a train of ten wagons coming in. "In front were eleven yokes of oxen driven by one man and dragging after them four large wagons, heavily laden. Two other teams, with seven yokes each, drawing three wagons, followed. There probably were 2,500 to 3,000 hides in the train."

Another Fort Worth observer that spring was impressed with one lot of 60,000 hides piled high on a platform near the Texas and Pacific Railroad. During the season, Fort Griffin sent about 200,000 hides, which brought the hunters about one dollar each. By that time, however, the Texas herds were almost killed off.

In January, 1877, a correspondent from Fort Griffin described the weapon and method of one hunter. He had "a regular hunter's rifle, a Sharps breech-loading, which shoots ninety-five grains of powder. The hunter, when he espies a herd, crawls on all fours until within range, then proceeds to shoot. When once the beasts smell blood, they stand still until the hunter shoots them down. Thousands of the animals are killed daily."

It took a big, heavy rifle for the shaggies. Many of the professionals used the expensive, long-range Sharps, made especially for buffalo hunting. With one of these rifles, weighing ten to sixteen pounds, a hunter could kill fifty or more buffalo in a day. With many hunters at work, the carnage was enormous. A surveying party found in one place 6,500 carcasses from which the hides had been stripped. A railway conductor said he could have walked a hundred miles along the right of way without stepping off the carcasses.

One of the most successful Texas hunters was J. Wright Mooar, who alone killed about twenty thousand head. Approaching a herd, he would stake his horse and go closer afoot, finally getting down on his hands and knees. He regarded a shot in the lungs as even better than one in the heart. "When you'd shoot a buffalo in the lights," he said, "he'd throw blood out of his nose. Then he'd step backward a step or two, flop over, and die. If you shot him through the heart, he'd run about four hundred yards before he'd fall, and he'd take the herd with him."

In camp the Mooar outfit varied their diet of buffalo hump with tongues. After being boiled until tender, the tongues were fried in marrow from the big bone of the animal's hip. "We pushed the marrow out with a stick," said Mooar. "It wasn't hard like tallow but was soft like lard. We used it to season biscuits. Sometimes we stuck bones in the fire and roasted them, then used the marrow as butter."

Mooar was one of the few hunters to shoot a white buffalo in Texas. The true white buffalo was an albino and was valued by some of the Indians for ceremonial use. A white buffalo robe might bring as much as one thousand dollars. Mooar shot this one near his camp in Nolan County in the fall of 1876.

The slaughter of the buffalo and the waste of meat did not go on without protest. After the legislatures of several states had passed laws to limit the killing, Texas lawmakers seemed about to adopt such a measure also. Then General Philip H. Sheridan addressed them. The hunters should receive medals instead of censure, he said. He declared that the hide men "will do more in the next year to settle the vexed Indian question than the entire Army has done in the last thirty years. They are destroying the Indians' commissary. Send them powder and lead. Let them kill, skin, and sell until the buffaloes are exterminated. Then your prairies can be covered with cattle and the festive cowboy who follows the hunter as a second forerunner of advanced civilization."

The General's prediction proved true. After the buffalo herds were gone, it was easier to keep the Indians on their reservations and soon the cleared ranges were populated with cattle.

In later decades, Texas had its annual slaughter of doves, quail, ducks, wild turkeys, and deer; and some communities held fox, wolf, coyote, coon, or rattlesnake hunts. But, except for a few scarce mountain lions and bobcats and an occasional golden eagle hunted by airplane, about the only game animal left to offer much excitement or hazard for hunters was that ferocious pig of the Southwest, the javelina. The name is pronounced "have-uh-lee-nuh," with the accent on the "lee." The animal is not to be confused with the familiar razorback, which is the domestic pig run wild.

The javelina, sometimes called the collared peccary or the musk hog, is one of the gamest animals of the Americas. Cowmen avoid its razor-like teeth as they do the fangs of a rattlesnake.

Early settlers in Texas were wary of this mean-tempered pig. One frontiersman described it as "a ball of fur with a butcher-knife run through it." Another pioneer, Noah Smithwick, said that he and his neighbors preferred hunting mountain lions, since javelinas cut up so many of the dogs.

Teddy Roosevelt came to Texas to hunt javelinas and went home with a full bag. Willis Van Devanter, retired associate justice of the Supreme Court, bagged two prize specimens in Texas in 1937. E. M. (Ted) Dealey, publisher of the Dallas *Morning News,* who had hunted grizzly bears in Alaska and mountain lions in Mexico, found some of his biggest thrills in shooting javelinas. "They're scrappers," he said. "The grizzlies are more dangerous, but the javelinas are the meanest little creatures you can find. They'll kill you if they can. I'd hate to get one in a corner."

The javelina, he pointed out, has no tusks: "He bites with his canine teeth. They mesh closely and are as sharp as razors. A javelina can take a man's leg off with one bite." Many a hunter has had to climb the nearest tree after wounding a javelina. Some have stayed treed for hours. The treed hunter is lucky if he has been able to bring a gun up with him. One had to kill twenty-six besiegers before he dared to slide down.

Although an unusual boar may weigh sixty pounds, the average is only about forty-six pounds. The ordinary sow weighs about forty-four pounds. Ted Dealey noticed that the tiny feet of the javelina do not hamper his speed. "When you jump a bunch of javelinas, it's just like flushing a covey of quail. They'll run in all directions. For the first hundred yards, they run as fast as racehorses."

Old-timers used to say that a wounded javelina would call others to his aid and that the embattled band would chase the hunter, who might be killed if he couldn't climb a tree in a hurry. James H. Cook, a frontier cowman, had several tilts with javelinas in Texas back in the 1870's. "When one squealed with pain," he said, "its comrades would come promptly to the rescue."

Anyone who goes after javelinas needs to be well armed. "It isn't safe to hunt them with anything but a high-powered rifle," declared Dealey. "You couldn't stop one with a shotgun. I shoot behind the shoulder, where the blade joins the neck. Usually this shot breaks the backbone. If it doesn't, it will break the legs and keep the javelina from running away. Sometimes a shot in the heart does the job."

Opinions differ on the edibility of javelina meat. Decades ago, when the animals were more plentiful, their flesh was common fare for Mexican ranch hands, many of whom liked it as well as venison. Some compared it to veal. "It tastes like nothing but javelina," said Ted Dealey; "but it could be called a cross between pork and lamb, with the accent on the lamb."

The animals have a distinctive odor. "You can't eat the meat of the boar," added the Dallas publisher. "It has too strong an odor. You hardly can stand to be within ten feet of him. He stinks. The odor comes from a gland in the back."

This scent gland or musk bag is located on the animal's rump.

53

The odor enables the javelinas to keep together and makes it easier for the young to follow their mothers through the dense undergrowth. The boars, by rubbing their backs against low limbs, map the range of the herd. The scent appears also to be a mating lure.

The javelina, which scientists know as *Pecari angulatus,* is the only wild hog native to the United States. The adult has a mane of long black hair. It has a grizzled appearance on its upper parts, from grayish white rings near the tips of the black hairs.

Once the javelina was found from the Arkansas backwoods to the steamy jungles of South America. In this country, it survives mainly in those parts of the Southwest that have dense thickets of prickly pear, chaparral, or other growths that offer protection. Sometimes it finds a home in rocky canyons or caverns. Where there is no water, it can obtain drink as well as food from the prickly pear, a common cactus. The herd has a small range, sleeping near its feeding grounds. There may be as many as fifty pigs in a herd.

Catching young javelinas has been a Texas sport for more than a century. In 1841 the Earl of Derby sent W. P. Smith to capture a few for his collection at Knowsley. Smith succeeded, catching some in hollow trees and others in pits. Pioneer settlers occasionally made pets of young javelinas. Some even trained them as watchdogs. In the latter capacity the pigs often showed too much zeal and chewed the dogs of friendly visitors.

When the javelina was more common, its hide was an important article of commerce. Stores in Texas country towns like Oakville and Tilden had their back rooms stacked as high as a man's head with piles of javelina hides. Hunting the animals for their hides was a boon to settlers when drouth took their crops and grass. Sometimes a hunter would bring in sixty or seventy pelts.

The hides make good leather and still are in demand. As recently as the season of 1936–37 a Uvalde dealer, Tom Neal, handled fifteen thousand javelina hides, most of them imported from Mexico. They were shipped to New York and to France to be made into purses, gloves, and shoes. The bristles were used in brushes.

This killing of javelinas for their hides finally made the animals so scarce above the border that in 1939 the Texas Legislature added

54

the javelina to the list of protected game animals. It set an open season, with a bag limit. The sale of hides taken in Texas was banned, although trading in those from Mexico was allowed. In recent years some Texans have hunted javelinas with bows and arrows.

Occasional drouths, which have hurt the deer crop in Texas by searing the grass, have had less effect on the javelinas. The wild pigs can live on cactus and other hardy growths not much affected by dry spells. The hunter who wants rugged sport can still find it in the javelina country. But he had better leave at home his fancy clothes and city-bred dogs. And a six-shooter in his belt might come in handy in case he has to climb a tree.

STATELY MOSS-LADEN OAKS in southeastern Texas could whisper many a tale of plantation balls. There were formal minuets, waltzes, and lively capers in which young couples cut the pigeon's wing to such tunes as "Rosin the Bow" and "Jin Along Josey." No lore on cowboys and the open range should obscure the fact that much of early Texas was a land of broad plantations ruled from patriarchal mansions.

Planters from the Deep South who sought cheap land farther west brought their slaves with them and established plantations like those they had known. Although the tradition of moonlight and magnolias was a bit less strong in Texas, ante bellum life in the lower valleys of the Trinity and Brazos rivers easily could have been mistaken for that of Georgia.

Settlers found the soil of the bottom lands unusually fertile and soon put their Negroes to work planting cotton, which quickly became the main cash crop. Some of the smaller plantations were worked entirely by white labor, either because the owners could not afford slaves or because, especially in the case of the German settlers, they did not believe in slavery. But on most of the plantations, the work of planting, cultivating, picking, and hauling was done by slaves.

William Bollaert, an Englishman who traveled through much of the Texas Republic in 1842–44, found that generally the slaves were well treated and were not overworked. On the better plantations, each slave family had its own log cabin, with half an acre of garden and some poultry and a few pigs. The Negroes had Saturday afternoon and Sunday off from field work, and those who grew old were kept instead of being sold to other masters. The women worked in the fields with the men, leaving their children in a log-cabin nursery in charge of an old woman who would stop a youngster's crying by giving him a lump of bacon.

Not all were that well off. Frederick Law Olmsted, who spent the early months of 1854 in Texas, described the slave quarters he found on a small plantation at the eastern edge of the state: They were "a rough enclosure of logs, ten feet square, without windows, covered with slabs of hewn wood four feet long. The great chinks are stopped with whatever has come to hand—a wad of cotton here and a corn shuck there. The suffering from cold within them must be great. The day before, we had seen a black girl of twelve or fourteen years sitting on a pile of logs before a house we passed, in a driving sleet, having for her only garment a short chemise."

On the larger plantations, bells called the slaves to and from work. Two brothers, Robert and David G. Mills, had bells cast in Philadelphia for their three plantations and several others. While at the foundry, they dropped fifty Mexican dollars into each bell as it was being cast. People said that, in a still morning, they could hear these bells five miles away.

Cotton was not entirely new to Texas. In a much earlier period, Spaniards at the missions had taught some of the Indians to grow a little cotton, but that cultivation had not lasted. Cotton was revived on a larger scale when, in the early 1820's, it was planted by Stephen F. Austin's colonists along the Brazos and by other settlers to the east.

The first cotton gin in Texas probably was that which Jared E. Groce built about 1825 on his plantation in the Austin colony. Many other gins were erected in the next few years. As there were no commercial gins, each large planter set up a small one on his land. The lesser growers, who had no gins, hauled their bolls to the nearest gin and paid one-tenth to one-eighth of the lint as a ginning fee.

The plantation gins were of many makes, all patterned after that of Eli Whitney. The typical one had two parts—the gin house and the press. Usually the former was a two-story frame building, with the machinery on the first floor and the gin stand and storage rooms on the second. Two teams of horses or a yoke of oxen powered the gin. The press was built in the open, just outside the gin house, and was operated with horses or oxen.

From a small beginning, the output of Texas cotton mounted rapidly. The planters sent about 500 bales to market in 1826, double that amount the next year, and 5,000 bales in 1832. In 1834 many of the growers received 14.5 cents a pound, and land prices rocketed. Ira Ingram, on the lower Colorado, estimated that "there is enough land in Texas, within the fine-staple region, to supply the demand, at present, of the whole civilized world."

Some of the growers suffered from lack of enough labor for planting and harvesting. Many grumbled at having to pay $2.50 a bale for bagging and rope, and the smaller ones winced at the ginning fee. Nearly all were at a disadvantage from poor processing. In 1844 a Galveston newspaper noted that Texas cotton, although often fine staple, "has frequently been placed in the lowest class solely on account of the slovenly manner in which it has been put up."

Moving the cotton to market was a task that often involved much time and expense. Sometimes boats came up the lower Trinity and Brazos and took down part of the cotton, but periods of low water and snags or other obstacles in the stream made them undependable. Most of the lint had to be hauled in wagons drawn slowly over long distances by mules or oxen.

At the eastern edge of Texas, Olmsted passed many cotton wagons, "two or three sometimes together, drawn by three or four pairs of mules or oxen, going slowly toward Natchitoches or Grand Ecore, each managed by a Negro driver. The load is commonly five bales of four hundred pounds, and the cotton comes in this tedious way, over execrable roads, 100 and even 150 miles. At night we met three or four teams half mired in a swamp." Sometimes this cotton could be shipped down the Sabine River, but when the water was low, it had to be hauled fifty miles farther to the Red River.

To the west, Olmsted passed more wagons loaded with cotton. "One carrying eight bales, drawn by ten lean oxen, was from San Marcos, bound for the coast. The teamster, who was on horseback, told us his best day's work was ten miles. In the creek near which we made our camp was a cotton team stalled, and it was late at night before the whipping and swearing came to an end."

Dr. John Washington Lockhart, who had a plantation of one thousand acres in Washington County, told of hauling cotton to Houston by ox wagon. Teamsters charged fifty cents a hundred pounds and regulated the loads by the number of oxen on each team. A five-yoke team would carry five bales, and a six-yoke team six bales. With good roads and mild weather, the round trip could be made in two weeks; otherwise it took nearly a month. The wagoner rode a Spanish pony and camped at night, using either a sleeping bag or a small tent.

Distances from markets and lack of transportation checked the spread of cotton plantations into northeastern Texas. Until the first railroads penetrated that section in 1872, farmers there had put most of their land in grain, used locally or sold to army posts. Yet some cotton had been grown as early as the republic period and smuggled into the United States. A little was shipped down the Red River on rare occasions when high water and freedom from log jams enabled boats to come up that far. Other cotton was hauled laboriously to Jefferson for shipment down the Red. During the Civil War, some went by wagon as far as Brownsville, where it brought fantastic prices and was run through the Union blockade.

For a time, sugar vied with cotton as a crop on the Texas plantations. In the lower valley of the Brazos—and, to a lesser degree, in the valleys of the Trinity, the Colorado, and the Guadalupe—some early settlers noticed that much of the soil closely resembled that of the sugar country in southern Louisiana. The flat, alluvial bottom land looked good for cane.

In the middle 1820's some of the settlers who had come from the Old South began planting patches of cane, each turning out a few hogsheads of sugar. By 1828 they were building sugar mills, confident that they could sell sugar cheaper than that which came from New Orleans. But the 1829 crop of 1,840 hogsheads was poor in quality, "little more than partially crystallized molasses."

In the early 1830's several planters along the Trinity and the

59

Colorado cultivated sugarcane, but the quality of the resultant sugar was mediocre. The first permanent sugar mill in Austin's colony was the one which William Stafford built in Fort Bend County, on the lower Brazos, in 1834. It was destroyed two years later in the revolution against Mexican rule.

The big spurt in Texas sugar growing came when hard times hit the cotton planters in the 1840's. Worms and wet weather struck heavy blows to the cotton crop on the coast in 1840, 1842, and 1843. Worse, cotton prices dropped to ruinous lows during that decade. As a result, many of the planters shifted some of their fields to cane. In 1843, Captain William Duncan built on his Caney Creek plantation Texas' first steam-powered sugar mill.

Some of the planters became enthusiastic. In the next year John Sweeny on the San Bernard harvested one hundred hogsheads of sugar of fine quality, while Duncan, using only fifty of his thirteen thousand acres, had an even larger crop. "The sugar-making business is going to bring Texas lands into notice," wrote Colonel James W. Morgan from his Galveston Bay home in 1846. "A few years hence, Galveston Bay and lands in the vicinity will be covered with sugar cane, leaving spots on the margin only for residences." Many other planters shared his opinion.

For a time this rosy view seemed justified. In 1847 the Brazos and Colorado valleys had a score of sugar plantations, and new ones were being established every year. In 1849 the Texas output jumped to 7,351 hogsheads of sugar and 441,638 gallons of molasses. Almost everyone who could obtain seed was planting cane. On his Waldeck Plantation Morgan R. Smith spent fifty thousand dollars in building a brick sugar house with a steam mill and a refinery.

The peak year in Texas sugar production was 1852. The crop was 11,023 hogsheads. At that time, Brazoria County alone had twenty-nine sugar plantations representing a total investment of $1,134,000. The Texas sugar country had fifteen horse-powered mills and twenty-nine steam mills. Still more were in prospect.

In Caldwell County in 1853, Hugh Withers put much of his land into cane. The yield was heavy, and many a vat of molasses was boiled for winter use. The syrup-making days were neighborhood events, one of his sons recalled. The men sat cross-legged or stood around the vat, telling yarns and tasting the liquid at various stages, while the boys chewed sticks of cane until they had aching stomachs.

The decline in Texas sugar growing stemmed from several unfavorable seasons but mainly from the large capital required. A first-rate sugar plantation called for a capital outlay of fifty thousand dollars. That was more than the average planter could afford. So most of the growers went back to cotton, although a few continued until the Civil War made shipments difficult.

While it lasted, the Texas sugar boom helped, along with cotton exports, to develop some of the state's finest plantations. The plantation homes varied widely in size, architectural style, and building materials. Often the original house was a double log cabin, with the breezy space between the two sections, called the dog trot, used to store saddles and other equipment. In summer the family might eat its meals there. The cabin walls were chinked with mud or mortar, and the roof was of oak or cypress shakes. Those planters who prospered built larger and more comfortable homes.

The Ellersley Plantation of John Greenville McNeel, in Brazoria County, became one of the outstanding show places and was noted for its Thoroughbred horses. McNeel's father had started it with "a good log house, on the verge of a pine grove, shaded by China trees." The son built, of handmade brick, a two-story plantation home of twenty-one rooms. It had large pillars on two sides and galleries for the whole length. The hearths and mantels were of marble, the floors luxuriously carpeted, and the furniture of walnut and mahogany. Also of brick were the overseer's house and the sugar house. The main products of the fields were cotton, sugar, corn, potatoes, and yams.

The Waldeck Plantation of Morgan R. Smith, in the same county, was one of the largest and most efficient in the Sugar Bowl. Its crops sometimes brought as much as seventy thousand dollars a year. In addition to the imposing home, it had a brick church for slaves, built in 1856 and one of the finest of its kind in the region.

The home of Dr. Lockhart in Washington County, in the Brazos

61

valley, was one and one-half stories and was built entirely of timber cut on the place. It had fluted pillars and dormer windows and was finished in plaster and walnut. In front of the house was a long row of crepe myrtles. The slave quarters faced a lane, with trees and rose bushes in front of each cabin. The plantation had its own store, blacksmith shop, and mule-powered cotton gin.

In the same county was the larger Glenbythe Plantation of Thomas Affleck. Its 3,500 acres of fields, pastures, and woodland were looked after by 120 slaves. The plantation home, in a grove of live oaks, had six bedrooms and two long galleries. Other buildings, in addition to the Negro quarters, included an overseer's house, a carriage house, a pigeonry, a church, a hospital, a sugar mill, a cotton gin, a sawmill, and a blacksmith shop.

On a high bluff on the east side of the Brazos, in Waller County, was the Bernardo Plantation of Jared E. Groce, from Alabama. The rambling home, built in 1822, was of cottonwood logs, hewn and counter-hewn. Polished walnut columns supported the house-length gallery. Each room had a fireplace of sandstone taken from the river. In addition to the main home, there were many separate buildings, including a kitchen, a dairy, a doctor's house, a guest house, and, off beside a small lake, quarters for home and field slaves.

In its first two years, the plantation depended for meat mainly on wild game—deer, turkey, and mustang, often without bread or salt. Much of the mustang meat was jerked—cut into strips and dried on a scaffold of small poles. Groce sent his first cotton to Mexico by muleback, trading it for coffee, tea, other provisions, and bags of Mexican dollars. Later he shipped cotton to New Orleans. His home, on the road from Houston to Austin, had many visitors, including General Sam Houston, a friend of the family. Houston's revolutionary army camped on the plantation for two weeks in the spring of 1836.

In the same county was the larger Liendo Plantation of Groce's son, Leonard W. Groce, which in time spread over 6,700 acres and was worked by about three hundred slaves. Bricks for the foundation and chimneys of the big Liendo home, built in 1852–53, were from the red clay of the Brazos. The house was colonial in style, with the outside walls of drop-lead siding painted white. The pine lumber had been shipped from Georgia by sea and hauled from the coast by ox teams. On the ceiling of the drawing room was painted a design of morning glories and roses. The kitchen, separate from the house, had facilities for roasting a whole beef at once. The outer buildings included a guest house and a school for the eleven Groce children and those of neighbors.

In good years Liendo's crops brought $80,000 to $100,000. During the Civil War, Union soldiers captured at Galveston were housed in a camp on the plantation. After the war, Major General George A. Custer and his troops were stationed there for three months. In the early 1870's the plantation home and part of the land were sold to Dr. Edmund Montgomery and his wife, Elizabet Ney, the sculptor.

Farther down, in a clump of live oaks on Oyster Creek, in Brazoria County, twelve miles from the Gulf, was the Eagle Island Plantation of Leonard Groce's sister and her husband, William H. Wharton. Developed as a sugar plantation about 1826, it had some of the richest alluvial soil in Texas. The original log house gave way to one of the most elaborate plantation homes, in which thirty guests could be entertained. Ships had brought its lumber and other materials from Mobile. The grounds were carefully landscaped, and the buildings included a brick sugar house.

Another noteworthy plantation in Brazoria County was Peach Point, west of the river, the home of Stephen F. Austin's sister and her husband, James F. Perry. Austin designed the house and encouraged the planting of orchards and a garden. In addition to cotton, this plantation grew corn, sugar cane, and a little tobacco. The house, at the edge of the woods, looked out over several miles of prairie to the Gulf. Rutherford B. Hayes was a guest there in 1848.

Brazoria County had many other large plantations. One was the well-developed Retrieve Plantation started by Abner Jackson and later improved by his partner, James Hamilton, with slaves brought from South Carolina. Its brick buildings included a two-story home, a sugar house, and a group of cabins. Another was Orozimbo, the home of Dr. James E. Phelps, one of Austin's early colonists. On this fine cotton plantation General Antonio López de Santa Anna, president of Mexico, was held as a prisoner of war for several months in 1836.

Near Cedar Creek on Galveston Bay was Evergreen Plantation, which Ashbel Smith bought from Moseley Baker in 1847. Smith raised corn, potatoes, sugarcane, and some livestock. In the present Grimes County, Jared E. Groce established Groce's Retreat to get away from the malaria of the Brazos River bottoms. Texas' interim president, David G. Burnet, stopped there with his cabinet for several days in March, 1836.

In northern Texas the Red River country had several noteworthy plantations. The 1,500-acre Pecan Point Plantation in Red River County was developed by Matthew Watson and his son John. The latter was noted for his lavish entertaining. The buildings included a cotton gin and press.

Even more famous was Glen Eden, built in Grayson County in 1845 by Holland Coffee, who had established a trading post at Preston in 1837. Although it was made of split logs, it was covered outside with clapboards and it had chimneys of local stone. With its wide halls, ornate banisters, and plastered inside walls, it was one of the finest homes in the region. Coffee kept his wine cellar well stocked and made his home notable for hospitality. Among the guests there were Sam Houston, Robert E. Lee, and Ulysses S. Grant. The home was dismantled in 1942 to make way for Lake Texoma.

In eastern Texas, plantations of note included Forest Hills, in Cherokee County, whose log mansion was built in 1847; Wyalucing, near Marshall, whose two-story brick home Beverly L. Holcombe built in 1850 and which later became the western postal headquarters of the Confederacy; and the 10,000-acre Monte Verdi of Julien S. Devereux in Rusk County, worked by about eighty slaves. The two-story home at Monte Verdi, for which lumber and many of the furnishings were hauled from Shreveport, became one of the landmarks of the region.

Also in Rusk County, three miles north of Henderson, was the Morris Plantation home, built by Judge William Wright Morris in 1849. This house of white clapboards had high-ceilinged rooms divided by a hall. Across the front was a porch with square white columns. Cooking was done in a huge fireplace equipped with iron pots and pans. The Negro cook, Aunt Ann, made soda-and-buttermilk biscuits in a Dutch oven with fire coals on the lid. Served with them for breakfast were butter, peach preserves, sausage, lye hominy, and fried apples or sweet potatoes. A colored girl used a brush of peacock feathers to keep flies off the table.

The Morris home, built near a spring, had in its dooryard white syringa, yellow jonquils, and red roses. There were rope swings for children. Spring brought the scent of apple and locust blossoms. Through the year the big smokehouse held home-cured hams and bacon, potatoes, dried fruits, and other food. Near the walled spring were crocks of fresh buttermilk for travelers.

The planters grew most of the food they needed, bringing in only coffee, tea, spices, and a few other items. Often potatoes, both Irish and sweet, would be piled on the ground for winter use and covered with corn stalks. The first cold spell in the fall would bring a butchering of hogs, followed by the curing of hams and bacon and the rendering of lard. Usually wild game was plentiful, and fish could be caught in most of the streams. Many of the plantations raised pumpkins and melons, but only a few grew fruit trees.

At Henry Austin's Bolivar Plantation on the Brazos, his sister, visiting there in 1838, noted: "They brought in a fine buck this morning. We get rabbits like chickens, and fish—great buffalo and perch—whenever we choose to catch them. There is a lake, too, fed by springs, full of fish."

Yet, while the larger and more prosperous plantations set fine tables, the smaller and more struggling ones fared less well. There was plenty of meat, whether beef, pork, or game; but sometimes it was accompanied by little more than corn bread, molasses, and milk. Often, too, the cutlery was primitive. Visitors on a plantation on the San Bernard River reported that the dinner served them would satisfy an epicure but added that it was handled with bowie and pocket knives and forks made from cane, while gourds were used for drinking.

But, whatever the smokehouse supplied, hospitality was open-handed and was not limited to relatives or friends. At his beautiful home on Pleasant Grove Plantation, Leander McNeel used to keep a slave out at the roadside to invite any belated traveler to stop for the night without charge.

Most of the clothing in the earlier days was made of homespun cotton and woolen cloth, dyed with the juices of local barks and berries. As means of transportation were improved, bolts of yard goods and even some "store-bought" clothes were brought in. Shoes made by slaves or itinerant shoemakers also gave way to factory-made footwear. The white women and girls had fancy dresses and silk stockings for parties and tried to keep up with the latest fashions.

Mail was carried by private conveyance. On the Brazos, Dr. Lockhart recalled: "Generally some man would volunteer, the neighbors paying his expenses, to go to Houston, the nearest post office, and bring the mail for all. Many a time I have seen a man mounted on a mule, if the roads were muddy—if dry, on a Spanish pony—with his blanket, rawhide rope, coffeepot, and wallet of provisions, with a pair of old saddlebags, start for Houston. In three or four days he would be back, bringing joy to all who wished to hear from the other states."

On Sunday the plantation families dressed up for church. Often the children went in the family carriage, sometimes accompanied by a colored boy who carried a silver cup to bring water to any who became thirsty. The parents followed in a buggy. Except for the married couples, the men and women sat in separate sections at church. In the early days, some families barred dancing, card games, and even piano playing, but later such restrictions were relaxed.

Some of the plantations, especially those near the Gulf Coast, had their own tracks for horse races. Other social events included camp meetings, dances, weddings, christenings, Fourth of July celebrations, and political barbecues.

In spite of their isolation, the Texas planters, like the small farmers and stockmen, were sensitive to political and economic winds. They rallied quickly to the War of Independence in the spring of 1836. After the fall of the Alamo at San Antonio on March 6, many joined the tattered army of General Sam Houston which, six

66

weeks later, defeated the large force of General Antonio López de Santa Anna at San Jacinto on April 21 and freed Texas from Mexican rule.

Decades later, as in the Old South, the Civil War brought drastic changes in plantation life in Texas. The planters had trouble getting the freedmen to work. In time they evolved the share-cropper system that in turn gave way to independent farms, many of them cultivated with machinery. After the plantations were broken up, most of the old manor homes were destroyed by fire, flood, or termites or fell to pieces from lack of repair. Only a few remained as symbols of a bygone era.

N<small>O ONE HAS DISPUTED THE TRUTH</small> that Berta Hart Nance put into one of her poems:

> *Other states were carved or born;*
> *Texas grew from hide and horn.*

The wind-bitten cowman, who did nearly all his work on horseback, became, rightly, the symbol of the state. The cotton grower, the oil driller, and the later industrial worker could not compete in glamour with the cowboy who wore a wide-brimmed hat and swung his lariat with a startlingly accurate aim.

Aside from glamour, cattle have been of major pocketbook interest to Texans ever since Spaniards trailed seed stock to the missions they established along several rivers in the area. Whether the cattle were leathery Longhorns or the white-faced Herefords of later days, they helped Texas to prosper.

Many of the early Spanish cattle escaped and ran wild in the brush country, where they multiplied. They learned to live on grass alone and to defend themselves against wolves, mountain lions, and other enemies. With a small mixture of blood from British cattle that later settlers brought, they formed the Longhorn breed, famous for its toughness and endurance. Early hunters stalked the wild Longhorns as game animals, finding some of the bulls as ferocious as any buffalo.

From the early settlements in eastern Texas, cowmen steadily pushed west, grazing their herds on lands wrested from the buffalo and the Indian. At first many lived in dugouts, sod houses, or log cabins near the streams from which their cattle drank. Although

68

far apart, they joined in defense against Indian raiders and white rustlers. Yet they showed open hospitality to visitors who gave no cause for suspicion. Veteran Charlie Goodnight recalled to J. Evetts Haley an old-timer's welcome to a stranger who rode up to his camp one evening. "After a frugal supper and a smoke, the cowman pulled a beef hide from a corner of the cabin, threw it on the dirt floor, turned to the traveler, and said: 'You sleep here. I'll rough it.'"

The cattlemen, who lived largely on beef, used strips or "whangs" of hide from their slaughtered steers for many purposes besides riatas and quirts. They found the tough hide suitable for horse hobbles, ox shoes, or camp stools. They used it to repair their wagons and other equipment. They had a saying that what one couldn't mend with rawhide wasn't worth mending, and another that Texas was held together with rawhide. Sometimes a sun-browned range rider was referred to as a "rawhide."

In the almost fenceless grasslands, Texas cowmen added new touches to the ancient practices of roundups, branding, and trail drives. They gradually developed the cowboy system of handling cattle, learning some of their techniques from the Mexican *vaqueros*.

Since the herds of many ranchmen often grazed on the same ranges of public land, spring and fall cow hunts were necessary to round up the cattle, brand the calves, and separate the herds. The cow hunt, which later developed into the more formal roundup, might last for several weeks. Usually it brought out ten to fifteen men, each with one to three spare horses. Each cowman took along a pack horse loaded with blankets and provisions. Wild game and an occasional unbranded yearling provided most of the food.

One such hunt was described by a stockman in Refugio County in 1860: "They sally forth, each man with a lasso at saddle bow and armed with an excellent six-shooter and bowie knife. They traverse a wide extent of country, driving into close herds large numbers of cattle at places most convenient to a pen. Then they cut out—select from the herd—such cattle as belong to the men who compose the crowd and those for whom they brand. They drive them into the pen and mark, brand, and alter the calves. Each man can tell his own calves by observing what cow the calf follows and sucks. But some calves among so large a number of cattle escape branding. These calves, when afterward discovered, if they have ceased to suck their mothers, are accounted common property and divided pro rata among the stock growers of the neighborhood."

Besides gathering and branding their own cattle, some of the stockmen added to their herds by capturing wild cattle from the brush. A group of them might ride out by moonlight and surround and drive off several hundred head. By keeping them on the move for several days, they would tire them enough to make them manageable. Others used small decoy herds to bring the wild cattle out with the tame ones. Some trapped wild cattle at water holes, tying the more obstreperous ones to work oxen that would lead them to a corral. A few of the more nervy hands might ride up behind a wild cow and throw it to the ground by twisting its tail around the horn of his saddle. Cattle thrown or roped sometimes were subdued by tying them to trees or tying their feet together.

For the cowboy, life on the range was rugged and often lonely. But on Saturday afternoon, when his work allowed, he would ride into town with some of his fellows. They would visit the barbershop, the saloons and gambling halls, and occasionally a dance hall or a bagnio. Often their departure from town was noisy. From Mexia they would leave at night "feeling their oats and often their corn and rye as well," recalled Blanche McCain Rimassa. "These country boys, who wouldn't have hurt a kitten, would jog along to the edge of town, then spur their horses, yell and whoop like wild men, and begin shooting at the stars. No home in Mexia showed a light on Saturday night, for a lighted candle or a coal-oil lamp looked too much like a star to take the risk."

For some, a ride with a trail herd brought a welcome diversion. Lack of railroads out of Texas had made the marketing of beef cattle a serious problem. Some small herds were trailed to ports on the Gulf Coast and shipped to New Orleans, Havana, or other markets. Others were taken on the hoof to New Orleans and a few to Northern cities. In the 1850's, when California's gold boom created a new market for beef, a number of herds were trailed to the Pacific Coast;

but this route was hazardous because of desert stretches and savage Apache raiders.

A new era in the Texas cattle industry opened soon after the Civil War. Ranchmen returning from the scenes of battle found their herds depleted. Mexicans and others left in charge had neglected the branding and had allowed many of the cattle to wander off into the brush and go wild. But the woods and the chaparral were bulging with wild and half-wild Longhorns that could be had for the taking.

Many stockmen determined to recoup their fortunes by capturing cattle and trailing them to the North, where beef was in strong demand. The prospect was inviting, since a steer worth only eight dollars in Texas might be worth twenty to thirty in Kansas or Missouri and the cost of trailing usually was only a dollar or so a head.

With an estimated five million cattle grazing in the Texas grasslands at the close of the war, it was easy to gather and brand enough of them for a trail herd. After a little taming, the Longhorns were almost ideal for trailing. Their toughness and endurance enabled them to walk a long distance in a day from one watering place to the next.

In the spring of 1866 the trailing of cattle out of Texas began on a much larger scale than ever before. Estimates of the number taken out of the state that year ranged from 200,000 to 260,000. A few of the herds went to Louisiana and others to New Mexico, but most of them were pointed north. Usually they went up the Shawnee Trail through Dallas, crossing the Red River near Preston. The trail led on, through the eastern edge of the Indian Territory, past Fort Gibson, and entered the southeastern corner of Kansas near Baxter Springs. The herds were headed for various Kansas and Missouri towns, principally Sedalia, Missouri, which had a railroad.

In Kansas and Missouri many of the drovers ran into trouble. Farmers in those states were up in arms because earlier Texas herds had brought what they called Texas fever. This was a serious livestock disease carried by ticks, but the role of the ticks was not yet generally known. The Texas Longhorns were immune to the fever, but they left on their bed grounds ticks which infected and made

71

unmarketable the cattle of Middle Western farmers. In some places, mobs killed or turned back the cattle and threatened the drovers. Jim Daugherty, a youth of sixteen from Denton County, in charge of a herd, saw one of his men shot dead. Jim was tied to a tree and whipped with hickory withes, but later he recovered and sold most of the steers.

This kind of trouble pointed to the need for a new trail farther west, beyond the settlements. The man with the vision and enterprise to open such a trail was a young Illinois cattle dealer, Joseph G. McCoy. In the summer and fall of 1867 he built cattle-loading pens and a hotel at the Kansas village of Abilene, on the Union Pacific Railroad. That fall Texas herds began using this new route, which came to be called the Chisholm Trail. For generations this trail would be celebrated in story and ballad. The cowboy would sing:

I woke up one morning on the old Chisholm Trail,
Rope in my hand and a cow by the tail.

Feet in the stirrups and seat in the saddle,
I hung and rattled with them Longhorn cattle.

Most of the men who went up the trail were young but were experienced in handling cattle. In September, 1867, a newspaper correspondent in Abilene wrote of the early arrivals: "Every man of them unquestionably was in the Rebel Army. Some of them have not yet worn out all their distinctive gray clothing." He described them as "keen-looking men, full of reserve force, shaggy with hair, undoubtedly terrible in a fight, yet peaceably great at cattle driving and not demonstrative in their style of wearing six-shooters."

Use of the new trail, which led through Fort Worth and crossed into the Indian Territory at Red River Station, increased rapidly. About 75,000 Texas cattle were trailed to Abilene in 1868, 150,000 in 1869, 300,000 in 1870 and 600,000 or more in 1871. After the season of 1871, which was the peak year, Abilene citizens asked the drovers to market elsewhere because of the crime and vice their business brought to the town. But the trailing continued—to Ellsworth and Wichita in the next few years and finally to Dodge City and Caldwell. Even after a railroad became available in 1873, the trails continued to be used because they were cheaper.

The Chisholm Trail made Fort Worth a booming cow town, filled with saloons, gambling casinos, variety theaters, and dance halls. In 1876 and later, many of the cattle herds went up a new Western Trail through Fort Griffin, crossing the Red River at Doan's Store and leading on north to Dodge City. Fort Griffin, on the Clear Fork of the Brazos River, although much smaller than Fort Worth, became equally wild. In addition to being on a cattle trail, it was the chief outfitting point and hide market for the Texas buffalo hunters.

In between the celebrating that many did at the start and end of the trail drive, the cowhands had long hours of hard, dusty work. The herd was strung out to prevent overheating and had to be guided by men on horseback—pointers, swing men, and flank riders—spaced along each side. The cattle in the lead set their own pace, munching a few bunches of grass as they walked along. In the rear were the unenvied tailers or drag men, who had to eat dust as they prodded the weaklings and laggards.

The men slept on the ground, in bags or rolled in blankets, subject to night-herding duty and, in the event of a stampede, an all-out chase. They took their meals while sitting or squatting around the campfire near the chuck wagon. The cook provided an abundance of roast beef and steaks, sourdough biscuits, and occasional son-of-a-gun stew. He couldn't offer much else except beans, canned tomatoes, or dried fruit. Always, though, there was plenty of hot, black coffee. Some called it six-shooter coffee, saying it was strong enough to float a pistol.

The trail had not only discomforts but dangers. In the earlier years there often was the possibility of an attack by Comanches or Kiowas. The Indians would try to stampede a herd at night and make off with some of the horses. In later years, the redskins were less warlike but would beg for a few steers and make trouble if refused. Usually the trail boss would compromise by giving them one or two lame or obstreperous animals or some with other brands that had wandered into the herd.

Stream crossings often were treacherous and perilous, especially during or just after high water. Floods brought delays and often caused sandbars to shift. Sometimes it was hard to start the herd across a stream. A cowboy might swim his horse ahead to show the way, or the herd might have an experienced lead steer that would do the job. In the river the men had to keep the herd compact to avoid gaps. At the same time they tried to keep the cattle from milling—churning around in a circle—which might cause some of them to drown. Untangling a mill was a hard job in which some cowboys lost their lives. But a smooth crossing, with the cattle swimming under water except for their head and horns, made an impressive picture. One cowman described the scene as "like a thousand rocking chairs floating on the water."

The worst and most dreaded of all the trail hazards was the stampede. It might be caused by the howl of a wolf, the breaking of a stick, a clap of thunder, or any unusual noise. Most often it took place at night, sometimes during a rainstorm. In an instant, the whole herd would be up and off in a panic, usually scattering in all directions.

A stampede brought all the trail hands into action. They got into their boots and on their saddles as quickly as they could and rushed after the frightened Longhorns. They tried to ride ahead of the leaders to head them off, or at least turn them into a circle. But the circle or mill must not be allowed to become too compact, lest the animals in the center be trampled or suffocated. Although some stampedes ended quickly, others continued for many miles, with a week or more required to round up the runaways. Some cattle might be lost and others killed by plunging over cliffs.

In any stampede the trail hand had to be careful not to be caught in front of the crazed cattle. They might split and go around him, but he couldn't be sure. For a cowhand unhorsed in front of a rushing herd, Mark Reeves had a bit of advice. All the fallen puncher needed to do, said Reeves, was to bend over, facing the oncoming beasts, hold his hat between his teeth, and shake his coattails over his back. But no one seemed eager to test that advice.

Trail driving was virtually ended in the 1880's, not by the new railroads but by the westward push of farm settlements and the fences that farmers and ranchmen set up. Barbed wire obstructed the trails that had felt the tramp of nine or ten million cattle, and grass reached across them. A romantic era had ended.

Barbed wire also brought on the most violent range clash of Texas history, the fence-cutters' war of 1883. Previously most of the vast grasslands of western Texas had been owned by the state and had been used freely by all stockmen. There had been few fences, since wood and stone were scarce. But for eight years barbed wire, a recently marketed invention, had been coming into Texas in increasing rolls. Resisted at first, fences of barbed wire soon were proved to be "pig tight, horse high, and bull strong." Then shipments of the wire began coming in by the trainload. In 1882 the Frying Pan Ranch in the Panhandle bought enough barbed wire to fence a pasture of 250,000 acres.

This fencing began to bring a change in ranching methods. Instead of grazing their herds on the open range, along with others, some cowmen began buying land from the state at low prices and enclosing it with fences. Naturally, the land along running streams went first. As more land was bought by individuals and fenced in, less was left for stockmen who clung to the open-range practices. Not only did they have less range, but they found more difficulty in watering their herds in dry spells. This was especially true in the severe drouth of 1883.

Advocates of a continued open range were mainly small cowmen who lacked the money or inclination to buy land and fence it. They regarded the open range as an inherent right and resented the fences that kept their herds from the best grass and water holes. The Texas Greenback party viewed barbed wire as a symbol of monopoly and encouraged resistance to fencing.

The open-range cowmen were especially enraged when they found some of the fencers enclosing land that they neither owned nor leased. Some of the fences took in public land and pastures belonging to other ranchmen or farmers. A few crossed roads and thus interfered with travel and the delivery of mail. Some ranchmen were accused of using the open range until its grass was depleted, then turning their herds into their own fenced pastures.

Opponents of fencing sent a deluge of protesting letters and telegrams to lawmakers and to the governor. When their pleas brought no action, they began making plans of their own. In many counties they formed small bands with passwords, spies, and messengers. Some of the groups gave themselves such names as Owls, Javelinas, or Blue Devils. They began destroying fences, usually working at night. After they had snipped the wire and destroyed the posts, they often left warnings against rebuilding.

On the coastal plains, one of the cattle kings, Abel H. (Shanghai) Pierce, who had built a fence around three leagues of land, found every strand of wire cut. Similar destruction occurred in other parts of the cattle country and in some of the sheep pastures. Fences that enclosed good streams or ponds were special objects of the snippers. In some instances fence-cutting was accompanied by pasture burning. In a few places the cutting was done in daylight, with guards posted to protect the men as they worked.

A number of the ranchmen suffered heavy losses. In Tom Green County, L. B. Harris had his fence cut between each pair of posts for nineteen miles and the posts and wire burned, causing a loss of six thousand dollars. C. D. Foote lost not only his fence but also ten head of fine Shorthorn cattle. Rewards for the conviction of fence-cutters went unclaimed, but in a few instances gunfire from enraged fence owners stopped them.

A Coleman County sheepman, Horace B. Starkweather, who had found his fence cut and two thousand cedar posts burned, along with his sheepfolds and herders' homes, rebuilt the fence only to have it cut again and scabby sheep turned in with his flock. He went to Chicago to borrow money, only to be met by newspaper headlines:

HELL BREAKS LOOSE IN TEXAS!

Wire Cutters Destroy
500 Miles of Fence
In Coleman County

Unable to obtain a loan, Starkweather hurried back to Texas, where he had so much trouble that he had to sell his ranch.

The cutters left warnings on many of the wrecked fences. One farmer near Gainesville found a card with a bullet hole through it and the threat: "If you don't make gates, we will make them for you." Snippers in Hamilton County left a picture of a coffin with a note saying that they were determined to have free grass and free water, even at the risk of their lives. In other instances, a coffin was nailed to a post of a cut fence and a grave was dug and a rope dangled from it.

Finally Governor John Ireland, who had tried to dodge the issue of fence-cutting, could do so no longer. He called the legislature to meet in special session on January 8, 1884. The lawmakers made fence-cutting and pasture burning felonies and made it a misdemeanor knowingly to fence public land or land belonging to others.

Although there were complaints that the new laws were too easy on illegal fencers, in view of the much heavier penalties for wire-cutting and pasture burning, enforcement of them gradually diminished the fence troubles. Sporadic snipping continued, however. As late as the summer of 1888, ranchmen in Navarro County had their fences cut by a group of small cowmen.

In an effort to stop this practice, two Texas Rangers, Sergeant Ira Aten and Jim King, were sent into the area. They arrived in a weatherbeaten farm wagon drawn by a horse and a mule and found jobs picking cotton and doing other farm work. In the evening King sometimes entertained a group with his fiddle. Before long they learned which men were doing the fence-cutting. Aten began making dynamite bombs to string along the remaining fences. He was ordered from Austin to stop this, but rumors of the bombs ended the snipping.

Fencing ended the era of the open range and made possible the development of the great Texas ranches. The King Ranch, largest of the surviving spreads, is a monument to Richard King, who arrived in the southern tip of the state in May, 1847, shortly before he was twenty-three years old. King, a son of Irish immigrants, was born in New York City, July 10, 1824. At eleven he was apprenticed to a jeweler, for his keep, to learn the trade. But, disgusted at having to scrub floors and mind the baby, he ran off and stowed away on a sailing ship, the *Desdemona*.

He worked as a cabin boy on the *Desdemona,* which was headed for Mobile, and later worked up to more responsible jobs on other ships. The master of one of them, Captain Joe Holland, sent young King back to live with the Holland family in Connecticut, where he went to school for eight months. After that, he joined the crew of a steamboat for service in the Seminole War in Florida.

In 1842, young King began working on steamboats on the Apalachicola and Chattahoochee rivers. The next year he met Captain Mifflin Kenedy, a Quaker, who, in 1846, asked him to come to the lower Río Grande to serve with a flotilla of steamboats in government service in the Mexican War. King became a pilot under Kenedy and helped move troops and army cargoes from the coast up the river.

After the war, Kenedy and King stayed on the Río Grande. In 1850 they and two other partners formed the firm of M. Kenedy and Company to operate steamboats on the river and a pack train to Monterrey. At that time Kenedy and King made their homes in Brownsville.

In the spring of 1852, Captain King made a horseback trip from Brownsville to Corpus Christi and return. He liked the fertile ranges, lush with tall grass, and decided to try his hand at cattle raising. He began buying land from Mexicans at a few cents an acre. In 1853 he acquired a tract of more than fifteen thousand acres on Santa Gertrudis Creek. This became the headquarters of his famed Santa Gertrudis Ranch. Kenedy, who began ranching in 1854, formed a partnership with King in 1860.

Late in 1854, King married a Presbyterian minister's daughter in Brownsville. He brought his bride by stagecoach over a trail of 120 miles to the small, simple building which served as the first ranchhouse for his broad, fenceless pastures. Lieutenant Colonel Robert E. Lee was a guest there several times from 1856 to 1861.

During the Civil War, King and Kenedy returned to the quarterdeck and carried cotton down the Río Grande to waiting British steamers. On resuming their ranch activities, they suffered from cattle rustling but continued to prosper, both before and after severing their partnership in 1868.

78

Captain King sent Longhorns to New Orleans under their own motive power and later had many herds pointed north over the long Chisholm Trail. In 1883 he used 190,000 pounds of barbed wire to fence some of his pastures. Undeterred by snippers, he continued to build fences, erected windmills, and otherwise improved his land.

After his death in 1885, his widow ruled the vast spread for forty years, with the help of her son-in-law, Robert J. Kleberg. She doubled the size of the ranch, improved its fences and other equipment, and introduced expensive beef and dairy herds. For watering the cattle, Kleberg drilled artesian wells. He also was a pioneer in developing the dipping vat as a weapon against cattle ticks.

Kleberg built an impressive twenty-five-room ranch house as a monument to Mrs. King's hospitality. Its dining table was made to accommodate forty people, and a guest was expected to sit down for a meal whenever he felt hungry. Many sportsmen were attracted by the ranch's wild game, which included animals from distant parts of the world.

Gradually the ranch lands were equipped with concrete bunkhouses, complex corrals, more fences and windmills, and later gasoline filling stations. A powerful machine was devised to clear the pastures of mesquite and other brush. This clearing made way for the planting of imported Rhodes grass and thus enabled a cow to graze on half the acreage formerly required.

When Captain King's widow died in 1925, at ninety-three, her will directed that the 1,250,000-acre ranch be administered by trustees for ten years and then divided. Her son-in-law, Robert J. Kleberg, survived her for seven years. After his death, his son of the same name, became the ranch manager. In 1933 the ranch sold oil-drilling rights to the Humble Oil and Refining Company.

The greatest achievement of the King Ranch has been its cattle breeding. More than two decades of scientific breeding and selective inbreeding brought America's first new and distinctive breed of beef cattle, the Santa Gertrudis. Cattle of this breed, with the King Ranch brand of the running W, were impressive animals with uniform coloring of cherry red, short hair, and smooth, pliant hides. They were unusually large and strong but ordinarily were gentle.

The failure of other breeds to thrive and fatten satisfactorily under conditions in southern Texas led to the experiments that resulted in the Santa Gertrudis. The aim of Robert J. Kleberg, Jr., was to develop a beef animal of large size and hardy constitution. He needed one that could fatten suitably on grass and could adapt itself to the climatic and grazing conditions of the region. The Santa Gertrudis breed represented an original cross of Brahmans from India with Shorthorns, then fixing of the type by scientific breeding. The new cattle were found to have the hardiness and endurance of the Brahmans and the beef qualities of the Shorthorns. After the breed was fixed, seed stock was made available to other ranchmen.

Also outstanding has been the King Ranch breeding of horses. Its scientific breeding of Quarter Horses was aimed to develop an all-sorrel horse that would resist sunburn. Starting with a sire later called Old Sorrel, in whose veins ran blood from both Steel Dust and Shiloh, the ranch used the breeding methods already begun with cattle. The results were highly successful. Later the ranch took up the breeding of Thoroughbreds and entered horses that won the Kentucky Derby in 1946 and 1950.

Another large and influential spread in southern Texas, was the Pierce Ranch, in Wharton and Matagorda counties, which included, at its peak, about 250,000 acres. This ranch was developed mainly by Abel H. (Shanghai) Pierce, one of the most colorful Texas cowmen. Born in Rhode Island in 1834, Pierce, at the age of nineteen, came to Texas as a stowaway on a schooner. He was described as "a tall, gangling boy with too-short pants." His first job after landing was splitting rails for a coastal ranchman, W. B. Grimes, at fourteen dollars a month and board.

Pierce fell out with Grimes after the latter paid him his wages in cattle, picking out old and almost worthless animals and charging him double the market price. He was all the more irked when Grimes refused to allow him to call on the Grimes daughter. The final break came when Shanghai returned after the Civil War. Before enlisting, he had left five hundred dollars with Grimes for safekeeping. On his return, Grimes paid him in worthless Confederate money.

Pierce acquired his nickname because he reminded someone

of a long-legged, long-necked Shanghai rooster. Soon after the war he married and, with his brother Jonathan, established Rancho Grande on Tres Palacios Creek. They paid gold for some of their cattle and captured wild ones from the brush. In the spring of 1871 they had more than 100,000 Longhorns and branded 25,000 calves and mavericks. They shipped some of the steers to Cuba to feed soldiers in the rebellion against Spain.

For several years, Shanghai trailed large herds to Kansas markets. Once, after he had arrived with 2,500 Longhorns, his steers had done so much swimming of rivers on the way that he referred to them as sea lions. On the trail his unusual height and his booming voice quickly caught attention. One Kansan wrote of his "ear-splitting voice, more piercing than a locomotive whistle, more noisy than a steam calliope." Charles A. Siringo, who had been with Pierce on the trail, said that people half a mile away could hear him. Shanghai always had a fund of salty talk and stories that made him a favorite in the cow camps.

In 1871, after some difficulties and the death of his wife and baby son, Shanghai sold out to his brother and two other men and went north for eighteen months. In the spring of 1872, the Santa Fe Railway engaged him to persuade drovers to market their cattle in Wichita instead of trailing them on to Ellsworth on the Kansas Pacific. The next season he worked for the city of Wichita, with the same purpose. For the 1874 season he switched his allegiance to Ellsworth, with less success for his efforts.

Back in Texas, Shanghai again began buying land, with his brother and a San Antonio banker, Daniel Sullivan, as partners. The firm was chartered in 1881 as the Pierce-Sullivan Land and Cattle Company and changed the next year to the Pierce-Sullivan Pasture and Cattle Company. The company was incorporated for one million dollars, with Shanghai as president, Sullivan as treasurer, and Jonathan as a director. The company bought land until it had a quarter of a million acres and sent big herds up the trails. Shanghai took special satisfaction in buying the public land on which W. B. Grimes had been grazing his herds, thus forcing Grimes to leave.

Shanghai Pierce sought ways to remove the ticks which caused cattle fever and toured Europe in search of cattle immune to ticks. He was one of the early Texas ranchmen to bring in Brahman cattle. Although he lost more than one million dollars in the Galveston hurricane and flood of 1900, he still was a millionaire when he died in December of that year.

Prominent among the big ranches in western Texas was the JA, established in 1877 by Charles Goodnight and his Irish-born partner, John G. Adair. Adair, a wealthy financier then living in Denver, backed the enterprise, while Goodnight, an experienced cowman, provided the foundation herd and managed the ranch.

As a boy of nine, Goodnight had been brought from Illinois to Texas in 1845. He rode bareback a mare called Blaze. With him, in two covered wagons, were his mother, his stepfather, his older brother, and his two sisters.

On the west bank of the Trinity River, across from the frontier village of Dallas, Charlie saw his first buffalo. Soon after the family settled, Charlie began riding a wild mustang that his brother had caught. At twelve he began working for neighboring farmers and stock raisers. At sixteen he started hauling freight by wagon, but two years later he turned back to farm work.

In 1857, Goodnight moved to hilly Palo Pinto County, which had good grass for cattle but was subject to Indian raids. Before long he was riding in scouting parties to help protect the scattered settlements from Comanche and Kiowa scalpers. During the Civil War, he served as a scout for a frontier regiment.

By the spring of 1866, when he was thirty, Goodnight had nearly one thousand head of cattle ready for market. As there was no local demand for them, he prepared to trail them to New Mexico and maybe to Colorado, where beef was needed for soldiers and miners. An older neighbor, Oliver Loving, decided to go along, taking his own cattle, the combined herd comprising about two thousand head.

Equipment for the drive included one of the earliest of Texas chuck wagons. Goodnight bought the gear of a government wagon, which had iron axles, and had a woodworker rebuild it with the

82

toughest wood he could find. In the back he built a chuck box, which served as the cook's cupboard.

The riders pointed the herd west to Horsehead Crossing of the bleak Pecos River, then up along the Pecos into New Mexico. After the steers were sold there, Loving trailed the cows and calves on to Colorado while Goodnight returned to Texas to gather another herd to be started on the trail in the fall. In 1867, Goodnight and Loving took a third herd over the same trail. After they started up the Pecos valley, Loving and a companion, who were riding on ahead of the herd, were attacked by Comanches and Loving was fatally wounded.

In 1876, Goodnight moved his 1,800 Shorthorn cattle to the Palo Duro Canyon in northwestern Texas. When he made his five-year agreement with Adair the next year, the JA Ranch was started there. At its peak, this ranch ran one hundred thousand cattle on one million acres. With his wife on the ranch and Mrs. Adair visiting it occasionally, Goodnight designed a safer type of sidesaddle, one that came into wide use.

Goodnight brought in Hereford bulls to improve the herd. He also crossed buffalo with cattle, but the resulting cattalo did not prove to be practical. In a country where sheriffs and courts were far apart, Goodnight was one of the leaders in ridding the ranges of cattle thieves.

After the death of Adair in 1885, Goodnight was a partner of Adair's widow until 1887. Then the land was divided, with Mrs. Adair retaining the JA brand. Goodnight sold his part of the ranch in 1890, but he lived on to the ripe age of ninety-three, a rugged patriarch of the Texas ranges.

Among the other large and well-managed ranches of western Texas was the Matador. Rustlers hesitated to rope a steer carrying the Matador's flying-V brand because they knew that everyone on the ranch rode a good horse and was expert with a lariat and a six-shooter, and would not hesitate to use either.

The Matador was started by Henry Campbell, of North Carolina birth, who had trailed Texas cattle north in 1878. In Chicago, Campbell met a banker and cattle trader, Colonel Alfred M. Britton, who financed him in establishing the Matador Ranch the next year, near the headwaters of the Pease River. Buffalo had just been cleared from that area, where land sold at ten to fifty cents an acre.

Campbell first bought range rights and a small herd from Joe Browning, who in 1878 had made his headquarters in a dugout left by a buffalo hunter. Next he bought eight thousand cattle which recently had been brought into the area. The first Matador brand was 50M, but the M was dropped because it was hard to heal on cattle. Later, when Campbell bought from John Dawson a herd already branded with a V, it was easier to adopt that brand than to rebrand the bought cattle. The 50 brand was retained for Matador horses.

Since money was needed to expand and fence the ranch, Britton went to Scotland, where many financiers were investing in American ranches. At Dundee he found an interested group who came over and visited the Matador. They liked it and, in 1882, formed the Matador Land and Cattle Company. For $1,250,000 this company bought the ranch and its forty thousand cattle. It expanded the Texas spread to 812,000 acres and leased ranges in Montana and South Dakota for fattening steers.

The new company kept Campbell as superintendent. In a few years it had about 100,000 cattle and 1,000 saddle and work horses. It used 100 to 150 cowboys and began replacing the tough Longhorns with British breeds—Herefords, Angus, and Shorthorns. When Campbell quit at the end of 1890 after arguments with the home office, the ranch was branding 18,000 to 25,000 calves a season.

A Scot cowman, Murdo Mackenzie, became the new manager. He reduced the cattle to seventy thousand and fattened many on northern ranges. He kept the chuck wagons but brought in telephone lines and trucks for efficiency. The ranch had a mansion, called the White House, for visitors from Scotland. In 1951 a group of American cattle companies bought the Matador shares for $18,960,000. Later the ranch was broken up into smaller ranches, but legends of the flying V continued around many a campfire.

Biggest of the Texas ranches was the XIT, strung along the western edge of the Panhandle. Its original 3,050,000 acres made it the largest fenced ranch in the world and almost as large as the whole state of Connecticut. It occupied former state land which the Texas Legislature exchanged in 1882 for the building of a new capitol in Austin.

The inception of the XIT went back to 1875, when Texas drew up a new constitution which voters ratified the following year. This constitution included a provision for setting aside three million acres to pay for a new statehouse. The Legislature had the land surveyed in 1879; and, when the old capitol burned in 1881, hastened to contract for a new building early in 1882. The successful bidder was Mattheas Schnell of Rock Island, Illinois, who soon afterward assigned his interest to Taylor, Babcock and Company, a Chicago mercantile firm.

This company built the Capitol in the next seven years. It formed the Capitol Syndicate Company, which established the XIT Ranch in 1885 to make use of the land until it could be sold profitably. The land was untouched by any railroad and was entirely unfenced. One of the owners, John V. Farwell, went to England, where he raised about ten million dollars to develop the ranch. Farwell became managing director of the ranch and soon afterward engaged Colonel B. H. (Barbecue) Campbell, an experienced cowman, as manager.

Campbell quickly began contracting for cattle. The first herd to reach the ranch was brought in from the Fort Concho country by Abner Blocker in July, 1885. At the suggestion of Blocker, Campbell adopted the XIT brand for the cattle, and the ranch soon took its name from the brand.

Despite Texas pride in the new capitol, taller than the one in Washington, before long some grangers complained that too much had been paid for it. They were answered by the fact that the cost of the building amounted to $1.07 an acre for the land which the contractors received—twice that which the state had been able to obtain for the choicest and best-watered land in the Panhandle. Land away from water brought only twenty-five cents an acre; as late as 1883, Charles Goodnight bought 170,000 acres at twenty cents.

The early history of the XIT was one of building windmills and almost endless fences, fighting prairie fires, and waging a long battle against cattle rustlers. For some time, the ranch sent 10,000 to 15,000 cattle a year over the trail to finishing ranges in the Black Hills or Montana, where they were fattened for the Chicago market. In 1889 it adopted a policy of bringing in Hereford, Shorthorn, and Angus cattle.

Eventually railroads penetrated the Panhandle, and with them came many farmers. The owners of the XIT, free from the antipathy of some ranchmen to nesters or "fool hoe men," had been working toward the day when they could sell their land at prices that only farmers could pay. In 1901 they began offering land for sale. Late in 1912 the last of the XIT cattle were sold; lands owned by the ranch were reduced to 460,000 acres in 1929 and to 20,000 in 1950. The last tract, 39 acres, was sold in 1963. Thereafter, only the annual XIT Reunion at Dalhart was left to remind old-timers of the days when XIT hands pounded leather and carried six-shooters in their belts.

Other large West Texas ranches, later broken up, included the Spur, which in its heyday included about 439,000 acres, and that of the Francklyn Land and Cattle Company. The latter spread, known as the Francklyn, the White Deer, or the Diamond F, made use of Panhandle land given to railroads to encourage construction. Both these ranches, although established by Americans, attracted British capital.

Resisting both foreign investment and the pressure for the parceling of land was the big Waggoner or Three D Ranch set up in 1851 by Daniel Waggoner, of Tennessee birth, and expanded by his son, Thomas Waggoner. This ranch profited from the discovery of oil and became famous for its Quarter Horses. With the breaking up of other spreads, it became Texas' second-largest ranch, surpassed only by the vast King Ranch.

Many Texan ranchmen, like the more progressive farmers, learned to obtain greater yields from their land. By checking overgrazing and erosion, planting better grasses, and eradicating useless brush that competed with grass for moisture, they increased their profits and lessened the toll of drouths. The 17,000-acre Flat Top

86

Ranch, southwest of Fort Worth, became a shining example of what could be done in reclaiming run-down land. It was developed by the late Charles Pettit of Dallas, who had grown up on a ranch and had made a fortune in oil. In 1936, Pettit bought the then 7,000-acre deteriorated Flat Top and a number of adjoining farms. With sound conservation practices, he made his spread a show place that demonstrated the value of scientific ranching.

T

HROUGH THE WOODED HILLS of the Edwards Plateau and across the brush country of southwestern Texas, one can drive for days without seeing a sheep or a goat. Yet many a flock is hidden in the dense growths of scrub mesquite, shin oak, and sprawling juniper. This seemingly forsaken land sustains more sheep than any other two states and enough Angora goats to provide 97 per cent of the nation's mohair output. San Angelo has become the country's largest inland wool market.

Sheep adapted themselves easily to this hilly land, even though their ancestors were not native to it. Except for the wild bighorns in the mountains, the New World had no sheep until Christopher Columbus brought a few on his second westward voyage in 1493. Later ships brought more sheep, along with horses and cattle. Most of the early Spanish sheep brought over were of inferior quality, the common *churros* still raised by the Navahos. They were hardy and made good eating; but they gave only a small yield of wool, and that unusually coarse.

In Texas the sheep industry began with the early Spanish missions. The Spanish sheepmen used the old system of *transhumante,* moving large flocks to seasonal ranges. The plan worked well for a time; but after the Texas missions were closed, most of the sheep ranches had to be abandoned because of Indian forays. The salvaged woolies were moved back toward San Antonio or the Río Grande.

In the period of the Texas Republic and the decade following annexation, sheep ranching made a new start and attained greater stability. This development was spurred by the bringing in of better breeds. German colonists along the Guadalupe River brought quality stock from their homeland, while both Anglos and Mexicans introduced Spanish Merinos, which yielded more and finer wool than the lowly *churros*.

Of the early Texas sheepmen, one of the most successful was George W. Kendall, who had been a schoolmate of Horace Greeley and editor of the New Orleans *Picayune*. Kendall, with three partners, bought and stocked a sheep ranch on the Nueces River in 1850. Two years later, Kendall, dissatisfied with the water, found a better site west of New Braunfels and moved his sheep there in the spring of 1853. Beginning in 1855, he operated a four-thousand-acre ranch at Post Springs, east of Boerne.

As protection against Indian raids, Kendall had to keep armed sentries on duty. He also had troubles from scab, drouth, and grass fires. But he improved and increased his flocks and in 1858 sheared nine thousand pounds of wool. Kendall is remembered for importing French Merino sheep. This breed later became the prevailing one in Texas. It came to be called the Rambouillet, taking this name from the fact that the breed was developed on an estate owned by King Louis XVI at the village of Rambouillet, forty miles west of Paris.

Another pioneer Texas sheepman was Captain Charles A. Schreiner, a former Texas Ranger of Alsatian birth. Schreiner resigned from the Ranger force in 1857 and the next year established a ranch near Turtle Creek, in Kerr County. In spite of hardships, he built up a ranch of more than 600,000 acres, on which he ran thirty thousand to forty thousand sheep. He chose the Delaine breed, another Merino type, over the Rambouillet as better suited to the rough and brushy hill country.

After the Civil War, Texas sheep ranching began expanding again. In 1866 wool valued at nearly two million dollars was shipped from Galveston. In 1880 Nueces County had one million sheep, and Corpus Christi had become one of the world's largest wool markets.

By that time, the ending of Indian raids and the slaughter of the buffalo had allowed the spread of sheep raising farther west. In the Texas Panhandle, Don Casimero Romero had established a profitable sheep empire on state land.

Lack of railroads caused some sheepmen to trail breeding

flocks all the way from California to Texas. Karl Anton von Schauer, son of an Austrian field marshal, started east from California with a flock of three thousand in 1859. Impeded by flooded streams, snowstorms, and Apache attacks and delayed by lambing seasons, he took three years to reach the Concho ranges, where he later ran about thirty thousand head.

Soon after the Civil War, Arthur G. Anderson, Tennessee born, rode horseback alone to California and trailed back, by way of Salt Lake City, a flock of French Merinos. Two years were required for the drive. Following the blizzard of 1888, which brought a heavy loss of sheep, Anderson sold his 125 sections of land near Colorado City and bought 225 sections to establish his Hat A Ranch in Pecos County, where he sometimes ran as many as forty thousand head.

Others who trailed foundation flocks from California to Texas included Jeff Moore, a pioneer sheepman on the South Concho; John Arden, who left with woolies in 1877, taking three years for his drive to San Angelo; and W. F. Holt, who trailed to Tom Green County in 1879.

Trailing sheep was especially hazardous in the era of Indian raiding, but one quick-thinking woman matched her wits against the redskins in 1868. Mrs. Robert Casey and her husband, with their five children, were moving from Menardsville to Fort Stanton, with ox wagons, a herd of cattle, and a small bunch of sheep. They were joined by three cowboys with a cattle herd from Mason County. When they were camped on a bank of the Pecos River, Indians swooped down and drove off most of the cattle. But as the raiders started to drive off the sheep, Mrs. Casey ran out, beating on a pan and calling, "Nannie! Nannie!" The sheep, hoping for salt or shelled corn, bolted from the Indians and ran back to the camp.

The sheep ranch lacked the glamour of the cattle spread. The pioneer herder worked alone with his wagon and his dog for long periods, cooking his own meals, mending his clothes, warding off wolves, and caring for sick or injured animals of his flock. In the early days, his appearance was anything but romantic. John Clay wrote of one herder: "An old weatherbeaten man—there he stood on a knoll, unshaven, a greasy hat on his head, his clothes worn and ragged, watching a flock of sheep as they kept slowly trailing a bench of rich grass."

On the Texas ranges, as elsewhere in the West, antagonism between cattlemen and sheepmen often was strong, although it did not bring as much violence as in some areas. To the frontier cowman the white canvas of the sheep wagon was as irritating as a red flag to a bull. The fact that both cattle and sheep were grazing on public land was disregarded. The cattlemen were determined not to be "sheeped out." They would not let alien flocks devour their grass or pollute their streams.

The cowhand, aboard a fleet horse, looked down on the shabby sheepherder, who usually was afoot, in a creaky little wagon, or on a shaggy burro. He regarded the herder as a pariah of the plains, an interloper who deserved no quarter. When he saw a herder in town, a cowboy likely would bleat derisively in imitation of a sheep. He would rather go hungry than eat lamb chops.

Seldom was a sheepman mentioned without a contemptuous epithet. M. W. Hickman, who grew up in Runnels County, was taught to hate sheepmen as "too low for a decent man's notice." Pomp Cutbirth said that in Callahan County a sheepherder was regarded as "lower down than a thief. He was just too low down for any use."

Economic competition was at the bottom of this social cleavage. Sheepmen and cattlemen were rivals for the use of public ranges. Cowmen tried to justify their antagonism by charging that sheep killed the grass by nibbling it too close and by trampling the roots with their sharp hoofs. They also complained that the woolies destroyed young trees and left on the range and in streams and pools an odor that was distasteful to cattle and horses.

Sheepmen pointed out that on some ranges sheep had been grazed for many years without hurting the grass, but the cowmen were not convinced. They called the woolies "hoofed locusts" and quoted the prophet Ezekiel: "Woe be to the shepherds of Israel! Seemeth it a small thing unto you that you have eaten up the good pasture, but ye must tread down with your feet the residue of your

91

pasture? And to have drunk the deep waters, but ye must foul the residue with your feet?"

Cattlemen sometimes banded together to terrorize the sheepmen and try to drive them off the ranges. Night riders, masked in some cases, would burn the sheep camps and kill many of the sheep by clubbing, shooting, dynamiting, poisoning, or driving them over cliffs. In his lonely camp, the sheepherder could do little to resist such sudden raids.

In Texas, acts of violence by cattlemen against sheep and their herders began soon after the Civil War. Charles Hanna, who brought the first sheep into Brown County in 1869, lost all his three hundred head in a night raid. When he went to his rock corral one morning to turn his woolies out on the pasture, every one had its throat cut.

Such incidents became frequent in the next dozen years. In the winter of 1875–76, when Charles Goodnight was in Colorado, one of his cowhands drove a flock of sheep into the Canadian River, where four to five hundred were drowned. Goodnight, who had to pay damages in court, made an agreement with the sheepmen on the division of the ranges and had no more trouble.

The rolling hills of the San Saba country were the site of several raids on sheep. Late in 1879, cowmen ordered young Peter Bertrand to move his sheep from the water hole they had been using on a creek. Bertrand, whose father had lived in Texas for more than fifty years, refused. Then the cattlemen set a dog on his sheep and returned later to fire a volley into the pen, killing some of the sheep.

A little later, in January, 1880, some of the seven thousand sheep belonging to the Ramsay brothers were resting quietly at night in two pens on the prairie near Fall Creek, in San Saba County. Suddenly a band of cowmen rode to the pens and began shooting at the woolies, throwing them into a panic. Next they dismounted, took out long knives, and began slitting throats. They left 240 sheep dead, many wounded, and the others scattered. This was the sixth such outrage in the county in two months.

On a public range below the South Concho River, a blustering cowman ordered C. C. Doty to leave with his sheep within three days or face hanging. On the third day, the cowman was back with two others, all bristling with guns.

"Why haven't you moved?" asked the bully.

"I like this country, and I've decided to stay," was the unexpected reply. Doty did stay, but not all sheepmen had his courage and rawhide tenacity.

In 1883, when drouth led to the cutting of many fences, several sheepmen in Brown County had their homes and pens burned and their flocks fired upon. All were ordered to leave. One who moved, with one thousand sheep, to Shackelford County, ran into similar trouble there. Raiders rode into his camp at night, fired into his flock, and cut the throats of twenty sheep.

In the same year, several sheep raisers in Hamilton County were ordered to leave but refused to go. One of them, Ed Pendleton, lost many of his woolies one night when eight masked men entered his pen and, after binding the herder, began killing and maiming his charges. Before departing, they told the herder he would be killed if he left the place before morning.

A dozen sheepmen met at Carlton a few days later to discuss their troubles and petition the governor for protection. They found about one hundred hostile cattlemen holding the hall and were ordered to leave. After some discussion, however, most of the cowmen agreed that the sheep raisers and their property should be protected.

For several more years, sheepmen in various parts of western Texas were subjected to violence and ordered to leave. On the Callaghan Ranch near Laredo, which ran more than forty thousand sheep, a Mexican herder was killed in 1884 after he had ignored an order to leave. In Stonewall County a cattleman scattered a flock of woolies, shooting many of them. He beat the herder with a rope and threatened to kill him unless he took the rest of the sheep away. In mountainous Jeff Davis County a gun battle between cowmen and sheepmen over range rights resulted in the death of a Mexican *vaquero*.

In 1888, Arthur G. Anderson was driving a band of California sheep from Alpine to his Hat A Ranch. He was arrested near Fort

Davis and ordered to pay a fine. Knowing that such a levy was unlawful, he refused. Since this frontier cow town, high in the mountains, had no jail, Anderson was placed in a dry cistern under the courthouse floor. After a week in this dungeon, he was released on a five-hundred-dollar bond for reappearance in court.

In time the antagonism lessened to the extent that putting cattle and sheep, and sometimes Angora goats, on the same range became common in some sections. In years of low beef prices, a number of cattlemen ran a few sheep, which they might call "mortgage-raisers." As old scars were healed, some cattlemen even learned to eat lamb chops.

Once it was firmly established, the Texas sheep industry grew rapidly. Many sheepmen brought in improved breeding stock and thus increased their wool clip. The Rambouillet, or French Merino, continued to be the most popular breed, especially after the publicity given to it at the Columbian Exposition in Chicago in 1893. Most of the other Texas sheep were of another fine-wool type, the Delaine, a smooth variety of Merino. Coarser grades of wool were obtained from mutton sheep grown on farms in eastern Texas.

Later decades brought a new breed, the Debouillet, developed by the late Amos D. Jones of New Mexico. In 1920, Jones began crossing Delaine rams with Rambouillet ewes to produce a breed that would combine the length of staple and character of the Delaine fleece with the larger body of the Rambouillet. In Texas, as elsewhere, a number of sheepmen adopted the new breed, and a Debouillet Sheep Breeders Association was formed in 1954.

Although most Texas sheep are shorn only once a year, in the late spring, the mild climate of the southern ranges gives ranchmen there the advantage of being able to shear twice a year. Spring shearing is done from about April 20 to June 15. Those bleating victims that undergo the power clippers a second time lose a summer growth from September 20 to November 1.

The sheepman gets cash from selling lambs as well as wool. Efforts to popularize lamb as a delicacy for the dinner table have enabled housewives to prepare it in a more appetizing manner. But periods of drouth hit the lamb crop along with the wool clip. When

94

the ranges are dry in the winter and spring, the ewes become poor in condition. Ranchmen have trouble inducing them to claim their lambs. Loss of lambs is high in such seasons, and many of those saved are pot-bellied from the small flow of mothers' milk.

Some Texas ranchmen found profit in goats. Introduced in South Carolina in 1849, the Angora was brought west after the Civil War, mainly to exterminate the brush. The goat and mohair industry of the Edwards Plateau dates chiefly from the beginning of the twentieth century, although some Mexican goats were there much earlier.

More a browsing than a grazing animal, the Angora has a wide range of appetite, which embraces green herbage, buffalo and mesquite grass, acorns, mesquite beans, and the young flower shoots of huisache and yucca. The goat thrives on land too barren for sheep, since it has greater diversity of taste, feeds at a higher level, and seems to have a better instinct for avoiding certain poisonous plants. The goats are shorn twice a year. The meat of the kid, called *cabrito,* is relished by Mexicans and by those Anglos who have tried it.

Repeated drouths and mounting competition from synthetic fibers and imported wool took a heavy toll in the sheep industry. Texas, which had 10,000,000 sheep on its ranges in 1940, dropped to 4,700,000 in 1957 but had 5,900,000 in 1963, producing more than 19.6 per cent of the nation's domestic wool. Ranchmen had some compensation in increased yields. In recent years, better care of flocks and the culling of ewes brought a greater weight of fleeces and a larger lamb crop.

Hazards of the sheep and goat raisers include not only drouths but predatory animals and sudden chilly winds in the wake of shearing. Yet profits from the fat years usually are enough to tide the ranchmen over the lean seasons. In recent decades the sheepmen have gained from the government policy of wool subsidies. Many also have added to the productivity of their land by using federal funds to check erosion and to eradicate the prickly-pear cactus and various kinds of brush that compete with grass for moisture.

AMBITION TO HAVE A HOME of his own, even if he had to build it himself, spurred the landless farmer who brought his family to Texas in a covered wagon. He might never own a big plantation house, but he could be happy in a snug cabin that kept out the rain and the north wind.

After arriving on the frontier and making a land claim or purchase, the pioneer family might have to sleep in their wagon for a few weeks until a cabin could be built. Some used a tent or a tipi temporarily or were taken in by a hospitable neighbor.

In a state as broad as Texas, frontier homes varied greatly in style. In arid sections of southwestern Texas, pioneers built homes of stone or adobe brick, as the Mexicans had done. On the high plains, where both stone and trees were scarce, dugouts and sod houses were fairly common. But in most parts of the state the log cabin was standard.

Usually the settler built his cabin near a spring or stream, since water had to be carried in buckets. But he liked to build on fairly high ground, in a bit of clearing. Such a site was less likely to be flooded and gave Indian marauders less opportunity for ambush attacks. In dangerous regions, small holes in the walls were used for watching the approaches and occasionally for defensive guns.

The cabin homes were of several types. A settler in a hurry and without much material or help might build a crude picket cabin of split logs, with the ends stuck in the ground. Others used round logs, laid parallel with the ground and fastened at the corners. Most of the cabins however, were better ones of hewed logs, which made a closer fit. The wood might be pine, oak, or cedar, depending on the region.

House-raising was a big community event. Neighbors for several miles, women as well as men, came to help. The owner had his logs already cut and hewed. They had been rolled to the site, if cut nearby, or dragged by oxen. Neighbors helped notch the ends and lift the logs into position. Occasionally there were men who liked to display unusual skill in this work. The women brought and set out food for a holiday feast. Often some of them helped the hostess with her quilting.

The typical one-room cabin was only about twelve by sixteen feet, although some cabins were a bit larger. It had a fireplace at one end. The walls usually were unpainted and soon became weatherbeaten. In summer the rough exterior might be softened by a trumpet vine, morning glory, or woodbine. There also might be a few flowers along the path, grown from seeds or slips brought from the wife's childhood home or given by a neighbor.

For the cabin walls, large, straight logs were needed. If crooked logs had to be used in places, small sticks were wedged into the cracks and the remaining crevices chinked with mud. In dry weather, this stuffing would fall out. It had to be replaced before winter blizzards struck. As nails were scarce and expensive, hardwood pins were used in putting the cabin together.

Some families whose cabins had good drainage preferred a floor of packed earth. Others had puncheon floors of split logs with the flat side up. A few had floors of whipsawed hardwood lumber known as rawhide. The chimney was built of stone in localities where stone was handy. Many isolated stone chimneys are still found on Texas prairies, the sole reminders of pioneers' cabins that burned long ago. Where there was no stone, the chimney was formed of sticks and lined with clay. Such a chimney smoked and was a constant fire hazard, but it had to do.

The cabin roof usually was of hand-rived oak or cypress shakes, although split boards were also used. The roofing was held in place with the aid of boards. The doors, hung on wooden or rawhide hinges, had no locks. Most of them had the proverbial latchstring hung on the outside for the use of visitors. Glass windows were rare in isolated homes in the early days. Sometimes windows were covered with treated rawhide that admitted part of the light.

Inside, shelves and pegs held spare clothes and linen. The fireplace, in addition to giving winter warmth and heat for cooking, helped to ventilate the cabin when doors and windows were closed. Usually it had a stone hearth. The better cabins had squeaky cranes for swinging heavy pots and kettles off the fire. Often there was a puncheon bench that could be drawn up in front of the fire on winter evenings.

Sometimes a bedstead or a chair or two had been brought from an earlier home, along with a spinning wheel. Most of the other furniture was crudely made on the frontier, often by the settler himself. Children slept in simple bunks softened with buffalo robes, feather beds, or mattresses stuffed with corn shucks.

Meals were served on a puncheon table. Until newfangled oil lamps became available, the only night light was from the fireplace or from homemade candles. Dishes usually were brought from a distance, but plates made of wood, which bore the polish of many scourings, were also used. Spoons were wood or pewter. In 1851 a visitor from the brush noted that in Austin people lived in comfortable, well-furnished houses and ate "with knives and forks."

Few pioneers were bothered by the crowding or the lack of privacy. In Hale County, a Baptist missionary, the Reverend J. W. Winn, built a dugout thirteen by twenty-eight feet. There, for the first winter, he lived with his wife, eight unmarried children, married son, married daughter, and six grandchildren—twenty persons in all. In many frontier homes, curtains or blankets were used to give a degree of privacy, especially for overnight guests.

The down-river and coastal towns had bigger homes and more elegant furnishings, even in the republic period. Some homes had mahogany hair sofas, rocking chairs upholstered with red velvet, marble-top tables, Franklin stoves, tin bathtubs, china dinner sets, and champagne glasses. But those luxuries were not for the hardy frontiersmen who cleared the land, broke the prairie sod, and followed the cattle herds.

Most clothing was simple. Noah Smithwick told of going to a wedding "resplendent in a brand new buckskin suit consisting of hunting shirt, pantaloons, and moccasins, all elaborately fringed." When Sam Houston was elected commander of the revolutionary Texas army in 1836, he was wearing buckskin breeches and a Mexican blanket. On another occasion he wore a hunting shirt of linsey-woolsey checks, a pair of cheap pants, and a broad-brimmed hat of smoky color, with the fur nap half an inch long. At a ball in 1837 he wore a fancy belt and trousers trimmed with gold lace, and a cravat about his neck; but as late as 1841 he was seen in a state procession in a beaded buckskin hunting shirt.

Yet, in spite of Houston's affecting it, buckskin was not commonly worn by whites except on the outer frontier. Pioneer Texas women, who carded, spun, and wove both cotton and wool, made clothes for their men and boys, as well as dresses for themselves and their daughters. Some even embroidered shirts for their husbands. When Jones Greene went from Dallas County to New Orleans, trailing to market a herd of surplus stock, he wore a dark, speckled suit made from wool grown on his own farm. His wife had cleaned and carded the wool, spun it, woven the cloth, dyed it with the juice of pokeberries and *bois d'arc* balls, and fashioned it into a durable suit.

Most of the country women's dresses were made at home and dyed with such items as logwood, sumac berries, boiled copperas, or onion skins. When they worked outdoors, many of the women wore sunbonnets to protect their eyes from glare. For trips to town or to church they usually had a dress or two of calico cut from a bolt at the store. Some had also a treasured silk for special occasions. In the larger towns, fashionable dresses of broadcloth, silk, and satin were more common.

Frontier food as a rule was plain and wholesome, although the menu often became monotonous and the cooking sometimes was faulty. Fried beef, venison, and salt pork were the most common meats of the republic years. For those living near the coast, fish and oysters offered some variety. There were roasting ears in season, and corn pone was on nearly every table. Most folks liked it, although a British diplomat called it "a modification of sawdust."

In the fall, hunters brought in fat wild turkeys, and those who lived near the grassy plains to the west often feasted on buffalo hump or roast tongue. Some of the wild game, however, was not always as appetizing as it later seemed in retrospect. Nestor Clay, after a long trip up the Colorado River and down the Brazos in 1832, told a friend that horse meat was "better than buffalo, wild cow, or venison."

A young man who arrived in Tyler County in 1845 found the fare a bit rugged. "I don't see how a man can live as you do," he wrote. "The ticks, the black mud, the sand flies, mosquitoes, dry beef, black coffee, and sweet potatoes of your country would ruin me. It is the perfect purgatory."

Tom Candy Ponting, on a cattle-buying trip in 1853, stopped overnight at the home of a ranchman in Hopkins County. All we had to eat," he recalled, "was corn bread that had been baked several days, and jerked dried beef."

When Frederick Law Olmsted traveled through much of Texas in the next year, he found a great variety of food. On struggling farms near the eastern edge of the state, he was offered little besides salt pork, corn bread, molasses, and milk. But on one of the more flourishing plantations farther west, he found "a clean table set with wheat bread, ham, tea, and preserved fruits, waited on by tidy and ready girls."

Noah Smithwick told of visiting a friend, Thomas B. Bell, whose pole cabin stood in a small clearing on the San Bernard River, where he grew a crop of corn. Bell and his wife and two children were dressed in buckskin. At supper, Smithwick recalled, "we sat on stools around a clapboard table, upon which were arranged wooden platters. Beside each platter lay a fork made of a joint of cane. The knives were of various patterns, ranging from butcher knives to pocketknives. For cups, we had little wild cymlings, scraped and scoured until they looked as white and clean as earthenware. The milk with which the cups were filled was as pure and sweet as mortal

On the Chisholm Trail
"Feet in the stirrups and seat in the saddle,
I hung and rattled with them Longhorn cattle."

Scribner's Magazine, *June, 1892*

A CAMP COOK AT WORK

On the trail or on roundup the chuck wagon was the cowboy's substitute
for home, and the camp cook was all-important to his well-being.

Erwin E. Smith photograph

AT THE SHEARING
Machines have replaced hand clippers for shearing the woolies.

LOOKING FOR A FARM SITE
The settler liked fairly high ground . . . in a bit of clearing.

Texas State Library Archives

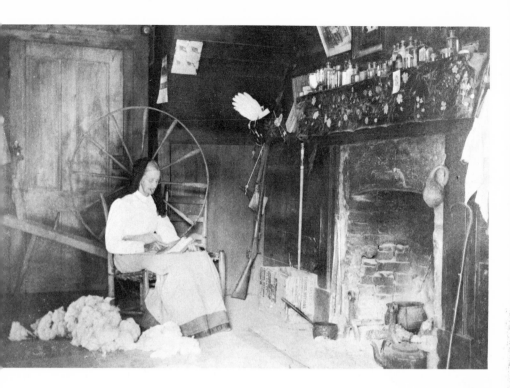

BATTING COTTON

Frontier women carded, spun, and wove cotton and wool.

Taulman Collection, University of Texas Library

BAPTIZING AT MOUNT CALM, 1901
A camp meeting or revival held by the Baptists usually was followed by
a group baptism in a nearby stream or pond.

Taulman Collection, University of Texas Library

MAKING MUSIC AT BLINN COLLEGE, BRENHAM
Since the days of dugouts, log cabins, and adobe huts . . . Texans have
shown an appreciation for music.

Kuehne Collection, University of Texas Library

THE COUNTRY DOCTOR
The frontier doctor drove in a buggy when roads and weather allowed—
often fifty or even one hundred miles—to treat the sick.

The Bettmann Archive

ever tasted. The repast was of the simplest but was served with as much grace as if it had been a feast."

Visitors to the towns of early Texas did not always find fancy fare in public places. In 1840, Dr. Francis Moore, Jr., editor of the Houston *Telegraph and Texas Register,* warned against "the ill-cooked, unwholesome food" of the taverns as a source of disease. "The heavy, sodden dough-balls, which in the shape of rolls are served at the hotels, are sufficient to create the worst remittent fever. They should be shunned by the hungry traveler as he would shun a charge of grapeshot."

When Olmsted was in Austin fourteen years later, he found the three hotels equally dirty and the food unappetizing. Of one of them he wrote: "Never did we see any wholesome food on that table. It was a succession of burnt flesh of swine and bulls, decaying vegetables, and sour and mouldy farinaceous glues, all pervaded with rancid butter."

When the first stagecoach traveled over the Butterfield Trail in 1858, only primitive food was provided at the stations where mules were changed. One of the passengers, Waterman L. Ormsby, reported: "We stopped at Abercrombie Pass to get breakfast, which consisted of the standard—coffee, tough beef, and butterless short cake, prepared by an old Negro woman, who, if cleanliness is next to godliness, would have little chance of heaven."

Other travelers fared better. In Dallas, Thomas F. Crutchfield built a log tavern in 1852, and his wife was such a fine cook that soon the Crutchfield House was famous for its dinners of venison, wild fowl, and catfish stuffed with cove oysters. Prince Paul of Williamsburg, Germany, spent two weeks there in 1852.

Gradually the planting of vegetable gardens and the coming of rail transportation added variety to Texas fare, though that of the more isolated families was slow to change. A man who toured Texas in 1873 liked everything except the food. "People in the interior still have a hearty scorn for anything good to eat," he wrote. "The bitter coffee and the greasy pork adorn most farmers' tables. One lady inquired of her guest, 'Won't you have a little bacon fat to wallop your corn dodgers in?' This was the acme of hospitality."

101

Even the well-to-do, he added, were "satisfied with the deadly pork and molasses, the clammy biscuits, and no vegetables whatever. The Negro is responsible for the introduction of such oceans of grease into Texas cookery."

A decade later the editors of *Texas Siftings* described a meal at the home of a cotton planter. The food "was spread on the plain pine table without a cover. We didn't at first know that it was a pine table, as it didn't seem to have been washed since the Revolution. Supper consisted of coffee without milk, flies without butter, corn bread, and fry. 'Fry' means rancid bacon charred by the fire."

The Texas farmer, they added, "lives on corn bread, bacon, and coffee the year round. Three times a day the same fare is set. Vegetables are not cultivated to any extent. As it is too much trouble to bring up the cows and milk them, Texans who own thousands of cattle don't have fresh meat, milk, or butter half a dozen times a year."

Many farm and ranch homes, of course, enjoyed better fare and more varied menus. Some women were good cooks before coming to Texas or had been well trained by their mothers. They kept their cabin homes as clean as they could, in spite of the flies from nearby stables; and, without refrigeration, they did their best to make plain food appetizing. In the spring, many gathered and cooked wild greens to help balance the heavy meat diet. In wooded parts of the state, women also dug sassafras roots to brew the tea their families liked to drink as a spring tonic.

Finally the tavernkeepers and the more affluent families in the towns no longer had to hang the milk in the well to keep it cool. A pioneer ice-making plant was started in San Antonio during the Civil War; and, a decade later, several other Texas cities had such plants. Ships brought Great Lakes ice to Galveston, and in 1873 trains began carrying St. Louis ice to other Texas cities and towns. In a few years, ice was being manufactured in all the larger cities.

As more settlers poured in from the Old South and the Middle West, eager for cheap land and a new start, primitive frontier conditions gradually gave way to more orderly and less strenuous life. Yield from the land increased, although calamities of nature and low prices for crops often brought unrest and protest.

The freeing of the slaves nipped the trend to grow cotton—and sometimes sugar—on vast plantations. But the extension of rail lines spread cotton growing over a much larger part of the state. Until the first railroad penetrated northern Texas in 1872, farmers in that section had put most of their fields in grain, used locally or sold to army posts. A little cotton had been shipped down the Red River or hauled by wagon to Jefferson—and some hauled even as far as Brownsville during the Civil War, when prices soared. After railroads were available to carry out the lint, cotton growing spread to large areas in which it had not been profitable earlier.

Expanding opportunities, however, did not free the Texas farmer from such hazards as predators, insect pests, and fires. In the pine country and across the prairies and plains, isolated families dreaded the hot breath and billowing smoke of blazes that raced before the wind. Some recalled fires that left several hundred sections of choice range and crop land black and seared.

Stockmen and farmers faced the danger of fire almost every year, especially in periods of drouth. Blazes sped across the dry grass to devour crops, winter forage, barns, farm homes, and sometimes even frontier towns. The start might come from a stroke of lightning or sparks from a train locomotive or a threshing-machine engine. Some fires spread from abandoned campfires or the burning wads from the discharge of a gun. Indians often set fires maliciously. Other blazes were thought to have come from the striking of a mustang's hoof on a flint rock.

Light in the night sky sometimes gave warning of the terror that approached. Smoke from burning grass might hide the sun for days; one prairie fire lasted for six weeks. Although such a fire might trap a traveler and one took four lives in 1860, most of the frontiersmen could take refuge in dugouts, coughing and sweating until the blaze swept over them. One farm woman, carrying a baby, found safety in a shallow well.

A number of early travelers left descriptions of prairie fires. "They are always spectacular and grand," wrote Albert D. Richardson, who was in the West in the late 1850's. "The sky is pierced with tall pyramids of flame or covered with writhing, leaping, lurid ser-

103

pents or transformed into a broad ocean lighted by a blazing sunset. Now a whole avalanche of fire slides off into the prairie and then, opening its great, devouring jaws, closes in upon the deadened grass."

Many plainsmen plowed strips around their homes and gardens, hoping that the fire would not leap over them. Others burned a space about their buildings for protection. Sometimes a traveler could save himself by starting a new fire ahead of the one he saw approaching. As soon as his fire had blackened a large piece of ground, he moved into it.

John C. Duval used this method when caught in the prairie soon after the Texas Revolution. "I took my flint and steel from my pocket," he recalled, "ignited some tinder which I wrapped in a wisp of dry grass, and swung it quickly backward and forward in my hand. It soon was in a blaze. With this I set fire to the grass ahead of me. In a few moments I had the satisfaction of seeing my counter fire sweeping the grass that grew in the direction in which I was going."

Cowmen taking their Longhorn herds up the Chisholm Trail needed to watch out for prairie fires. George W. Brock of Lockhart, while trailing a herd north in the spring of 1879, had to move his cattle into rough country because his cook accidentally had set fire to the grass. Later Brock saw lightning start a grass fire, which rain soon extinguished.

Sheepmen, too, had to contend with fires that roared across their pastures and endangered their flocks. In 1882 a fast blaze swept from the South Concho across the Edwards Plateau to the headsprings of the San Saba. It left a swath of black, charred stubs forty miles wide. Herders caught in its path drove their flocks into the bed of a dry lake and battled the flames for five days until help arrived from the outside.

In the Texas Panhandle the vast and almost unimpeded spread of the XIT Ranch had several disastrous blazes, despite the plowing of fire guards. In 1885, flames from a carelessly set cooking fire spread to the pastures. The blaze raced from the Beaver to the Canadian, leaving many cows and calves dead and others severely burned or blinded.

On the XIT, as elsewhere on the plains, cowmen sometimes fought prairie fires with drags. First, they killed a yearling or a two-year-old, cut off its head, and skinned one side. Then, with ropes tied to their saddle horns, two men—one on each side of the blaze—dragged the carcass down the line of fire. This drag, with its loose hide flapping along behind, put out most of the blaze. Men following on foot with wet gunnysacks or blankets batted out any small flames that remained.

Even the grizzled buffalo hunters who cleared the plains for the cowmen had trouble occasionally from prairie fires. In 1875, when Jack Bickerdyke was taking hides near the north edge of the Texas Panhandle, he looked up and saw a fire sweeping down between the Beaver and the North Palo Duro. When he ran to catch his horse, he found that his mount, frightened by the oncoming blaze, had run down the creek, leaving him afoot. By the time he returned to the buffalo he had killed and half skinned, he was surrounded by fire. To save himself, he ripped open the carcass, pulled out the entrails, crawled inside, and put the hide down to cover himself and his rifle as well as he could. Although the smoke choked and almost smothered him as the fire swept past, he staggered out uninjured a few minutes later.

Invasions by hordes of ravenous grasshoppers left the stricken farmers almost as helpless as did the fires. Pioneer settlers never knew when the sky would be darkened by clouds of "Rocky Mountain locusts," landing on crops and pastures. Often the hungry visitors would strip the fields of every green leaf. Nothing succeeded in driving off the pests or lessening their destructive greed.

Texas began suffering from such blitz attacks in the early days of settlement. Navarro County had such a visitation in 1853. Every green sprig was destroyed by the hungry horde, wrote a local historian, Annie Carpenter Love. "The reddish green cloud of insects rolled over the country like a flood until there was a heavy coating on the ground. After the third day, Navarro County looked as though a fire had swept over it and had singed every plant."

Two years later Fort Belknap, to the northwest, reported a mass of 'hoppers that came in "like a dense snow storm." A similar cloud swept down the valley of the Colorado River in 1858. Noah Smithwick said the insects devoured every green thing except the ragweed, which apparently was too bitter. The grasshoppers used the denuded bushes and weeds as roosts. "When the cold nights came, they were frozen on their perches. In this state they fell easy victims to the hogs, which devoured millions of them. But enough were left to seed the ground for the next season's crop."

No farm or ranch was safe from the swift-moving plagues. The flutter of grasshoppers' wings as they came in made a roar that was almost deafening. In a field of corn they devoured the tender leaves and newly formed ears, leaving the stalks as bare as tent poles. Sometimes they beat on cabin roofs with the sound of hail, then pushed inside and ate the window curtains. They ate family washings hanging on lines. Men working outside had to tie strings around the bottoms of their pants legs to keep the voracious pests from crawling up inside.

In gardens the looters not only devoured everything above the surface but went into the ground after onions and turnips. In the fields they cut the bands to open sheaves of grain. They ate the paint off buildings and left the handles of implements so rough they could not be used. They contaminated creeks so badly that often cattle refused to drink from them.

In army camps the 'hoppers ate holes in wagon covers and the tarpaulins covering supplies. One soldier, who had been marching all night, lay down on the prairie at midday for a nap. Soon his fellows noticed that he was covered with grasshoppers and woke him. His throat and wrists were bleeding from bites.

Along the pioneer railways the insects would alight on the rails and ballast in the evening, apparently attracted by the warmth of the steel, until they were four to six inches thick. They made the rails so greasy that locomotive wheels spun instead of pulling. Trains could not move until after workmen had shoveled off the 'hoppers and sanded the rails. In one frontier town in 1866 the pests stopped horse races by covering the track one to three inches thick.

Embattled farmers fought the grasshoppers with clubs and brush brooms. They beat on tin pans to drive them away with noise. They put out poison. But nothing seemed to do much good. Usually the greedy insects stayed until everything green was gone, then moved on. Sometimes a heavy rain drowned many of them. Chickens and turkeys ate themselves sick.

Many areas of Texas reported invasions. "A stranger in Dallas on Wednesday last," said that city's *Herald* of September 26, 1876, "might have imagined that a clear sky was distributing a snow storm over the fertile fields of northern Texas. Untold millions of locusts dotted the firmament with circling flakes which, falling by thousands, gave the appearance of snowfall. Parties walking along the streets were surprised to see swarms of locusts rise almost at their feet.

"In the suburbs there are complaints of their depredations on grass and vegetables. In shrubbery they are fastidious, devouring the verbenas but ignoring the other flowers." The *Herald* advised citizens to keep their wells and cisterns tightly closed and to wrap cotton around the trunks of their fruit trees and shrubs.

In Fayette County in February, 1877, grasshoppers were reported to be hatching by the millions and eating everything they could find. A month later they were devouring early gardens there and starting to eat the young corn and cotton plants. By the first of April many discouraged farmers had quit planting. A week later the 'hoppers had denuded the gardens of their second plantings.

In 1879 the skies over Denton County were darkened by clouds of grasshoppers. X. Carson of Dallas, then a nine-year-old boy on a farm nine miles west of Denton, recalled his family's fear that the insects would destroy the wheat crop. Luckily, the cloud swept on southward toward the Gulf of Mexico. Will Williams of Denton, a still younger boy at that time, remembered that swarms darkened the sun and were so thick on the ground that "the steps over the fence to our cow lot were made slick by the mashing of grasshoppers under our feet."

Some discouraged farmers put their belongings in their wagons, hitched their scrawny horses, and headed back east. They had had more than their fill of the Promised Land described attractively in emigrant circulars. On one creaking wagon was scrawled, "Hoppers et all but the wagon sheet."

Later visitations, if less tragic, often brought serious destruction of crops. One in western Texas in the early 1880's was described by Anson Cox in a brief account that Mary L. Cox quoted in her history of Hale County:

"One of our farmers near Estacado had a beautiful field of wheat. The 'hoppers were more numerous in the grass but soon left the grass as the wheat began to grow. The farmer, having a large family of children, armed each child with a brush broom to kill the 'hoppers as they passed a furrow he had plowed around the field. Then he hitched his team to a large log and drove the horses at a trot along the furrow, crushing the 'hoppers. But all in vain. After an hour or two, he gave up.

"The 'hoppers grew fast and ate every green thing in sight except the bull thistles and yucca plants. They crawled right over sod houses or into them if the doors were opened. I thought I could save my garden. I had a large earth tank two or three feet above the level of the land. I made a ditch around it and let the water in; but the 'hoppers marched in, filled the ditch with drowned 'hoppers, then the others marched over them and feasted on my garden. There was desolation everywhere—everything green gone as bare as though there never had been any vegetation."

In later years, modern methods helped to check the pests but did not banish them. The summer of 1937 brought the worst grasshopper plague since 1880. Thousands of acres were eaten bare, and crops worth millions of dollars were devoured. Some farmers and ranchmen fought the invaders with shallow tanks of kerosene. Others had their fields dusted from airplanes that could scatter poison on 250 acres in an hour. Most depended on poison bait. Drifts of grasshoppers against some buildings were more than a yard deep.

In the frontier period, such misfortunes as drouths and grasshopper plagues led the more restless settlers to pull up stakes and move to sites that seemed more promising. The last request of J. Brit Bailey was that he be buried standing, facing the west, with his rifle by his side, his powder horn on his shoulder, his lead bullets ready for reloading, and a jug of whisky at his feet. He had been going west all his life, he said; and, when awakened, he wanted to continue.

Even in the days of sod-busting on the prairies and maverick branding on the plains, frontier life in Texas wasn't all work. Hunting and fishing provided sport as well as food. And there were such social gatherings as house raisings, quilting bees, taffy pullings, box parties, and dances.

The towns had baseball games, fairs, an occasional visiting circus or balloon ascension, and, on the Fourth of July a chicken fry, fish fry, or barbecue, with calf-roping contests, political speeches, and fireworks. Some of the men engaged in billiards or bowling or attended wrestling matches, dogfights, rat killings, and deadly combats between dogs and badgers. For the serious-minded, the larger communities offered lyceum lectures and, in later years, summer chautauquas in big tents.

In the range country, dances were infrequent in the early days but were not limited entirely to weddings and Christmas. Sometimes a cowboy would go two hundred miles to attend a big dance that might last three days. Since there usually weren't enough girls to go around, the men had to await their turns. Occasionally, a few of the men would tie a white handkerchief around their arms to tag themselves as "lady fair" or "heifer branded." Women would bring their children and babies if they had no one with whom to leave them. The women, and maybe some of the men, would take turns watching the babies in the wagons. The dancing started about sundown and lasted until the roosters began to crow.

Noah Smithwick, an early settler, recalled a wedding party in the Austin colony. After the ceremony, performed by the *alcalde* from San Felipe, and a fine supper, the puncheon floor of the cabin was cleared for dancing. The young folk, he noted, didn't glide around. "They shuffled and double shuffled, wired, and cut the pigeon's wing, making the splinters fly.

"Some of the boys were not provided with shoes. Moccasins were not adapted to that kind of dancing floor, and moreover they couldn't make enough noise. But their more fortunate brethren weren't selfish or disposed to put on airs. When they had danced a turn, they generously exchanged footgear with the moccasined contingent and gave them the ring; and we kicked every splinter off that floor before morning. The fiddle manipulated by Mose being too weak to make itself heard above the din of clattering feet, we had in another fellow with a clevis and pin; and we had a most enjoyable time."

Smithwick described another dance at which an old Negro performed on a clevis as an accompaniment to his singing, while another scraped on a cotton hoe with a caseknife. The favorite chorus was:

> *Oh git up, gals, in de mawnin,'*
> *Oh git up, gals, in de mawnin,'*
> *Oh git up, gals, in de mawnin,'*
> *Jes at de break of day.*

At the conclusion, he added, "the performer gave an extra blow to the clevis, while the dancers responded with a series of dexterous rat-tat-tats with heel and toe."

A fiddler who could play "The Arkansas Traveler" and "Turkey in the Straw" was in frequent demand for frontier dances. Also popular was any good caller for square dances. Standing on the floor, sitting beside the fiddler, or sometimes taking part in the dancing, he called out in a loud voice such directions as:

> *Choose your partner, form a ring,*
> *Double eight, and double L swing.*

> *First swing six, then swing eight,*
> *Swing 'em like swinging on a gate.*

> *Ducks in the river going to the ford,*
> *Coffee in a little rag, sugar in a gourd.*

110

Square dances were popular in and around Parker County, especially in settlements along Bear Creek and the Brazos River. The most popular dance fiddler in that region just after the Civil War was Arch Bozzell, a six-footer who stuffed his breeches into his boots. He was recalled as having "a small mustache, a winning smile, and a deft hand with the bow." His favorite pieces included "The Arkansas Traveler," "Cotton-Eyed Joe," "Sally Gooden," "Turkey in the Straw," "Leather Breeches," "The Buffalo Gals," and "Black-Eyed Susie."

Most of the dances were held in homes, but an unusually big affair might be staged in a public building. In the Panhandle at times the Texline Courthouse was converted into a dance hall. A typical ranch dance at Buffalo Springs, to the music of a couple of fiddles, was described by Mrs. C. R. Duke. The XIT cowboys left off their spurs and wore dancing shoes, she said. "We danced in a room about fourteen by sixteen. Everyone came to the ranch in a wagon or buggy. There were not many women or girls—and not a bobbed head in the bunch. Most of them wore their hair in the latest pompadour and curled their own hair by heating the curlers over a coal-oil lamp. Our dresses almost touched the floor and were tight as beeswax. Lipstick, rouge, and permanents were unknown.

"We danced the schottische, waltz, glide, polka, and all kinds of square dances. We waltzed to the tune of 'Good-by, Old Paint' until the early hours of morning." At midnight the hosts served a supper that ended with cake and coffee.

Even before Mexican rule was overthrown, many Texas towns began holding celebrations on the Fourth of July. Harrisburg had one such celebration at least as early as 1833. Mrs. Dilue Harris recalled a big one of 1834 near Stafford's Point on the Brazos, about fifteen miles from Harrisburg. The whisky gave out early in the evening, but there was a wealth of food, including barbecued beef, fowls, vegetables, corn bread, honey, and coffee. A shortage of flour explained the absence of cakes. Music was provided by three Negro fiddlers who played in turn and by another who beat time with the fiddlers, using an iron pin and clevis from the end of a cart tongue or plow beam. The young people, Anglos and Latins, danced the

Virginia Reel and waltzes from three in the afternoon until morning. A similar Fourth of July barbecue, with a dance, was held in frontier Sherman in 1847. For the feast, men built a large brush shed, in which long tables were loaded with roast beef and other delicacies. For refreshment there was a barrel of whisky with a tin cup beside it. The people danced in the log courthouse, about twenty by twenty feet, to the hoe-down music of a stalwart Negro.

Of a Fourth of July barbecue at Marble Falls in 1854, Noah Smithwick recalled some of the food. There was a wagonload of roasting ears, along with loads of other vegetables, watermelons, and cantaloupes. "Huntsmen brought in venison and wild turkey, and beef and pork galore were advanced. There were pound cakes, wild-grape pies, dewberry pies, and wild plum pies. As yet there was no cultivated fruit except dried fruit, which was scarce and high."

Later celebrations of Independence Day often included a barbecue, political oratory, a rodeo, fireworks, and a dance. At frontier Ozona, Allan R. Bosworth recalled, the merrymaking lasted three days, and everything was free. "Ranchers donated beef steers for barbecue, merchants provided bread and a barrel of pickles, and men on the committee cooked vast quantities of Texas-style *frijole* beans. There were gallons of scalding coffee, strong enough to float a horseshoe, and a barrel of ice-cold lemonade." After the spread-eagle speaking and the contests in riding and roping, the celebration ended with a grand shirtsleeve ball.

Another event that attracted farm families and cowboys to the towns was the traveling circus. Of the several which toured frontier Texas, the most frequent and most popular was that of Mollie A. Bailey. From winter quarters in Houston she took her three-pole tent show to the towns of Texas and nearby states by wagon for thirty-six years until she put it on a train in 1905. The show's trapeze and tight-wire performers, musicians, clowns, and trained canaries were popular wherever the show went; and Mollie, who knew thousands of Texans by name, was a welcome guest in many homes.

County and state fairs were also popular. In 1852, Colonel Henry L. Kinney, the founder of Corpus Christi, sponsored a Lone Star Fair to promote the city. Entertainment included stock shows, fireworks, cockfights, horse races, bullfights featuring the celebrated Don Camerena of Mexico City, and the noted Maltby's Circus. Dallas, with a more central location, began holding a state fair intermittently in 1859 and regularly in 1886. It offered horse races, political speeches, musical shows, ice-skating extravaganzas, and many carnival attractions.

Children in the country towns, and even on the farms and ranches, seldom found time heavy on their hands, despite the scarcity of store-bought toys. When they were not in school or doing chores set by their parents, they usually could devise games. The girls had rag dolls, and their brothers seemed never to tire of playing cowboy. "Little children, as early as they can walk," wrote a newspaper correspondent from the brush of DeWitt County, "pilfer their mother's tape and make lassos to rope the kittens and the ducks. The boys, as soon as they can climb on a pony, are off to the prairie to drive stock. As they advance toward manhood, their highest ambition is to conquer a pitching mustang or throw a wild beef by the tail."

The late John Hendrix recalled that when he was a young boy in Gainesville, he and his neighbors played with sticks as horses, corncob cattle, and string corrals. "Our pastures and corrals were fenced with twine in which we kept our herds of corncobs, each marked with his father's brand. The brands were placed on the cobs with branding irons made of hay wire by our elders or old hands in from the ranches for a layoff."

Also popular with Texas boys was playing at battles between settlers and Indians and, after 1878, skirmishes between Texas Rangers and the train-robbing band of Sam Bass.

Matching horses in short races was a favorite sport on the Texas frontier. Racing a pair of fast mounts on a straight, grassy track appealed to almost every pioneer settler. Hardly any man was too poor to have a saddle horse or two, and even a teen-age youth could find someone to match ponies with him. Watching a pair of nags in a sprint gave him a chance to toss his sombrero and air his lungs.

Any horse that wasn't crippled was a potential racer; but for the Sunday afternoon matches that townsmen, farmers, and cowmen

113

would ride miles to see, the small, chunky Quarter Horse, bred and trained to run a quarter of a mile, was the favorite. Maneuverable and intelligent, he also was the most dependable type of cow pony in the Longhorn roundups and trail drives.

Quarter racing, popular in Virginia, Kentucky, and Tennessee in earlier days, was common on the Texas prairies by the time of annexation. Some of the matches attracted so many visitors that part of them had to camp out. Most of the spectators, however, came from short distances. Usually they came on horseback and remained in their saddles to watch the matches, their faces shaded by the broad brims of their hats. Frequently the mounts of the onlookers formed a solid line on either side of the grassy or harrowed course.

At a track one mile north of Denton, cut-ups often had a bit of fun at the expense of fans who came to the races on mounts hired from the livery stables. One of the sportive youths would snatch the reins from an unsuspecting fellow and toss them over the horse's head. At the same moment, his confederate would give the livery horse a swat on the rump. At that, the startled but discerning pony would tear out for the stable in town. The rider, hanging on as well as he could, would try without success to stop his rushing steed. Sometimes three or four of these livery horses could be seen capering down the road from the race track to Denton.

Scrub races on the prairies had few standing rules. For each match the owners of the contending ponies made a separate agreement. Although sometimes more horses competed, the typical race was a match between two mounts, often representing rival ranches or towns. Before the start, the judges would line the ponies with a tree or a post or some other fixed object. Even the end of a wagon might do. Judges had to be chosen carefully, since charges of foul play sometimes led to fights. One Indian judge, determined not to be tricked, stretched across the finish line a light rope smeared with red paint. The winning horse, he ruled, would have to show a paint mark to claim the prize.

Racing men used various methods in starting the horses. One was a pistol shot. Another was called the lap and tap. Under this rule, the mounts were led about fifty feet back from the starting line, where they whirled and began running. If the judge found them sufficiently close "in lap" as they crossed the starting line, he "tapped them off" by shouting, "Go!" If they were too far apart, they had to be taken back for a new start.

A third method, common in Texas and the Indian Territory, was by "ask and answer." The starter would ask, "Are you ready?" When he heard the jockeys answer, "Yes," he would shout, "Go!" and the match would be on. For important races in the larger towns, the start sometimes was made from chutes built of narrow poles cut in the woods. The stalls were devised in an effort to allow the rivals an even getaway.

The most celebrated of all the racing Quarter Horses of the Texas frontier was the bay stallion Steel Dust. Brought from Illinois as a yearling just before annexation, Steel Dust quickly developed into an amazing sprinter. From his stable on Ten Mile Creek, southeast of Lancaster, in Dallas County, the renown of Steel Dust spread to adjoining counties.

To the north, in Collin County, was another noted sprinter. He was Monmouth, a Kentucky short horse owned by Harrison Stiff. One of the biggest racing events of the period was the match between Steel Dust and Monmouth at McKinney in 1855. Steel Dust won readily and, later that year, was matched in Dallas against Jack Batchler's famous Tennessee stallion, Shiloh. But Steel Dust, injured in the stall at the start, went blind. He never raced again but lived to sire colts that won on many tracks.

Even though few frontier women approved of cockfighting, many of their menfolk liked to slip off on Sunday afternoon to a bare spot in the woods where lively matches were promised. Others watched rooster duels in the towns—in the back streets or, down toward Mexico, in the plazas. Some kept a pet gamecock in the barn, feeding him extra corn and training him for combat.

Although George Washington had been a patron of the cockpits, most of the Anglos in Texas acquired their taste for cockfighting from men of Mexican ancestry, who had a passion for the sport. In a season that lasted from Thanksgiving to July 4, one could find chicken fights in San Antonio, El Paso, and other places. In the plazas

115

the belligerent birds would be tied to stakes or held by their owners until the contests began. Each cock had the spur of his left leg cut off and a slasher attached. This was a long steel knife, shaped like a saber but concave toward the cutting edge. It was two to four inches long, sharp as a razor, and pointed as a needle.

Some of the pigmy roosters were scrawny and bore the scars of earlier fights; others were beautiful in their plumage of black and gold. They would peck eagerly at each other as the handlers held them close to each other to whet their appetite for blood. For two weeks most of them had been penned and deprived of female company. They had been given workouts a week earlier, with chamois muffs on their spurs. They had had no food that day. Their combs had been trimmed closely, and the steel gaffs with which they had been heeled glinted in the light.

To the north the gaffs tended to be a bit shorter and less deadly than the Mexican slashers. But the standard length was two and one-quarter inches, and most of the clashes ended in death for at least one of the roosters.

Breeders and cockers from distant states flocked to Dallas in February, 1886, to attend the great cocking main between that city and St. Louis. Chicago and St. Louis newspapers sent sports writers to cover the event, which lasted several days, with five hundred roosters participating. An entire forenoon was required for weighing and matching the birds. The Dallas *Morning News* observed that this main "firmly established Texas supremacy in the cocking world."

The most brilliant match in the tournament, on the result of which $2,500 changed hands, was a four-round go between Shawl-neck, a Dallas Redquill with a ragged gill, and Spooner, the St. Louis champion, a dark red-ginger bird with a high comb. They weighed even at 4:15. In the first round, both birds jumped to the scratch, the dark one showing the better judgment, the Redquill cock going low. On the turn they came together, hung, and were separated. In the second round, the birds jumped to a hang. St. Louis came up groggy in the fourth and, at the first shock, lay down to his punishment. The Dallas champion shattered his steel at the second blow, ending the battle in three minutes and six seconds.

116

Dallas continued to be an important cocking center, although some citizens frowned on the sport. Late in 1888 the *News* published a letter from a reader who protested that "to take these poor birds, armed with steel, and allow them to cut and kill each other for the amusement of men should not be allowed."

Dallas' last big cocking main was held in 1905. The next year the legislature outlawed the sport. But as it did not ban the breeding and training of gamecocks, hundreds of Texans continued to prepare birds for competition in other states and in Mexico and the Philippines. With so many gamecocks available, it was inevitable that rooster fighting should continue surreptitiously, usually at a bare spot in the woods on Sunday afternoon. A bigger cocking main might be held in a pit with an earth floor and a canvas wall, or in an isolated clubhouse with sawdust and bleachers.

Before the start of each match, the referee weighs the cocks at the edge of the pit. Most of the birds balance the scales at five pounds or a little more. Usual rules stipulate that birds matched to each other must not vary more than two ounces in weight. As the match is about to start, bets are shouted across the pit. Most of the wagers are for only five or ten dollars, but some go much higher.

"Get ready," the referee calls; and the handlers place their birds on lines facing the center of the ring and about six feet from each other.

"Pit your birds!" he says a few seconds later, watch in hand. The handlers let go their fowls, and the cocks rush at each other like demons, pecking and clawing and beating with their wings. "Watch 'em shuffle!" fans shout from all sides.

Soon one gaff makes a strike, and the cocks are entangled. "Handle," the referee calls, and two men pull out the steel spur, untangle the birds, and take them back to the lines for the second pitting of the match. Both birds are panting from the heat and excitement, and the handlers blow on them to cool them. A wing of one bird may be broken and bleeding, but he still is game.

Again the two cocks rush at each other, half-running, half-flying. This time one gets his gaff into his enemy. "He's got a rattle," backers of the stuck bird say hopelessly as he is carried back to his side of the pit. The gaff has gone through his back and into his lungs, and he is coughing up blood.

The handler wipes the bloody head with a wet cloth and holds a finger in the cock's beak to help him breathe easier, but most of the fight has gone out of him. In the next pitting he makes only feeble resistance, and in a few moments he is carried off dead as other cocks are being heeled for the next match.

In the larger Texas towns, horse racing and cockfighting vied with baseball and soon had to compete with other outdoor sports, including lawn tennis, golf, football, and bicycle riding. In the 1880's and 1890's, cycling was especially popular among the men, young men, and some of the young women. Texas saw its first bicycle not long after this new vehicle had been popularized at the Centennial Fair at Philadelphia in 1876. The strange velocipede with wooden spokes and iron tires aroused great curiosity. In 1882, Gross R. Scruggs of Dallas paid $162.50 for that city's first bicycle with solid rubber tires.

The Dallas Wheel Club, said to have been the first of its kind in Texas, was formed in the spring of 1886, with twenty-three men as charter members. An early action of the club was to adopt a uniform consisting of a white shirt, blue knee-breeches, low white shoes, and the regulation cap of the League of American Wheelmen.

Rival clubs were formed in Dallas and other Texas cities as the more fashionable young men took up cycling. Mounting and riding one of the high-wheeled contraptions required almost the skill of a bronc buster. Usually the main wheel was forty-eight to sixty-four inches high. It had a much smaller wheel behind, although in a later variation called the star the small wheel was in front.

Outstanding among Dallas' daring young cyclists was Tom L. Monagan, who brought with him from St. Louis early in 1886 not only his bicycle but several racing medals and the further distinction of having taken part in that event of nationwide importance, the annual bicycle race from Chicago to Pullman.

Remaining strictly an amateur, Monagan soon became captain, and later president, of the Dallas Wheel Club and brought it fame by winning repeatedly the state championship in bicycle speed. Monagan and his mates performed in many Texas cities but gained their most spectacular victories at the State Fair of Texas. A quarter-mile dirt track was provided for bicycle races at the fair in Dallas in 1886, and championship races were held there for years.

In 1887 four members of the Dallas Wheel Club pedaled their high-wheel bicycles to Waxahachie, thirty miles to the south. The trip took three hours and forty-five minutes. The men had to push their bicycles up sandy hills and, ten miles from their goal, took time to rest a few minutes under shady trees.

The first century run in Texas was made in 1891, when C. T. Daugherty of Dallas covered 103 miles in thirteen hours and ten minutes running time. Two years later the Dallas Wheel Club, headed by its bugler who flourished a silver instrument, led the long parade that greeted the steamer *H. A. Harvey, Jr.*, which had come up the Trinity River from the Gulf of Mexico.

In June, 1895, Dallas cyclists expressed displeasure at a new city ordinance requiring bells on all bicycles. They obtained the loudest bells they could find and made enough noise to rouse people from their homes. In the following month, 125 elaborately decorated bicycles appeared in a lantern parade in Dallas on the eve of the meeting of the Texas division of the League of American Wheelmen. In that decade the efforts of cyclists greatly spurred the movement for better roads.

The advent of the safety bicycle, whose wheels were of equal size, made cycling even more popular, and many young women joined in the sport. Dallas' Cycle Park, built in the fall of 1898, had a half-mile board track and became a favorite gathering place for cyclists for several years.

By that time, newspapers were complaining that the bicycle fad had overrun the state; and Jim Hogg, former governor, was declaring that cyclists would become "a race of people running around on all fours like monkeys." The boys, he said, "won't wear coats, and the women want to wear breeches all the time. Tell your folks not to learn to ride the things and thus avoid deformity."

Such warnings went unheeded, but it was not long until chasers after mechanical fads and lovers of speed had their attention diverted to a newer and even more fascinating contrivance—the horseless carriage.

Meanwhile, baseball continued popular in the towns, as it had been for several decades. As early as 1872, the Robert E. Lee team from New Orleans had invaded Texas, playing in several towns. From Waco to Austin the squad had to travel by stagecoach for lack of other transportation.

Men who boasted that they could shoot a bumblebee off a thistle at five hundred yards or plug the bunghole of a barrel rolling down a hillside tested their skill in hunting and shooting clubs. In the Trinity valley the Dallas Hunting and Fishing Club, formed in 1885, bought one thousand acres of land three miles east of Hutchins. The Texas Fox and Wolf Hunters' Association, formed in 1892, began holding a spring wolf hunt and an autumn fox hunt.

In 1896, when William Jennings Bryan was campaigning for free silver, two Dallas businessmen introduced golf into Texas. They were H. L. Edwards and R. E. Potter, who had tried the game in their native England. Obtaining clubs and balls from Boston, they laid out a crude six-hole course on a prairie at the edge of town, thus giving Dallas a taste of what later became a popular pastime.

CHAPTER NINE

HORSEMEN FOR THE LORD

A CROSS THE PRAIRIES and plains of Texas, religion never was far away. Even the most primitive Indian tribes believed in a Great Spirit, whose favor they sought with dances and other rites. When the Spaniards came, priests and friars rode with the conquistadors. Near the garrisoned forts, called presidios, rose more than a score of missions, where efforts were made to convert Indians to the Christian religion and the white man's ways.

The typical mission brought a pleasing Spanish architectural style to Texas. It was built with Indian labor, sometimes with help from soldiers. Besides a church and a house for the missionaries, it included small houses for the Indians, a granary, a blacksmith shop, and other buildings, all of them forming a quadrangle. Surrounding the mission was a protecting wall with fortified gates. Outside were a garden, an orchard, and a cemetery. Still beyond were cultivated fields and pastures for horses, cattle, and sheep.

With gifts of food, clothing, tobacco, beads, and other trinkets, Indians were induced to come to the missions to live and work. There they were taught the Spanish language, the Christian religion, and such trades as gardening, weaving, leather work, and the making of pottery and baskets. Schools were provided for the children.

The day at the mission began at dawn, when bells called all adults to morning worship, followed by instruction in the catechism. Then came breakfast and work in the fields or elsewhere. At night the Indians were locked in to keep them from running away.

Some of the missions acquired large flocks and herds. By 1770 the Mission of Espiritú Santo, near Goliad, had forty thousand cattle grazing between the Guadalupe and San Antonio rivers, while the nearby Mission of Rosario claimed thirty thousand ranging to the west. Sheep also were held in large numbers at most of the missions, where their wool was used in making clothes and blankets.

Although the padres treated the Indians kindly, some of the converts found mission life confining in contrast to the freedom of the plains. When an Indian failed to attend church or tried to run away and was caught, he was flogged in front of the others and required to kiss the priest's hand.

The Spanish missions in Texas, in contrast to those in some other parts of Mexico, were handicapped by the fact that most of the Plains Indians, instead of being concentrated in villages, were in roving bands whose members disliked anything that interfered with their hunting, warfare, or freedom of movement. Thus their willingness to live and work at the missions wore off after a brief time.

Another handicap was the hostility of warrior bands that frequently attacked the missions and drove off many of their horses, cattle, and sheep. This opposition caused some of the missions to be abandoned within a few years after they were built. The fierce Comanches, who had little use for the missions from the start, were further alienated when a number of the missions took in Apaches, traditional enemies of the Comanches. An army of Comanches and other Indians, with faces painted black and crimson, attacked the San Saba Mission in March, 1758, killing everyone found there except three who escaped, and set fire to the buildings. After killing Fray José Santiesteban at the foot of the altar where he was praying, the Comanches cut off his head and tossed it about like a ball.

Still another drawback to the success of the missions was the frequent antagonism of the soldiers sent to protect them. At the San Xavier missions, trouble with the military came to a head in 1752. The situation there was described by an early Spanish historian, Juan Agustín Morfi: "Lust, selfishness, cruelty, and unbearable pride were the dominating passions which these men set as examples to the Indians they were charged to defend. Girls, single or married, were made to serve the captain in his pleasures. Modesty was banished from the missions. The most lascivious soldiers were the most successful; there were no other merits for promotion than to secure new subjects for the satisfaction of the captain. Scandal found its way into the walls of the temple. The neophytes saw themselves deprived of their wives and daughters by the soldiers, oppressed by excessive labor, insulted every moment of the day, and denied the right to voice their misfortunes. The religious tried to correct or modify the abuses."

This trouble led Fray Miguel Pinilla to declare Captain Felipe de Rabago and his whole garrison excommunicated, an action that led to still further quarreling.

Yet, although they did not achieve lasting conversion of many of the Indians, most of whom later were moved north of the Red River, the missions helped to push forward the Spanish frontier in Texas. They planted new churches, some of which survived and a few of which later were restored as historical shrines. Their influence modified for the better that of the military forces, whose interest was largely in conquest and plunder.

Protestant ministers in Texas had to await a later period, since they were not allowed under Spanish or Mexican rule. Some came anyway under the Mexicans, and more followed after Texas gained its independence in 1836. They preached not to the Indians but to the white settlers. The typical pioneer preacher was a circuit rider, dependent, no less than the cowman, on a sturdy horse. If he lost his mount, he had to borrow one or give up his circuit until he could buy another. Often his circuit extended for hundreds of miles. Horse thieves, white as well as bronze, were no respecters of the clergy. At Weatherford, in November, 1874, while a Methodist conference was in session, someone stole the horses of several preachers, leaving them afoot.

Often the steed that carried the circuit preacher had an arduous job. In the republic period, one Methodist in the marshy coastal country, the Reverend Jesse Hord, was thankful for a horse that carried him across a prairie that "nothing but a duck or a goose ever crossed."

The long circuits, with few stopping places for food and shelter, were hard on horses and men. A pioneer Methodist, Benjamin Lakin, wrote in his diary on a Friday in January, "Preached in a cold and open meeting house, then rode about ten miles in the cold." On Sunday he recorded, "Snow falling fast. Rode and preached." On Monday the roads were worse: "Last night it rained and froze to a sleet. Today I rode an unbroken way. The ice cut my horse's legs until the blood came." On Tuesday the ice was so much harder that Lakin had to walk in front of his horse and break the way.

Early Texas was a fertile field for the circuit rider. Accounts of the republic have much comment on heavy drinking, profane language, and disregard of the Sabbath. The Methodists, the first to develop the practice of circuit riding, took an active lead in Texas. An Austin man noted in his diary in 1843 that "the panther is scarcely more keen-scented for the backwoodsman's blood than the Methodist preacher is for his soul." Another Texan, in Washington County, observed in 1849 that "the Methodist preacher is far in advance of the Yankee clock peddler."

The flexible circuit system was easily adjusted to population in motion. Some of the early preachers had twenty-five to forty preaching places. Where there were no churches, they held services in the cabins of settlers or, in summer, under the trees. Often the preaching was set for midday, since many of the families had no clocks or watches. The early Texas circuit preacher received only one hundred dollars a year, or little more than that, but was given free meals and lodging most of the time in the homes of his parishioners. Bishops discouraged the preachers from marrying because so many of the married ones had to give up their circuits for work that would better support their families.

Horses of the itinerant preachers were of various types. The Reverend W. Y. Allen of Houston wrote in his diary in 1839 that he had bought an Indian pony. The mounts needed a great deal of endurance for long rides over rough trails. Some of the riders were keen judges of horseflesh and could hold their own in a trade.

The equipment of the circuit rider included a pair of saddlebags that held his Bible, hymnbook, spare clothes, toilet articles, and writing materials. Rolled behind the saddle was a sheepskin blanket or buffalo robe. In winter the stirrups might be faced around and lined with sheepskin to keep the rider's feet warm. In dangerous

124

country some preachers carried a long-barreled rifle, a pistol, and a bowie knife.

Occasionally a strange horse made trouble, even for an expert rider. That pioneer West Texas Methodist, the Reverend Andrew Jackson Potter, had been a jockey in his youth; yet even he was thrown once by a spoiled horse. He was in bed several weeks with a damaged hip, had to preach on crutches for a while, and was left with a slight limp. Potter, a sturdy fellow with a reputation as a fighter, had no fear of scoffers or troublemakers. Once he took a gun and a dangerous knife from a ruffian who had abused and chastized his daughter-in-law while her husband was bedridden.

Sometimes a swollen stream kept the circuit preacher from his appointment. When an early Methodist missionary, the Reverend Robert Alexander, tried to cross the San Jacinto River in 1837, his horse refused to swim with the load. The preacher then made a raft of saplings, put his saddle on it, and got on himself. Two years later another Methodist, the Reverend Littleton Fowler, had to cross the swollen San Jacinto in a similar manner.

In western Texas even the wind could be an impediment. The Reverend J. W. Winn, a Baptist missionary, who spent his first Texas winter in a dugout with nineteen other people, often had to change his route in order to have the Panhandle gale at his back. The frontier Baptist clerics did not do as much circuit riding as the Methodist, but many of them were farmer-preachers whose crops and livestock helped to support their religious work. A number became expert with the calf rope and the branding iron.

Wild animals were a hazard in some sections. One Baptist, the Reverend Edward B. Featherston, learned that while on his way home from Dickens one night. At the Salt Fork of the Brazos River, he thought he would stake his horse, Ned, and take a nap. But then he heard a scream that sent a chill down his spine. He thought it was the cry of a panther. It was long and loud, he recalled, "and sounded like the wail of a woman in distress. It wound up as I imagine a woman would scream if she were being dragged into a den by some vile man.

125

"Ned gave a Spanish snort and wanted to trot in that sand; but, to save his strength, I held him back. I changed my plan about resting! So did Ned, and he went home with renewed vigor."

In the early days, hostile Indians might be lurking in the bushes. The Reverend William L. McCalla, a Kentuckian who visited Texas in 1840, would build a large fire at night in an effort to fool any scouting redskins. Before turning in, he would stalk boldly to a nearby thicket, as if he had companions there, and shout, "Now, boys, keep a good lookout tonight and take unerring aim at every villain who shows his face."

The Reverend Pleasant Tackett, who arrived in Parker County with his family in October, 1854, had to be wary of attack by savages. On one occasion he and three of his sons were charged from ambush at close range. They killed four of the redskins, wounded one, and drove off the others. One of the Tackett boys carried the steel spike of an arrow in his skull for eight weeks, but he survived. One of the preacher's first professional duties after his arrival was to hold funeral services for an adopted daughter, who had been bitten by a large rattler coiled under her bed.

White brigands were a frequent menace. In 1833 the Reverend Sumner Bacon, a Presbyterian who distributed thousands of Bibles between the Sabine River and the San Antonio, was captured by two assailants, dragged into a thicket, and threatened with instant death. He begged to be allowed to pray first, and his captors granted his request. Bacon knelt and prayed so loudly and so fervently that the thugs went off and left him alone. Later, while another Presbyterian, the Reverend John McCullough, was preaching in southwestern Texas, a band of men rode into the building and began shooting at him. He saved his life by dodging behind the books that were piled around him.

Not all the circuit preachers rode horseback. In West Texas a pioneer Methodist, the Reverend Ed R. Wallace, better known as Parson Hanks, discarded his saddle horse for a cart to which he drove a rondo trotter. After his horse ran off and smashed the cart, Wallace obtained a buggy, for which he bought a pair of black horses. Later he got a team of Spanish mules, which he drove across the plains

126

for four years, covering thousands of miles. One of his circuits required him to travel three hundred miles a month to meet appointments. A man who lived in the cedar brakes asked him to drive twenty-five miles to perform a wedding ceremony. He went.

Wallace, who often had to drive through blizzards and to preach in dugouts, sometimes had to sleep out on the prairie. He recalled one occasion when he camped out with some wagon drivers: "The wolves howled all around the wagons. This was a lonely experience. Amid the still, dark hours of the night, no sound could be heard except the howling of the droves of wolves. Even if one lone wolf undertook a howl by himself, he would bark so fast and chop it up so there would seem to be a dozen or more with him. They kept up this racket all night."

Once, while he was driving with his wife and baby to a conference, his team floundered in quicksand in crossing the Salt Fork of the Brazos. The team finally pulled loose from the buggy, after breaking tugs and singletrees, and got out on solid ground. The buggy had sunk to the axles. After carrying everything out of it, Wallace finally extricated it with difficulty from the quicksand. By wiring the broken pieces, he was able to go on, with his family, to the conference.

The worst enemy of the circuit preacher was disease. Contaminated drinking water, swarms of insects, and contact with the sick often imparted more germs than he could throw off. Dysentery, typhoid fever, malaria, cholera and other plagues took a heavy toll. Only the hardiest of the circuit riders lived to a ripe age.

Yet these horsemen for the Lord traveled almost incredible distances and preached in nearly every community they visited. One East Texas Methodist, the Reverend Francis A. Wilson, estimated that he had traveled 150,000 miles and preached seven thousand sermons. The aforementioned Andrew Jackson Potter, when assigned to the Uvalde circuit in 1871, found that he had to make a two-hundred-mile circuit in wild Indian country. The nearest point on the circuit was fifty miles from his home.

For this traveling, preaching, comforting the stricken, and burying the dead, even in the latter days of circuit riding, the preach-

127

er might receive one hundred to six hundred dollars a year, but he seldom collected all that was promised him. Often he had to take part of his pay in produce. In Brown County, members of the Oak Baptist Church could raise only eight dollars a month in cash for their pastor, Ben Wilson, who "would accept meat, meal, potatoes, and corn but would much prefer to have money." It was little wonder that married preachers had to do farm or ranch work part of the year to support their families. Being a saint of the saddlebags in frontier Texas called for strong faith in heavenly rewards.

While meeting in cabin homes or a country school, the pioneer congregation planned the building of a church. The early churches were small and often crudely finished, but the members tried to keep them clean and attractive. A church in Austin, soon after the Civil War, had at its door a placard asking the men to discard their chaws of tobacco before entering and to refrain from spitting on the floor.

Hymnbooks were scarce, and often there was only a tuning fork instead of an organ; but the spiritual songs came out with vigor. J. Marvin Hunter, in his memoirs, told of a country deacon who, while in town on jury duty, attended church there and heard an anthem for the first time. Back home, he tried to explain to his wife: "If I'd say, 'Ma, the cows is in the corn,' that would be no anthem. But if I'd say, 'Ma, Ma, the cows—the cows—the Holstein cow—the muley cow—the Jersey cow—the spotted cow—all the cows—the cows—is in—is in—the cows is in—is in—the corn—the corn—corn; ah, men,' that would be an anthem."

The building of individual churches on the frontier lessened the need for the circuit rider but left intact for a time that other potent institution of backwoods Protestantism, the camp meeting. Usually held in the late summer or fall, the camp meeting was a big social event for rural families and was attended by evangelistic fervor. In the days of the Texas Republic, and to a diminishing degree in the decades that followed, the camp meeting outdid even the political rally in excitement.

Hundreds, and sometimes several thousand, persons gathered on horseback or in oxcarts or covered wagons for the outdoor revivals. An ordinary camp meeting might last only from Thursday through Sunday, but a big one continued through two weekends. Families brought their own food, which they cooked over camp-fires. At some of the meetings in Parker County a beef would be killed every day and the meat divided free among the campers. Noah Smithwick reported that in Burnet County, where camp meetings were held each fall, the handing out of free food "induced many not overthrifty people to become regular camp followers. As most of them were forehanded with children, they became a heavy tax on the good brethren."

In the earlier days, most of the people came in homemade clothes, some of the men in buckskin suits and caps of deerskin with the hair side out. The men carried their rifles and pistols for protection on the way. The campers slept in tents or small arbors or in their wagons. All of them found time to visit relatives and friends they had not seen for some time.

Usually the meeting place was a clearing in the woods. In the center was built a gigantic brush arbor. Benches were made of hewn logs or of rough planks laid across logs, in either case without back supports. Sometimes a rail fence down the center separated the men from the women. The pulpit stand was made of slabs, poles, or even a dry-goods box. Several times a day the blowing of a horn or the ringing of a bell called the congregation to the arbor.

The preaching was loud and earnest, with much contrasting of heaven and hell and with many an "Amen!" from the listeners. No one could sleep through a sermon by the Reverend Francis A. Wilson, one of the Methodist stalwarts of East Texas in the republic period. Appearing in a flowing robe and with disheveled hair, Wilson would describe the Last Judgment so vividly that nearly everyone in his audience quaked with fear.

One night, while conducting a meeting on Little Cow Creek, near the Sabine River, Wilson had the campers roused in the middle of the night. The preaching lasted until after 4:00 A.M. Then, said Wilson, "I heard a sound of rushing in the southwest corner of the tents. A horse that was tied near the house was alarmed. After making several powerful efforts, he broke loose as if the Devil were after him. With that, shouts commenced in the tents over the camp ground."

129

This backwoods preacher knew how to rout the Devil's helpers, those Shelby County rowdies who tried to break up his meetings. "Now, Lord," he prayed, "if any Regulator or Moderator makes an effort to revive their disturbance, curse him with the loss of eyes, destroy his limbs that he may never be able to walk, curse him when he sits down to eat, curse his fields; and if this will not stop his hellish career, kill him and send him down to his own place."

The camp meeting, which had sprung in part from the Great Revival of 1800 and had followed the frontier down the Ohio Valley, reached Texas even before the Revolution of 1836. Meetings held before that had to be surreptitious because of the law banning Protestant activities. Yet some of the *alcaldes* and Mexican military commanders winked at camp meetings as long as there was no attendant disturbance.

In the spring of 1832 two Methodist preachers held a meeting in the woods near Milam. In the following year one was held ten miles east of San Augustine, with three preachers and about eighty listeners. In 1835 a second meeting near San Augustine boasted twelve tents and about two hundred people. A whisky dealer set up a shanty at the edge of the site, but the campers drove him away.

In the fall of 1837, after the ban against Protestantism had been lifted, two Methodist preachers, Littleton Fowler and John B. Denton, held a camp meeting near Clarksville. By 1843 such meetings had become more common—and more rousing. Houston Methodists, wrote an observer in 1845, "are in a state of frightful excitement, which has lasted eight or ten days and attracts crowds of spectators. No pen or tongue could give an adequate description of these riotous scenes."

Religious frenzy evoked at the camp meetings took many forms. Some of those affected by the preaching and singing would engage in wild dancing and shouting. Others rolled on the ground, went into trances, or had cataleptic fits. Some, after feeling a constriction of blood vessels and a shortness of breath, would drop prostrate. With their hands and feet cold, they would lie inert from an hour to a day. Often scoffers, as well as those seeking salvation, were struck down in such fashion.

Writing of Cumberland Presbyterian camp meetings held by the Shiloh Church in Ellis County, an observer reported that "it was not uncommon to see persons fall as dead. They would lie for hours and sometimes for days unconscious of surrounding events. I have seen persons who were affected by the jerks perform feats that were incredible. A man would be so affected mentally that his body would be so wrought upon that he would move head foremost on his back so rapidly that it could not be perceived how it was accomplished. When thus spasmodically affected, he was so strong that half a dozen men could not hold him."

The "jerks" were a fairly common manifestation. These attacks came suddenly, sometimes outside the meetings. A woman's head might jerk so violently that the braids of hair down her back would crack almost like a whip. Some persons would spin like a cartwheel. Grasping in vain at nearby trees, they would be carried helplessly on. Some kicked up the earth like a horse beset with flies. One preacher, in the midst of his sermon, began jerking so violently that he rolled off the platform and down a hill.

Camp meetings caused others to go into convulsions of barking. The victim would jerk, foam at the mouth, and roll into a hog wallow. Then he would throw up his arms, begin to bark, and rush off into the woods. One such was found barking up a tree half a mile away. "I have treed the Devil," he shouted.

Camp meetings, Texans used to say, were "hell on women but paradise for children and dogs." At one Texas meeting two youths stole some watermelons from a load that a farmer had brought to sell to the campers. The next night a doctor injected tartar emetic into the biggest of the remaining melons and placed them on top. About midnight he was called to a tent where the culprits, who thought they were dying, confessed and begged for prayer.

As churches in the frontier towns became more common and better staffed, camp meetings lost out. Frequently there was criticism of fighting, gambling, and whisky peddling in the groves about the grounds. On the lower Brazos, John W. Lockhart noted that a fellow known as Old Scratch, although routed from the camp, often lingered nearby in the brush with a jug of whisky, where some of the deacons visited him.

Some churchmen also observed that many camp converts soon backslid and that cavortings of some of the young people in the woods on the fringe of the camp brought a crop of unfortunate woods colts nine months later. For decades the expression "camp-meeting baby" was common in eastern Texas.

A camp meeting or other revival held by the Baptists usually was followed by a group baptism in a nearby stream or pond. Some of the converts showed remarkably changed lives, but others soon slumped back into their old ways. John Hendrix recalled a baptizing at Blue Hole which he and a neighbor ranchman saw from a nearby bluff. Among those immersed was an old cattle rustler who had preyed on many herds. As the preacher raised him to his feet, the neighbor turned to Hendrix and said: "John, if one of us had the nerve to shoot that old so-and-so before he dries off, he might go to heaven. But if the sun ever hits him and dries him off, he'll be a cow thief the rest of his life."

Most preachers and laymen concluded that it was better not to try to scare people into religion. In 1876 the Fort Worth *Democrat* criticized the woodland revivals as undignified. "Camp meetings are not potent agents for the conversion of the heart," it said. "We have little faith in them." Final prevalence of this view virtually ended one of the most amazing institutions of the frontier.

U NENVIABLE WAS THE PERSON who became ill or injured on the Texas frontier. There were no hospitals except in distant cities, and the nearest doctor might be at least a day's journey away. Early accounts of Texas, written to attract settlers, had eulogized the climate as most healthful. But colonists soon learned that such claims were exaggerated. Dysentery was common, especially in summer. Other ailments were more frequent and often more deadly then than later, and there were occasional visitations of yellow fever and cholera, with tragic results.

Not only were doctors scarce, but many of them were deficient in training. Unaware that malaria was caused by a virus carried by mosquitoes, they attributed it to bad air from stagnant water. Probably malaria was mainly responsible for the pallor of Texas faces noticed by many visitors in the years of the republic. Of Brazoria County women a young New Yorker wrote in the spring of 1842: "I can't say that I admire their looks, generally their complexion being mostly of a sallow hue and wanting that mixture of red and white so common at the North."

In the older towns, some citizens were making a brave beginning at sanitation. In Houston, in the summer of 1839, a grand jury denounced the filthy condition of the jail, where "the effluvia for feet about it are so potent as to sicken the stoutest stomach." In October, when many Houstonians were dying of yellow fever, a newspaper there took the board of health to task for the condition of the streets, where carrion "has been suffered to lie unremoved, to impregnate the atmosphere with its putridity."

In that year, and again in 1844, Houston and Galveston were

133

struck by epidemics of yellow fever that took hundreds of lives. In Houston, lime was spread where the disease had raged, and bonfires were made from tar and tar barrels at the street corners.

Overindulgence in intoxicants and the Texas diet of beef, bacon, potatoes, and corn bread may not have been conducive to the best health. At Fort Phantom Hill on the Clear Fork of the Brazos, a drouth in 1852 made vegetables so scarce that eighteen soldiers became sick with scurvy and one died. The post surgeon added pickles to the diet in hope of remedying this condition. Other soldiers came down with diarrhea and dysentery from drinking brackish water from green-scummed pools and sluggish streams.

When anyone in a farm home became ill with a contagious disease, other members of the household were likely to catch it. Most frontier people slept with windows closed, usually two persons in each bed. They drank from the same cups, and many even took turns chewing the same wad of wax. Homes had no refrigeration for food and milk, which often were exposed to flies and other insects.

For many ailments, some doctors still bled their patients; but that practice was becoming less common. Calomel, Epsom salts, and castor oil were frequently used remedies. Quinine was replacing Peruvian bark for malaria. Most chills and fevers called for purges. Mustard plasters and flaxseed poultices were used in treating throat and chest troubles.

Often the pioneer doctor had to ride fifty or even one hundred miles on horseback or in a buggy to treat the sick, remove bullets, or set bones. He might have to operate on a kitchen table, in a crude bunk, or on the ground beside a chuck wagon.

Fees were low and collections poor. Many physicians had to take their pay in farm produce or livestock. A large number had to operate drugstores or other businesses or engage in part-time farming or ranching to make ends meet. Some peddled patent medicines and a hair tonic made of bear oil.

The difficulty in collecting fees was reflected in an item in the Denison *News* in 1873. A doctor who had ridden fifty miles to attend a farm wife presented a bill for fifty dollars and prepared for the journey home. As he was about to mount his horse, the patient's husband appeared, rifle in hand.

"Doctor," he said, "I reckon we'd better settle this matter right now." Taking him aside, he added, "I don't want to owe no man nothing. Here's a ten, which is about a square thing, I reckon. Now if you ain't satisfied, just git your weapon and come behind the hill thar, so's the old woman won't be riled up, and we'll settle it. I don't want no man to go away from my house dissatisfied, especially you, Doc."

Long rides to visit patients were the rule rather than the exception. On Thanksgiving Day of 1877, Dr. Henry F. Hoyt was out hunting buffalo with James Campbell, a sheep rancher. Just before sundown, a Mexican rode into the hunters' camp, leading a saddled mustang. He had been sent by Don Casimero Romero, a wealthy sheepman, to bring the doctor to his fifteen-year-old foster daughter. The girl, Señorita Piedad Romero, called the "Belle of the Panhandle," was suffering from smallpox.

As the hacienda of Don Casimero was at Tascosa, one hundred miles away, the doctor left at sundown with an escort and rode all night. Late the next afternoon they reached the Canadian River opposite Tascosa. There some Mexicans called the doctor into an adobe shack at the ford. Inside was a Mexican on his back, in severe pain from a dislocated shoulder wrenched in buffalo hunting.

Hoyt had no anesthetic, but went ahead to try to help the ailing man. Pulling off one of his boots, he used his heel as a fulcrum and, by main strength, reduced the dislocation. Then he fastened the hunter's arm to his body with an improvised bandage and told him to keep quiet for three days and then to come over to Tascosa for examination. But the Mexican was too curious to wait. The next morning he slipped off the bandage. This allowed his shoulder to pop out again, thus requiring a second operation.

On the Tascosa side of the river, Dr. Hoyt found the beautiful Señorita Piedad covered with pustules and suffering from a torment of itching. He had little medicine with him and the dusty town had no drugstore. Then, recalling that gunpowder contained charcoal, saltpeter, and sulphur, he made a paste of gunpowder and water and had it spread over the whole body of the girl, who recovered in time to make her debut in Panhandle society on Christmas.

Dr. Hoyt found the Panhandle too thinly populated to provide enough patients for him to make a living as a physician. Besides, so many of the cowboys there died in their boots that they made more work for an undertaker than for a doctor. So Hoyt took a job as a cowhand on the LX Ranch, where, after helping to build a large corral, he learned the art of roping with a cowhide riata.

In 1885, as more families came into the Panhandle, several ranchmen paid Dr. Jerome D. Stocking a bonus to induce him to settle in Clarendon. The doctor found in the surrounding plains plenty of patients to keep him busy. He drove in a buggy when roads and weather allowed, but had to ride horseback much of the time. As happens to all doctors, he sometimes arrived too late. Joe Heflin Smith reported that, when a young woman died of tuberculosis, her grieving husband remarked to Stocking, "Doctor, I would rather have lost my best team than my wife."

From his office in Colorado, Texas, Dr. P. C. Coleman covered a territory that spread forty miles south, one hundred miles west, and shorter distances east and north. On wagon beds or other rough equipment he set broken bones and removed bullets. Before the day of local anesthetics, he used ether or chloroform for operations.

On one occasion Dr. Coleman rode forty miles through the night to treat a sick baby in a dugout. After he had taken care of the baby, the family allowed him to sleep for the rest of the night on the ground under the bed of the ailing baby. He was one of twelve persons in the dugout that measured about fifteen feet square.

Another of Coleman's patients was a boy who had become entangled in the harness of a runaway plow team. The sharp point of the plowshare had cut into the youth's abdomen, leaving his intestines "out of the body cavity, covered with dirt and trash." But after the doctor cleaned and replaced the parts and stitched the cut, the boy recovered. In another runaway case, a woman had been thrown from a cart into a wire fence, dragged through sand, trash, and burs, and her scalp almost torn from her head. Yet after the doctor cleaned and stitched the scalp, the woman was as good as ever.

The scarcity of doctors on the frontier led many farm and ranch families to rely most of the time on patent medicines or home remedies for ordinary ailments. The medicine shelf often contained quinine, calomel, Epsom salts, castor oil, and a variety of proprietary cures. The last might include Lee's Bilious Pills, Hooper's Female Pills, Rowan's Tonic Mixture, Dr. Hull's Worm Lozenges, Dalley's Magical Pain Extractor Salve, and Indian Vegetable Elixir and Nerve and Bone Liniment. The last-named bore the guarantee: "Rheumatism and lameness positively cured, and all shriveled muscles and limbs restored."

Local newspapers and farm publications used much of their space for advertising such tonics and remedies as Hostetter's Bitters, Peruna, and Simmons Liver Regulator. Manufacturers of many of the medicines indulged in extravagant claims that they would cure a large number of ailments. Dr. Radway's Sarsaparillian Resolvent was recommended for twenty-two diseases. Simmons Liver Regulator was advertised as a remedy for dyspepsia, diarrhea, dropsy, sick headaches, bilious fever, bilious colic, costiveness, and jaundice. An advertisement in the *Texas Almanac* for 1867 promised that Argyle Bitters would strengthen and invigorate the entire system and effectively cure "dyspepsia, liver complaint, nervous debility, disordered stomach, disgust for food, heartburn, loss of appetite, general debility and prostration of the system."

Some patent remedies were dispensed through traveling medicine shows which might offer a small brass band, Negro minstrels, or other entertainment. The spieler, after depicting the horrors of tapeworms, would offer silverware or other bait to sell his medicine at one dollar a bottle.

Many home remedies were popular. The pioneer woman made use of "loosenin' weeds" and on occasion made a brew of green gourds as an emetic. Any member of the family who had boils would be given sulphur and molasses or at least large doses of sassafras tea. For a sore throat, asafetida was hung on a string about the neck. For snakebite the men took generous doses of whisky. For rheuma-

137

tism some swallowed red ants in vinegar, while others merely carried a potato in a pocket.

The credulous had still other backwoods remedies. A baby that had a fit might be given a dose of scrapings from pewter spoons. Mare's milk was recommended for whooping cough and milkweed for warts. A chest cold called for a red flannel soaked in turpentine and grease, or a plaster of dry mustard and the whites of eggs. Or a child with a cold might have to wear around his neck a piece of meat sprinkled with pepper.

A more popular cold remedy was a mixture of rock candy and whisky. Another common one was a bitter horehound tea made by boiling horehound leaves in water for several days. Some made this tea more palatable by mixing it with wild honey. A recommended remedy for diphtheria was a pinch of gunpowder in a glass of warm water or sour milk.

Sassafras tea, in addition to being used as a medicine for certain ailments, was drunk regularly in many pioneer homes in East Texas from Groundhog Day until late spring. Frontiersmen dug the roots in the woods because they thought the pale-rose brew helped them by thinning their blood.

Young boys sometimes rebelled at the home remedies which their parents or others concocted for them. A frontier newspaper editor, the late J. Marvin Hunter, recalled that as a youth in East Texas, working on a paper and living with an elderly couple, he was attacked by the chills of malaria. "I woke up at four o'clock in the morning with my teeth rattling like castanets. Cold shivers crept up and down my spinal column as though someone had poked the sharp end of an iceberg down my back. My first impression was that the bedroom floor had caved in and let the bed down into the cellar. The enamel was getting loose on my teeth."

After he woke his landlady, she built a fire in the kitchen stove and gave him a gallon of warm water to drink. Then she had him soak his feet in hot mustard water and wrap them in an old flannel petticoat. She put a square yard of mustard plaster on his chest and another on his back. Next she had him drink a warm bran mash in which ground mustard, ginger, paregoric, peppermint essence, molasses, catnip tea, and vinegar were mixed with water. By that time, young Hunter didn't care much whether he lived or died, but his landlady wasn't through. She bundled him with hot water in bottles, jugs, and fruit jars. Wedged so tight that he couldn't move, he felt as if he had fallen into the crater of a volcano.

As if these remedies were not enough, neighbor women came in after daybreak with other suggestions. On their recommendations, the landlady put a flaxseed poultice on his stomach, tied a bag of boiled onions under each arm, and wrapped him in old blankets soaked in arnica and camphor. When the next chill came on, she and her two grown daughters "got a couple of red-hot flatirons, wrapped them in a cloth, and strapped them to the bottoms of my feet. Presently the cloth came loose and slipped off. I gave one wild yell of agony and drew my feet up so they collided with the headboard of the bed. The next instant those flatirons were flying across the room, but not until they had raised a blister the size of a watermelon on the bottom of each foot."

Meanwhile the mustard plasters on the back and chest of Hunter had done their work. "I was as sore as a rare beefsteak. The only way I could rest was by standing on one elbow and hanging to the bedpost to steady myself." In the evening the patient was visited by a physician, who prescribed quinine and rest, which, with good food, restored his strength.

One of the most nearly universal and most controversial of frontier remedies was the madstone, used as a cure for hydrophobia or rabies. As late as the 1890's, some persons would apply a madstone, if one could be found, to the bite of a rabid dog, or skunk, or to that of a poisonous snake.

Some believed that this stone came from the stomach of a cow or a white deer. If a person had hydrophobia, they said, this stone would cling to the wound for several hours and, when taken off, would change the color of milk to bilious green.

In San Antonio in the days of the republic, Ben Milam had a madstone about the size of a goose egg. He cut off one-third of it and gave the smaller part to Collin McKinney. The remainder he kept until his house burned. McKinney later divided his part and gave a small piece to each of his sons.

In Sherman in 1875, W. M. James was bitten by a mad dog loose in the streets. A piece of the McKinney madstone was applied for thirty-one hours. Four times, said a newspaper account, the stone dropped off and was relieved of its poison by being soaked in hot milk.

An early Dallas newspaper reported that "Mr. Ledbetter, living on Duck Creek, about eighteen miles east of Dallas, was bitten by a mad dog. He came to the city immediately in search of a madstone. If he has not succeeded in finding one, the following item from the Denison *Cresset* may interest him:

" 'The boy recently bitten by a mad dog has returned from McKinney, whence he was taken by his father to test the virtue of the madstone. It adhered to the wound for twenty-two hours and then dropped off. A remarkable thing is that it will not stay on when applied to a person bitten by a nonrabid dog.' "

In Decatur in 1873, twelve-year-old Charlie Terrell was playing in his back yard when a house cat jumped on him. The cat bit him on the wrist and knee before he threw it off and ran crying into the open door of the smokehouse. Next the cat got into a fight with a small dog, ran into a grocery store, and leaped from one counter to another before it was driven out. From there it ran down Main Street, bit a carpenter on the leg, and engaged in a fight with a pack of dogs that killed it.

People knew that the cat was rabid because the carpenter died of hydrophobia and a cow nipped by one of the bitten dogs went mad. Charlie's father called a doctor who suggested cutting off the bitten hand; but the father reminded him that there also was a bite on the knee. Finally someone told him that Ab Stepp, who lived near the mouth of Oliver Creek, had a madstone. The next morning the elder Terrell hitched a horse to his buggy and took Charlie to the Stepp home, arriving just after noon.

Charlie recalled in later years that Stepp put him to bed, took his wrist, scarified it, and applied a small porous stone. "He would let it remain on the wound for half an hour or more, then take it

140

off and put it in a cup of warm milk. This he continued until just before dark, when it seemed to adhere no longer to the wound. He then said that all the poison was out and began on my knee. The next morning we returned home, after paying him twenty-five dollars." Stepp claimed he had seen only one case of rabies that his stone failed to cure; that time the victim was having convulsions, and the treatment came too late. The Terrells were uneasy for a time, but nothing came of the bites.

Use of the madstone ceased gradually after the bearded Louis Pasteur developed his antirabies vaccine in 1885. The brilliant French bacteriologist had prepared an emulsion from the spinal cord of a rabbit dead from rabies. Seventy years later the Texas State Department of Health was making antirabies vaccine at the rate of more than five thousand shots a year.

COUNTRY SCHOOLS in which "readin' and writin' and 'rithmetic" were "taught to the tune of the hickory stick" were unusually hard to maintain on the Texas frontier. Settlers' homes were often far apart, qualified teachers hard to find, and textbooks scarce. The pupils had to trudge across the prairie or ride horseback, carrying their lunch pails.

While in Harrisburg, in May, 1834, Dr. Pleasant W. Rose found a teacher, David Henson, who had just arrived by schooner from New Orleans. Rose immediately engaged him to start a school in his neighborhood on Oyster Creek. The school was opened June 1 in a log house that had been used as a blacksmith shop. It had a puncheon floor but no windows and no shutter for the door. Only a few books, donated from homes, were available.

The school was started with ten pupils, a daughter of Rose recalled. The teacher and three of the older boys lived in the school, except for week ends, doing their own cooking. The mothers of the pupils brought them food, including milk, butter, and eggs. Without arithmetic books or a blackboard, the teacher had to write the multiplication tables on cardboard from a bandbox donated by Mrs. Rose for that purpose.

A frontier school in Stephen F. Austin's colony in 1835, taught by an Irishman named Cahill, was recalled by M. M. Kenney. One of the pupils was Kenney's older brother, about eight. On the first day, the mother went along over the two-mile trail, using a hatchet to blaze the path so that it would be easier for youngsters to find their way home in the evening.

Kenney recalled a later school, which he attended about 1838 or 1839, taught three or four months a year by an old Irishman named Dyar. What impressed young Kenney most was an array of switches of various sizes and types for disciplinary use.

On one side of the room was a row of small, straight, and limber switches made apparently of Osage orange or *bois d'arc,* for use on the small boys. "I remember meditating on the feasibility of destroying all that kind of timber growing near the schoolhouse. My terror was a little red switch that I caught often, usually for laughing in school.

"The larger switches were graded, partly by the size of the boys and partly by the gravity of the offense, the gravest of which was an imperfect lesson. The third size of rods was of hickory—tough sticks which the teacher did not use on the little boys but which he did use on the larger scholars, without the least hesitation or reserve, if they failed to get the appointed lesson or were derelict in any of their duties. The fourth size was of oak and would better have been called clubs. These he applied, more in the style of the shillelagh than of the ferule, to the largest boys.

"Some of the boys ran from him; but no one ever struck back, it being a point of honor not to strike the teacher. I do not remember that he ever whipped any of the girls."

The school had Webster's spelling book, a text called *The English Reader,* and books brought from homes, including Defoe's *Robinson Crusoe,* Weems's *Life of George Washington,* and Goldsmith's *Natural History.* The pupils had a variety of arithmetic books and did their figuring on slates. Occasionally the bellowing and fighting of nearby cattle disturbed the recitations. Some of the trees outside had swings for the girls. At noon, in favorable weather, the boys rode their horses to a swimming hole in the creek.

Education had been a primary aim of early colonists from the United States. In the Spanish period, schools to give basic training to the children of soldiers and colonists and to convert the Indians and teach them trades had met with little success. Stephen F. Austin showed his interest in education as early as 1823, when he drew up a proposed constitution for the Republic of Mexico. One article made it the duty of Congress "to provide for the speedy establishment of

143

schools and colleges throughout the nation." Another empowered Congress "to establish a general system of education and to appropriate public funds for the endowment and support of schools."

In the following year, a legal code drawn up by Austin for his colony provided that all fines be applied for the use of schools and other public purposes. It was several more years, however, before public schools were opened in the colony. Meanwhile, some of the wealthier colonists sent their children to schools in the United States or to private colonial schools supported by subscription and occasionally subsidized with local funds. The best school of this kind was one established in Bexar in 1828.

More neighborhood and public schools were started in the period of the Texas Republic and the early years of statehood, some of them taught by women. The frontier Texas schoolmarm usually did a good job, even though she had to arrive early in winter to build a fire in the stove. One pioneer teacher joined her pupils in fighting a prairie fire all morning to save the school building.

A lady teacher who arrived in Texas in the early 1850's described her school thus: "It has one door and a window without sash or glass. But there is no lack of ventilation, the spaces between the logs admitting lots of air."

On the opening day, a dozen wasps dropped from a nest in the roof, sending everyone scampering out. Then, after she had restored order, the teacher noticed that the children were looking into the rafters. Glancing upward, she saw "an enormously long snake, coiling and uncoiling with the utmost sang-froid and gazing with a twinkle in his eye at the scene below."

In that era, some of the plantations had their own schools. Early in 1851, Laura J. Clark, a recent arrival from Maine, began teaching in a school on the Reese Plantation, ten miles from Brazoria. The small schoolhouse, finished inside with red cedar, stood in a grove of live oak and wild peach trees. The ten pupils were children, nephews, and nieces of the planter, who grew cotton and sugar cane.

In Caldwell County, Mark A. Withers recalled that his first school, in the early 1850's, was a one-room log house with a puncheon floor. The seats also were of split logs, with pegs driven in for legs. "Nothing was so hard to sit on, but they had one redeeming feature—splinters prevented the pupils from sliding. Later this log school was replaced with a frame one built with lumber hauled from Bastrop. It had pine benches and, for the teacher, a table on which was a hand bell, a small dictionary, and a long switch. Back of this was a homemade chair with a rawhide bottom.

"Two things we gloried in—a two-by-four blackboard, fastened to the wall too high for the younger ones to reach, and a heating stove. The only privilege I had was helping to build fires and bring water.

"On opening day each child brought all the schoolbooks that could be found at home. If he couldn't use them, somebody else could. We had Webster's blue-back speller, McGuffey's readers, and Ray's or White's arithmetic. The spelling books were thumbed until they were so dog-eared that, instead of being only half an inch thick, they were two or three inches."

As the frontier moved westward, the schoolhouse followed, although the Civil War made teachers scarcer again and sometimes there was danger of an Indian attack. In 1862, settlers in southeastern Parker County started a school and asked one of their number, Stephen Heffington, to teach it. He agreed on condition that the neighbors cultivate his crops. The men split logs from along South Bear Creek to make benches, which were without backs and were of the same height for all pupils, of whom there were only nine at first.

The only books used were those which the children brought from home. As the school was without a blackboard or slates, Heffington went to the creek and found some flat, slab-like rocks. He smoothed their surfaces and had his pupils use them as slates, with some pieces of softer rock as markers. At home the youngsters did their studying by the light of tallow candles made by their parents.

After the war a larger school was built on Bear Creek and had about twenty pupils. It used such standard textbooks as Webster's blue-back speller, Ray's arithmetic, and McGuffey's readers. The event there recalled most vividly by one of the students, Tom Taylor, was a clash between the fat teacher and his biggest pupil, Jim Romans. Jim habitually chewed tobacco in school but moved his jaw so quietly that he was hard to catch. One day the teacher asked, "Jim, what is it that you have in your mouth?" Jim swallowed his quid and answered, "Meat."

Later, Taylor recalled, Jim was required to stand on the end of a bench for another offense, with the teacher on the other end. "Jim quietly stepped off his end. Suddenly his end of the bench went into the air, and the teacher went sprawling on the floor and rolled nearly to the middle of the room. He jumped to his feet and dashed after Jim and started beating him with his fists. Jim returned the blows, and finally they clinched and were rolling on the floor.

"The children all dashed out of the room, screaming. Jim got the upper hand, rushed out of the room into the yard, grabbed a big rock, and came back to brain the teacher. The teacher grabbed Jim's arm and finally took the rock away from him and threw it out of the window. It whizzed by my older sister's head, missing by two inches.

"The children all ran home, and by the next morning the fight was all over that part of the country. It was talked of for years. Jim left school and boasted that he had whipped the teacher."

One woman teacher faced even greater danger. In Hamilton County, on July 11, 1866, Indians attacked a school on the Leon River while the children were out at recess. When they rushed in to tell their teacher, Miss Ann Whitney, she thought the visitors were cowboys.

The teacher discovered her error when she saw the men cut loose a staked horse. She told the children to get away if they could. By this time the redskins were at the door. Most of the youngsters escaped by a window and hid under the floor, but the Indians wounded a girl and captured a young boy, John Kuykendall.

While the frantic teacher bolted the door, the Indians began shooting arrows at her from windows on both sides of the building. One brave said that if she would come to his window, she would not be shot. But a barrage of arrows into her face left her dying on the floor. The Indians carried off John Kuykendall. Later they sold him to an agent for a gallon of whisky.

In the fall of 1877, five-year-old Edna Turley, living on a farm south of Austin, joined her older brothers and sisters in attending a subscription school on Onion Creek. The youngsters had to walk two miles through a pasture, keeping an eye out for belligerent bulls. Three years later they enrolled in the district's first public school at the old Rock Church, which was near their home. They enjoyed the church benches, which had backs, but still had to use their laps as desks. Among the songs they sang were "Shoo Fly," "Baa, Baa, Black Sheep," and "All Around the Maypole."

In her memoirs, Edna Turley, long after she had become Mrs. Thomas Carpenter, recalled the day when her sister Alpha drew on one side of her double slate a picture of the bald, fat teacher, A. H. Decherd, and on the other a likeness of a huge local fat man named Kelly, noted for eating fish. After the pictures and the verse she wrote under them had started an outburst of tittering, the teacher grabbed the slate before she could rub out anything. He turned pink with confusion as he read:

> *Good Professor Decherd*
> *And fish-eating Mr. Kelly—*
> *It's hard indeed to tell*
> *Which has the larger belly.*

As the towns acquired larger and more advanced schools, many added such activities as competitive sports and glee clubs. Some also found occasional excitement in pranks by the larger boys. At Ozona, out in the dusty chaparral country, Allan R. Bosworth recalled such incidents as tying a dead skunk to the bell rope, putting a cow in the belfry, and hoisting a buggy to the roof of the two-story schoolhouse.

In many of the towns and cities, especially after Texas joined the United States, private schools, academies, and colleges sprang up. Often their impressive names were misleading since some of the academies included elementary grades and many of the colleges included preparatory or high-school training, some not extending above that level. But the private schools often were better equipped than those of the frontier communities; and, while some lasted only a year or two, others grew and expanded into well-financed and enduring institutions.

The regulations of the private academies, military schools, and colleges, as published in their annual catalogs, show that care was taken to insure the good behavior and moral conduct of the students, especially those who boarded at the school. Regulations at the Texas Military Institute at Rutersville in 1858 included: "Arms, other than those in military use, are peremptorily prohibited on the institute grounds on pain of dismissal. Dueling or fighting a pitched battle will be punished by dismissal or expulsion of all concerned. The possession or use of playing cards and games of chance are prohibited on pain of dismissal." Each cadet, in the presence of a parent or guardian, signed a pledge to abide by the rules, to avoid bringing or using weapons or any kind of intoxicating drink.

Teachers in the academies, although relieved of having to take part of their pay in board, moving from one home to another each month, as many had to do on the frontier, often had other problems. At Seymour Academy in the early 1890's the teacher was D. R. Britt. One of his former pupils, Ott Black, later described him as "a heavy-set man with a black mustache and a sour disposition."

Britt, Black recalled, "expelled a cattleman's girl one day because she had gone to a dance against his wishes. When the cowpunchers heard of it, they rode in from miles around and, during a recess, shot twenty-four holes into the Seymour Academy. The last I ever saw of Professor Britt, he was neck-and-neck with a jack rabbit running out of the country."

The school board, added Black, hired a local man who was handy with a six-shooter to complete the term.

At the Texas Military Institute at Llano, rules for the school year of 1897–98 included: "Cadets must bathe at least once a week. Cadets must report ten minutes after leaving the bath, to the officer of the day, and have their bath recorded. Otherwise they will be marked as absent from that duty. Hair must be cut as often as required; and, when necessary, cadets must shave each week. Finger nails, cuffs, collars, shoes will be under special inspection each day."

148

At Burnetta College at Venus at the turn of the century, the boys and girls wore uniforms and were forbidden to visit race tracks, billiard parlors, and saloons. Match games of baseball or football with other teams were not allowed, on pain of expulsion. Students were ordered not to keep in their possession "pistols, dirks, bowie knives, or other dangerous weapons. Pupils of the opposite sex, whether boarders or not, must not receive calls. Note writing will not be tolerated. Giving or receiving calls also applies to teachers during weekdays."

At Weatherford in 1902–1903, the Texas Female Academy and Conservatory of Music, operated by the Cumberland Presbyterians, required resident pupils "to attend church and Sabbath school each Sabbath."

A year later the Wall School at Honey Grove, "an academy for boys and young men" which also admitted "a few ambitious girls and young ladies," required male boarders to sign a rigid pledge. Each promised to attend church and Sunday school each Sunday morning, to keep no firearms, to avoid drinking even a drop of any intoxicant, to refrain from visiting the town or the railroad station without permission, to avoid leaving his room at night, to refrain from playing any game in his room at night or cards at any time, and not to call on a young lady without permission.

Work toward a state school system for Texas and state and private institutions of higher learning began early. The state constitution of 1845 at the time of annexation provided for the establishment of free schools and called on the legislature to set aside from tax revenue a perpetual fund to support them. Such a fund was started in 1854, and an ex officio state board of education was created in 1866.

The University of Texas, although not opened until September 15, 1883, had its origin in an action of the Congress of the Republic of Texas in 1839, which ordered a site set aside for a university. Financing through grants of land was provided in 1858, but the Civil War delayed the start of the university. On November 17, 1882, at the laying of the cornerstone of the first building in Austin, Ashbel Smith made an address that proved prophetic: "Smite the rocks with the rod of knowledge, and the fountains of unstinted wealth will gush forth." Later discovery of large reservoirs of petroleum under lands owned by the university made it one of the wealthiest institutions of its kind in the country.

Rice University was opened under the name of Rice Institute in Houston in 1912, as a nonpolitical and nonsectarian university endowed from the estate of its founder, William Marsh Rice. From its beginning, it had limited enrollment and maintained a high standard of scholarship through selective admission.

Southern Methodist University was opened in Dallas in the fall of 1915. With the University of Texas and Rice University, it became one of the three institutions in Texas to have chapters of Phi Beta Kappa, national academic honor society.

The four additional Texas members of the Southwest Conference achieved academic, as well as athletic, eminence. They are the Agricultural and Mechanical University of Texas, opened at College Station in 1876; Texas Technological College, opened at Lubbock in 1925; Texas Christian University, an outgrowth of an earlier institution, which took its present name in 1902 and moved from Waco to Fort Worth in 1910; and Baylor University, Baptist, opened at Independence in 1846 and moved to Waco in 1887.

As Texas grew, scores of other worthy institutions of higher learning were added to the list. Most of them, along with many of the public school systems of the state, were racially integrated in the early 1960's, in nearly all cases without friction.

IN THE FRONTIER TOWN OF AUSTIN, when much of Texas still was a fenceless buffalo range and when almost every Texan carried a six-shooter, the editor of the *Southwest American* had a peculiar but effective method for insuring his freedom of expression. When he saw a stranger or a troublemaker approaching, he signaled for his printer in an adjoining room to poke the barrel of a Winchester through a hole in the wall, taking close aim at the visitor. If the man proved to be friendly, the rifle was quietly withdrawn; but if he became wrathful or threatening, the editor had only to point to the protruding muzzle to cool him.

Similar precautions were taken by another Texas editor, J. Guy Reid, who published a little weekly at Cotulla and once was wounded in a gun battle. Reid had a habit of popping off in print at people he didn't like and on one occasion referred to a sheriff as the offspring of a razorback hog sired by a ringneck buzzard. He kept an arsenal in his office and guarded against surprise visits by means of carefully placed mirrors and a device by which anyone who entered would step on a mat and ring a hidden bell. When he went out into the street, he wore two pistols, a dirk, and two pairs of brass knucks.

Assaults on pioneer editors were common enough to warrant such defense measures. The frontier had many fearless editors— men who didn't hesitate to proclaim boldly the truth as they saw it, even though their words might get them into trouble. The independence of the editor did not stem from financial security. On the contrary, it may have been enhanced by the fact that he had little worldly goods to lose.

In the farm settlement or the cow town, the newsman not only

151

could hear the wolf's howl at night but knew every day that the wolf wasn't far from his door. He issued frequent appeals for readers to pay their lapsed subscriptions. The *Telegraph and Texas Register,* after having to move from town to town several times during the Revolution and once having its press captured by Mexican soldiers and thrown into Buffalo Bayou, was especially in need. "How thankful we would be," the owner said, if everyone "would pay his subscription in advance!"

But if cash were not at hand, the publisher would take almost anything else. Many subscriptions were paid in vegetables, fruit, or poultry. At Jacksboro the *Frontier Echo* said in 1875, "Cord wood taken at this office for subscriptions." Two years later the newspaper announced, "We will take wheat at the market price in payment for subscriptions."

One Texas editor, Harry P. Hornby of the Uvalde *News,* often lacked the dollar to pay the express charge on a shipment of paper. He and his bride took their honeymoon on railroad scrip and furnished their home with goods obtained from a San Antonio store in exchange for advertising. "One farmer friend," Hornby recalled, "brought 150 pounds of cotton seed to pay for his subscription. It helped to feed our cow. Honey often was exchanged, as well as peaches, pears, and other fruits. The most unusual exchange I ever received was a pint of rattlesnake oil. It helped grease printing machinery."

Yet being hungry never kept the frontier editor from being fearless. He insisted on exercising freedom of the press, even if it might cost him his life. His outspoken words might be directed against some lawbreaker, a political candidate, a lax official, or even a rival editor. In the village of Birdville, near Fort Worth, John J. Courtenay started the *Western Express* in 1855, and A. G. Walker followed with the *Union* two years later. The two became bitter opponents on secession and on the location of the county seat. Finally, in a street encounter, both reached for their pistols. Courtenay, who drew too slowly, fell dying.

Early in 1869 similar antagonism arose in Houston between J. G. Tracy, editor of the *Union,* and Somers Kinney, editor of the

152

Times. In a street fight the two exchanged pistol shots. An innocent youth who happened to be standing nearby received a serious wound, but neither of the dueling newsmen was hurt.

Apologies were rare in those days; but later in 1869, the Houston *Union,* as reported in the Austin *Republican,* "expressed in sensible and manly terms its regret for the vituperative and personal style it had too frequently used with regard to political opponents and promised for the future a larger measure of self-restraint and dignity. We believe that the editor was sincere in his resolution. Although a subsequent number contains needless and ungracious personal allusions, we are willing to attribute them to haste and a neglect of revision."

To the north, the editor of the Denton *Monitor* was under no such self-imposed restraint. "The editor of the San Antonio *Herald* says he smells a rat," he wrote in 1870. "If the rat smells him, the poor creature will decidedly have the worst of it." Early in 1875 another Denton newsman, the editor of the *Times,* made the error of libeling someone closer to home, as a result of which he was horsewhipped by a woman.

The next year brought a newspaper quarrel in the old town of Jefferson, to the east. Frank J. Patillo of the *Leader* picked up a cowhide whip and went out after Ward Taylor, editor of the *Jimplecute.* But before he could strike his rival, Taylor drew a pistol and shot him through the heart, killing him.

In the same year, in the mesquite country west of Fort Worth, two angry readers of the Fort Griffin *Echo,* published in a wild town of buffalo hunters and cattle drovers, went to the newspaper office to shoot the editor, G. W. Robson. When they learned that he was away from the office, they consoled themselves by killing the owner of the paper instead.

Ready for such visitors, Albert Tyson, editor of the *X-Ray* at Rising Star, boasted that he was a fighting editor with a quick trigger-finger. A contemporary, Alvin S. Peek, claimed that he had issued newspapers in nine states and territories and had shot eleven men who took exception to his editorial opinions. But Peek, at fifty-one, died with his boots on.

153

In 1878 the Comanche *Chief* and the Eastland *Review* engaged in a long editorial duel of words. Said the *Review* in one of its outbursts: "Boil down two or three curs and pour them into a mold the shape of a monkey. Take out as soon as cold, and you will have an animal similar in smell, form, and substance to the editor of the Comanche *Chief*." The latter editor could be equally caustic. "The present governor of the great state of Texas," he wrote in 1879, "has been dog drunk several times since his election."

In 1882 J. B. Cranfill started the Gatesville *Advance* and soon afterward ran into trouble. While he was in a neighboring town on business, his printer-partner took too many drinks and, while under their influence, wrote and published a highly libelous attack on a rival Gatesville editor, W. B. Scott of the *Sun*. When Cranfill returned and went to his rival's office to try to straighten the matter out, the two armed editors engaged in a fight that easily might have become fatal.

The next year the editor of the Vernon *Guard* wrote that the sheriff was not "the proper kind of official." The sheriff replied that if the paper ever again said anything against him, he would shoot the editor full of holes. At this, the editor promptly called the sheriff everything from a liar to a would-be murderer. "Rather than surrender our rights and liberties," he thundered, "we will strike a blow for freedom of speech and honest citizens of Wilbarger County, even though our life pays the forfeit before the sun sets tonight."

In Abilene in the 1880's bitterness arose between W. C. Gibbs, editor of the *Magnetic Quill,* who defended the cowmen and the open range, and C. E. Gilbert, editor of the *Reporter,* who spoke for the farmers and wanted to cut the big ranches into family farms. Once Gilbert went out looking for Gibbs and struck at him with the butt of a buggy whip. Gibbs drew a pistol and fired at Gilbert, inflicting a slight wound in his face. The latter paid a small fine for fighting and creating a disturbance.

Any slight to a sensitive editor might bring retaliation in his next issue. In 1884 the editor of the Albany *News* wrote: "The old crank that presides over the hotel on the south side of the square, who recently slandered another hotel and was soundly thrashed therefor, objected to our looking over his register this morning."

In 1896 a Populist editor in Pearsall made strong accusations against officials of Frio County and attacked the sheriff, a former Texas Ranger. A little later the editor was shot to death in his office.

Soon afterward Waco became the principal Texas graveyard for gun-toting editors. Six-shooter Junction—that was the name which many cowboys had given to frontier Waco. Guns often barked in the streets, and many a man died there in his boots. The city had two editorial gun fights in 1897 and 1898, battles in which four men lost their lives and a fifth lost an arm.

Both street shootings stemmed from the rape of a young Brazilian girl in Waco and attendant scandals. Involved on one side of the controversy were officials of Baylor University and their partisans. On the other side were caustic critics. One was G. B. Gerald, who had been a Confederate colonel, a county judge, and Waco postmaster, as well as a newspaper editor. Another was William C. Brann, fiery editor and publisher of the *Iconoclast,* a monthly magazine that had attained a national circulation of 100,000.

Judge Gerald, who was called Big Sandy because of his reddish beard and hair, had become associate editor of the Waco *Examiner* in 1872. Two years later he had bought the *Advance* but had sold it soon afterward. In the fall of 1897 he quarreled with J. W. Harris, editor of the Waco *Times-Herald.* He accused Harris of having failed to return a letter which Gerald had written him on the controversy between Brann and the Baylor partisans.

After Harris threw him out of the *Times-Herald* office and down the stairs, Judge Gerald issued a circular stating his side of the quarrel. He said that he was not gunning for anyone but that he refused to be intimidated. Each man, thinking the other was out to kill him, began carrying a gun. The *Times-Herald* editor's brother, W. A. Harris, also borrowed a pistol and began practicing marksmanship.

The three men met about 5:00 P. M. on November 9, at Fourth and Austin, when the streets were crowded. J. W. Harris, the editor, was standing at the corner drugstore. His brother was across the street near the Citizens National Bank. As Judge Gerald crossed the street, the firing began.

When the smoke cleared, W. A. Harris was dead and his brother mortally wounded. Judge Gerald had bullet holes in his right ankle and his left arm, which was later amputated. Gerald, known as a man with a high sense of honor, was tried and acquitted.

A second battle took place on South Fourth Street the next spring, on April 1, 1898. The participants were Tom E. Davis, son of a pioneer lawyer and brother of a lady teacher at Baylor, and Brann. A tall, broad-shouldered fellow with an intellectual look, Brann was forty-three. Before moving to Waco, he had been a newspaperman in Galveston, Houston, Austin, and San Antonio. He spent some of his time lecturing and was preparing to leave on a speaking tour when the shooting started.

Waco's young city attorney, Tom L. McCullough, was coming out of a barbershop when he heard the guns bark. "Brann had been shot through and through," he recalled, "but he made two shots. I was astonished at his fortitude."

Brann was shot in the spine. The bullets struck him in the back, entering, as one of his friends put it, "where his suspenders crossed." Brann was walked by friends to the city hall, a block and a half across the square, where the marshal took him. Both he and Davis died the next day.

In the new century, the language of editors became more polite and their persons safer. Yet the late Boyce House found frontier conditions persisting in the West Texas oil-field town of Eastland in the early 1920's. When he arrived there in 1921, one of the first bits he heard was that the preceding editor, just fired, had threatened to whip him. He also learned that an advertising man had quit because he did not like the atmosphere of gun smoke. "To thunder," he said, "with a job where they use six-shooters for paperweights!"

After House had exposed a road-building scandal in which some money stuck to the wrong hands and the roads were substandard, he was subjected to anonymous threats and physical attacks but kept his skin whole. His last scrap there was with a sheriff who had struck him in the face in public because of a news item that the officer didn't like. But after the sheriff was involved in a knife fight in a nearby town and was caught patronizing a bootleg dive, he was forced out of office and gave the newspaper no more trouble.

The pioneer editor, of course, did not spend all his time exposing wrongdoing or quarreling. He was an inveterate booster for his town. He knew that his own chance for success depended on the growth of the new community he had chosen, and he used much of his space to extol its climate, its people, its prospects, and the fertility of the surrounding area.

Although much of the local and state news was routine, sometimes there would be an exciting event to report. It might be a fight with Indian marauders, a bold train robbery, or a street battle between law officers and a band of desperadoes.

News columns included many brief personal items, some of them sent in by country correspondents. If a farmer suffered a fall from a horse, if his wife lost her chickens from cholera, or if his daughter went to town and bought a bridal dress—all were grist for the editor. The papers reported weddings in detail, sometimes including a list of the gifts. G. W. Robson, editor of the *Frontier Echo* at Jacksboro, wrote up weddings with such flourish and with such compliments to the bride that it became customary to reward him with a big cake with white frosting. In addition to their news, busy editors used their shears to fill columns with stories, essays, or poems from other papers.

Advertisements offered little to startle the reader. Medicine advertising, with extravagant claims, was prominent in almost every paper. It paid a low rate but was welcome because the pay usually was in cash. A few local ads were well written, but often they lost much of their punch by being run too long without change.

Except among the advertisements, illustrations were few; but one Texas paper, the Albany *News,* attained distinction by having its news pages enlivened with pictures. Its editor, Edgar Rye, was adept at carving woodcuts with his pocketknife and illustrated many of his articles and editorials. He ran cuts of cattle barons he interviewed, pictured an attempted bank robbery, showed the town mar-

157

shal exterminating a den of skunks, and depicted defeated political candidates boarding a steamboat to go up Salt Creek and drown their sorrows.

Perhaps the most amusing picture by Rye was one based on the fact that Albany had plenty of water but no whisky, while neighboring Cisco had much whisky but was short of water in that drouth season. The illustration showed Cisco people gazing longingly at the Albany water tank while swapping an express car full of hard liquor for a supply of clear water.

Some publishers found ingenious names for their papers. Although Texas had none quite as striking as Arizona's Tombstone *Epitaph,* it had memorable ones in the Comanche *Chief* and the Jefferson *Jimplecute.* The latter name was made up of the first letters of each word of an involved slogan, "Join-Industry-Manufacturing-Planning-Labor-Energy-Capital-[in]-Unity-Together-Everlasting."

Mortality among the frontier newspapers was high. Often a town acquired more papers than it could support, and the weaker ones had to fold. In other cases the town itself failed to survive, perhaps because a rival won a battle to become the county seat or to be on the line of a new railroad. When a publisher-editor saw that he had made a bad guess or that his town was hopelessly dwindling, he might move to a more promising community.

Western Texas saw many such moves. The *Frontier Echo* was established at Jacksboro in 1875, but three years later, after that town had ceased to be an important shipping point for cattle, the paper was moved west to become the Fort Griffin *Echo.* After a few more years, when a railroad was built through Albany instead of Fort Griffin and the military post was abandoned, the paper was shifted again and became the Albany *Echo.*

Another Texas publisher of that era hopped from Palo Pinto to Mineral Wells and thence to Albany, while still another went from Blanco County to Bertram and later to Burnet. An 1881 item noted that "the Coleman *Courant* has pulled up stakes and moved to Colorado City, the new and growing city on the Colorado River at the crossing of the Texas and Pacific Railroad."

This moving from place to place was the lot also of a colorful editor whom Northwest Texas acquired in 1876. He was Asa S. Mercer, who had been the first president of the University of Washington and who had received nationwide publicity by importing a shipload of young women from New York to Seattle. In his seven years in Texas he published and edited four newspapers: the Wichita *Herald*, the Vernon *Guard*, the Bowie *Cross Timber*, and the Mobeetie *Panhandle*. In 1883 he moved to Wyoming, where he edited the *Northwest Live Stock Journal* and, in 1894, wrote and published a famous pamphlet, *The Banditti of the Plains*, a biting account of the Wyoming cattlemen's war of 1892.

One of the Texas newsmen who moved most frequently was restless Don H. Biggers, who began his long career as a printer for the Colorado City *Clipper* about 1884, when he was only fourteen. He went from there to a job in Cisco and in 1890 bought the Midland *Gazette*. When that newspaper's building burned soon afterward, he went back to Colorado City briefly, then in 1891 started the Ranger *Atlas*. After a few months he sold that paper and went to work for the Albany *News*. In 1893 he left Albany and, for a time, edited the Breckenridge *Texian*. Later he was a newspaper writer, editor, or publisher in other Texas communities, including Cleburne, Abilene, Rotan, Lubbock, Eastland, and Fort Worth.

Although he engaged in no gun battles, Biggers was a writer of irascible temperament who might have needed a pistol in his belt in earlier years. His death in 1957 removed the last of the personal editors from the Texas scene. The others long before had discarded buckskin for store suits and left off their pistols, but a few still carried memories of rawhide days when the smell of printer's ink sometimes was smothered by the odor of gun smoke.

In the frontier period, as later, the country editor was a constructive force and a community leader. Along with politicians, lawyers, and others, he served on civic and promotional committees. He was generous with his newspaper space not only in attracting settlers, railroads, and industries but in building roads, schools, and churches and upgrading cultural life. Without the economic rewards of the banker, the land speculator, or the ranchman, he worked as hard as any of them for the progress of his community.

159

SETTLERS ON THE TEXAS FRONTIER had to contend not only with redskin raiders but with paleface scoundrels who lost no opportunity to make trouble. In the wake of valiant pioneers who braved hardship to make new homes were ruffians who had gone west to escape jail or to seek easy fortunes from the work of others. Many of them made a precarious living as horse thieves or cattle rustlers.

Such unwelcome elements were noted in most frontier communities. It was not uncommon to ask a man why he had run away from home, wrote W. B. Dewees, an early Texas settler. "Few persons feel insulted at such a question. They generally answer for some crime or other which they have committed. If they deny having committed any crime or say they did not run away, they are looked upon suspiciously."

An eastern visitor to Texas in 1853–54, Frederick Law Olmsted, pointed out that "in the rapid settlement of the country, many an adventurer crossed the border, spurred by love of liberty, forfeited at home, rather than drawn by a love of adventure or of rich soil. Probably a more reckless and vicious crew was seldom gathered than that which peopled some parts of eastern Texas at the time of its resistance to the Mexican government. 'G.T.T.'—gone to Texas —was the slang appendage to the name of every man who disappeared before the discovery of some rascality. Did a man emigrate thither, everyone was on the watch for the discreditable reason to turn up."

"If your life would be of the slightest use to anyone," Olmsted added, "you might be sure he would take it. It was safe only as you were in constant readiness to defend it. Horses and wives were of as little account as umbrellas in more advanced states. Everybody appropriated everything that suited him, running his own risk of a penalty."

To handle such culprits, both in the farmlands and on the cattle ranges, justice had to be rough and ready. This was especially true in the open grasslands to the west, before barbed-wire fences and windmills marked the advance of civilization. Early cowmen could not always wait for formal courts. They had to act boldly to rid their range of horse thieves and cattle rustlers.

Most despised was the horse thief, who was looked upon as even worse than a killer. He not only took property but deprived the ranchman of the mounts he must have in his daily work. Without them, the cowman could not make a living. If unhorsed out on the plains, he was exposed to many dangers. He might die of thirst or hunger. He might be frozen stiff in a sudden blizzard. He might become prey to snarling beasts or scalping Comanches.

Stockmen wanted to be sure that the ponies they turned out to graze at night would be within reach the next morning. Anyone caught with a stolen horse could expect no mercy. In the range country, horse thieves were the most frequent objects of the committees of vigilance formed to stamp out lawlessness. Any good calf rope could be used in decorating a tree.

Held in almost equal contempt was the cow thief. Anyone caught stealing calves or altering brands likely would be given a ticket to the hereafter. Lack of fences made the brand the sole badge of ownership, and no tampering with this mark was tolerated. Even possession of a running iron, used by rustlers in changing brands, was enough to cause grave suspicion.

The Texas vigilance committees, although they seldom held formal trials, were made up of leading citizens who moved carefully and arrested no one except culprits against whom the evidence was overwhelming. Their verdicts, usually banishment or death, were fair. Since there was no appeal, technicalities offered no escape.

In the decades just before and after the Civil War, almost every Texas county had vigilante hangings. In the spring of 1857, seven

161

horse thieves were hanged at different places along the San Antonio River. In each case, the thief's weapons and outer clothes were carefully placed at the foot of the tree. In August, 1864, citizens hanged three horse thieves in Smith County, in northeastern Texas.

In 1869 the Denton *Monitor* reported that the business of horse stealing there had played out. "Horse thieves have been swung to limbs whenever caught, and cow thieves have not been slighted." But, in spite of such hangings, the thefts continued. Early in 1878 a Houston newspaper estimated that 100,000 horses had been stolen in Texas in the preceding three years and that not one thief in ten had been caught.

Texas' most active vigilance committee was that of Fort Griffin, the wild town on the Western cattle trail and an outfitting point and hide market for buffalo hunters. So many horses had been stolen without any of the thieves being caught that ranchmen formed a committee of night riders in the spring of 1876. On the night of April 9 they caught a man stealing a horse and quickly left him swinging from the limb of a pecan tree along the Clear Fork of the Brazos River. Below the body they left a pick and shovel for anyone who might want to dig a grave. "So far, so good," wrote a local newspaper correspondent. "As long as the committee strings up the right parties, it has the well wishes of every lover of tranquillity."

The committee was busy all that spring, hanging some of the most notorious horse thieves and banishing others. Its work had a deterrent effect, but the group had to be revived two years later. This was after a former sheriff was found stealing steers from his neighbors, butchering them in his pen, tossing the hides with their tell-tale brands into a deep hole in the river, and selling the beef to the nearby military garrison. The vigilantes ended the former sheriff's career with a volley of rifle shots. In a little more than two years, they had done away with nearly a score of stock thieves and had driven out many others.

Some of the early Texas courts followed procedures scarcely more formal than those of the vigilance committees. Out in the prairie-dog country, one elderly justice of the peace was called Old Necessity because he knew no law. The only book on his bench was

162

a mail-order catalog bound in sheepskin to make it look like a law tome. In each trial he consulted this volume diligently before giving his verdict.

One day a stranger was brought before Old Necessity for a misdemeanor to which he pleaded guilty. The defendant's lawyer mentioned a mitigating circumstance and asked the court to be lenient. The justice put on his spectacles, opened his bound volume at random, looked at it a moment, and announced, "I fine you $4.88."

The accused man jumped up to protest, but his attorney yanked him back to his seat. "Sit down," he ordered. "Be thankful he opened it at pants instead of at pianos."

Another dispenser of justice in the chaparral allowed a lawyer's bluff to hide ignorance of the law and of court procedure. In one case the prosecutor was outraged when his opponent quoted the law. Unable to disprove the citation, the prosecutor nevertheless declared boldly, "Your Honor, that ain't the law."

When the defending lawyer refused to give in, the prosecuting attorney finally threw a ten-spot on the table and declared, "I'll bet you ten dollars it ain't the law."

The opposing lawyer, who didn't have a ten with him, received no sympathy from the justice. "Yes, money talks," he said. "If you ain't got the nerve to cover his ten, I guess you're wrong. The court rules against you."

In such a court a defendant from outside the county often had little chance. In the Cooke County village of Callisburg, early in 1875, a man from Grayson County was haled before a justice of the peace and accused of stealing a cow. The defendant showed a bill of sale, attested by two witnesses who had seen him pay money for the cow. Nevertheless, the expounder of law and justice held the accused man for trial and refused to take anyone from outside Cooke County on his bond. The justice said that, since there had been so many unpunished cow thefts, he was forced to take action, even though he was satisfied that the defendant had bought and paid for the cow.

Texas' most celebrated frontier justice was bearded Roy Bean, who dispensed law of a sort in the dusty country west of the Pecos

River. Still standing in the village of Langtry, at the edge of the primitive Big Bend country, is the boxlike board cabin in which Bean sold beer and handed out judicial rulings.

Kentucky-born Bean had had a checkered career as a trader on the Chihuahua Trail and as a bartender in California and New Mexico before he settled in San Antonio during the Civil War and married an eighteen-year-old Mexican girl. In the early 1880's, Bean followed the Southern Pacific Railroad westward, taking along a tent from which he sold whisky to the hard-drinking Irishmen of the construction crews.

Although Bean had had little schooling, his beard gave him a dignified appearance. Soon he was being called on to settle disputes or to say what should be done with the body of someone who had been killed in a shooting affray. Then, in 1882, at the request of the Texas Rangers, who had no court in that part of the state to which they could take offenders, Bean was appointed a justice of the peace.

Bean had a battered law book, but it was more for show than for use. Once he acquitted a brawny Irishman because he found no law against killing a Chinaman. In 1892, the body of Pat O'Brien, killed in a fall from the high railroad bridge over Myers Canyon, was brought before Bean. The dead man had a six-shooter in one pocket and forty dollars in another. So the justice fined him forty dollars for carrying a concealed weapon.

With no jail for many miles, Bean kept prisoners chained to a nearby mesquite tree. They slept on the ground, with gunnysacks for pillows, and occasionally worked at jobs that Bean wanted done. The judge pocketed the fines he collected and frequently recessed court to sell refreshments at the bar.

Little more formal than that of Roy Bean were some of the early Texas courts above the level of justice of the peace, even in the larger places. William Bollaert, an Englishman who visited Texas in the latter days of the republic, was shocked at the conduct of a Galveston judge. He found this jurist chewing his quid and resting his feet on his desk while the lawyers, "ready at speech and loads of references, from Magna Charta upward," chewed, smoked, and whittled.

With law enforcement weak in many sections of the frontier, the curbing of lawbreakers often depended on the bringing in of Texas Rangers. This fighting outfit, the outgrowth of a small mounted force formed by Stephen F. Austin in colonial days to defend the settlements against Indian raids, soon earned a world-wide reputation. The Texas Ranger, said John S. Ford, "can ride like a Mexican, trail like an Indian, shoot like a Tennessean, and fight like a devil."

In the early days the Rangers provided their own horses and wore buckskin, corduroy, or khaki, with leather boots and large felt hats. Often they had to sleep in the open. They were especially effective after they began using the new Colt revolvers. Colt called his first successful gun the Texas and, about 1842, named an improved military model the Walker, for Captain Samuel H. Walker of the Rangers, who had suggested some changes. The Rangers quickly gave the revolver the name of six-shooter.

When they were not busy chasing Indians or horse thieves, the Rangers might be called on for other chores, as in the comic-opera "archives war" of 1842–43. When a Mexican army appeared at San Antonio and demanded surrender of the town, the unprepared Texas force withdrew and President Sam Houston called an emergency session of Congress, not in Austin, the capital, but in Houston. Austin citizens, fearing loss of the capital, set vigilantes to guard the archives, which Houston sent Rangers to move to Washington-on-the-Brazos for safekeeping. Before the Rangers took the archives away, Mrs. Angelina Eberly fired a cannon at them. Later, on January 1, 1843, vigilantes from Austin overtook the wagons along Brushy Creek and seized the papers from the Rangers, who had orders to avoid bloodshed.

One of the early Ranger captains was John C. Hays, better known as Jack Hays. A young Tennessean who had settled in San Antonio, Hays engaged in surveying but soon joined the Ranger force, in which he was made a captain in 1840. He fought many battles with the Indians, including one in the summer of 1844 when his Ranger force of sixteen men encountered between sixty and seventy warriors near the Llano River. The Rangers, who closed in with their new revolvers, killed twenty-three Indians and lost only one man and had four wounded.

165

Following the Mexican War, in which the Rangers served valiantly as scouts and guerrilla fighters, the force was virtually disbanded on the supposition that the United States Army would defend the frontier. But, although a few military posts were set up along the Río Grande, Indian raids and forays of Mexican cattle thieves became so serious that Sam Houston thundered in the Senate in 1858: "Give us one thousand Rangers and we will be responsible for the defense of our frontier. Texas does not want regular troops. Withdraw them if you please."

In 1875, Captain L. H. McNelly of the restored Rangers led thirty of his men across the Río Grande after Mexican cattle thieves when United States cavalrymen refused to cross although they had orders to do so. The Rangers stood their ground against repeated attacks by the Mexicans, who had about 100 cavalrymen and 150 to 200 foot soldiers. In the evening the Mexicans asked for a truce, but McNelly refused until the stolen cattle were returned. Without any help from the American soldiers across the river, he threatened to resume fighting the Mexicans, who then had what looked like 800 or 900 men. The Mexicans sent back 65 of the 150 stolen beeves, and the Rangers retired to the Texas side of the river.

In December of the following year, Lieutenant Lee (Red) Hall and sixteen of his Rangers were sent out from Clinton in a cold drizzle one evening to bring in seven men indicted for murders linked with the Sutton-Taylor feud. At a farm home near Cuero they found the wanted men and others dancing at a wedding party. With his men surrounding the house, Hall stepped unarmed into the doorway. As those inside recognized him, the music stopped. Women screamed, and men reached for their guns.

"Do you want anyone here?" asked the bridegroom, one of the indicted men.

Yes, I want seven men," he answered, naming them.

"How many men you got?" asked one.

"Seventeen, counting myself," Hall replied calmly.

"Well, we've got seventy. I guess we'll have to fight it out."

"That's the talk!" shouted the Ranger. He gave the feudists three minutes to get their women and children out of the house and ordered his men to shoot to kill. Before that time was up, however, the men inside decided not to fight. They gave the Rangers their guns and, after the party ended, the seven men went off as prisoners.

In 1877 another Ranger lieutenant, John B. Armstrong, single-handedly went after one of the state's most wanton killers, John Wesley Hardin, accused of more than a score of murders. Armstrong followed Hardin to Alabama, where he learned that the desperado had gone to Florida. A few days later the Ranger entered a passenger car at Pensacola Junction and saw Hardin facing him. As Hardin reached for his gun, one of his four companions put a bullet through Armstrong's hat and received a fatal shot in return. Armstrong then grabbed Hardin's gun and kicked the killer back into his seat, giving him a blow on the head with his six-shooter. He then disarmed the other three. Later he brought Hardin back to Texas, where the bandit was tried, convicted, and sent to prison.

In the summer of 1878, a special company of Rangers chased the notorious brigand and train robber, Sam Bass, through the woods and across the prairies of northern Texas without catching him, although one of his men was killed. Finally, after an associate of Bass had betrayed him, Rangers and local officers closed in on Sam and two of his band at the village of Round Rock. In a street battle on July 19, Bass received a mortal wound. He was picked up the next morning and died on the twenty-first, his twenty-seventh birthday.

In the era of James E. and Miriam Ferguson, the Ranger force deteriorated, its tough, trigger-fingered men dismissed to make room for drugstore cowboys who happened to be on the right side of the political fence. But, in 1935, Governor James V. Allred induced the legislature to reorganize and modernize the force in an attempt to restore its old traditions. The new Rangers rode streamlined cars but sometimes took horses in a trailer to use in the mountains.

As the Texas frontier became more populous, the enforcement of order and law became easier. Vigilance committees were dispensed with, and Rangers were called in less often. Many communities acquired marshals and sheriffs who showed both courage and efficiency, prosecutors became bolder, and judges and juries were more severe.

167

Before he joined the Texas Rangers, Lee Hall had been marshal at Sherman. From early 1873 until the fall of 1874, he was deputy sheriff of Grayson County and assigned to keep order in Denison, then a wild railroad and cattle town and a den of vice and crime. Denison was just outgrowing its status as a tent and shanty town, and some of its houses still were on rollers. On Skiddy Street, south of Main, anything went.

Skiddy Street, later called Chestnut, was lined on both sides with tents, shacks, and board houses of saloons, gambling joints, hurdy-gurdy houses, and "dovecotes" that offered sex for all races. Brawls and holdups were everyday events. Cowboys shot up the streets, and Indians full of firewater filled the night with their whoops.

Yet Hall, a youth of twenty-three from North Carolina, showed himself a match for any outlaw. Edward King, who wrote of Denison in *Scribner's Magazine*, said: "He moved about tranquilly every day in a community where a hundred men would have delighted in shedding his blood. He was called on to stop brawls at all hours of night, yet his life went on." Although threatened, ambushed, and shot at many times, Hall stuck to his job until he had driven out the worst of the border scum.

In 1874, frontier Dallas acquired an able marshal in Junius (June) Peak, who had served earlier as a deputy sheriff. In his four years as marshal, Peak had to quell the ebullience of visiting cowboys and keep an eye on shady characters attracted by the boom of a town that had two railroads. Yet—tall, thin, and mustached—he was a quiet and unassuming officer who did his work without fanfare. His record as a marshal led Governor Richard Coke to appoint him to head a special company of Texas Rangers to chase Sam Bass and his brigands.

Fort Worth, an outfitting town for drovers going up the Chisholm Trail, had as marshal in 1876 a tall, icy-nerved fellow, Tim I. Courtright. Courtright, born on an Illinois farm, was thirty-one and a Union veteran. Almost everyone called him Long Hair Jim because he often let his hair grow to his shoulders, as did Wild Bill Hickok and some of the Indian scouts. Courtright, who wore two pistols in his belt and was quick on the draw, had two policemen for day work and two others for night patrol.

Jim and his helpers were especially busy on Saturday nights, when many cowboys were inclined to go wild and shoot out the street lights. On such nights they sometimes had to crowd twenty-five to thirty lawbreakers in the two cells and dungeon of the log jail at Second and Commerce streets. Although rough on killers and horse thieves, Jim was easy on gamblers. He allowed his policemen to loaf in the casinos and variety theaters when they might have been patrolling, and often he tried his own hand at the gaming tables.

Texas had many other fearless law officers, most of them receiving scant recognition for their work in quieting feuds, checking cattle rustling and horse thieving, and capturing those who too easily reached for their guns. One who stood out was James B. Gillett, who, after six years with the Texas Rangers, was elected marshal of El Paso and helped tame that border town. Another was J. J. Spradley, who, as sheriff of Nacogdoches County for thirty years, was relentless in bringing lawbreakers to justice.

Less credit is deserved by Texas' most-celebrated law officer, Ben Thompson. After operating gambling halls in several towns in Kansas and adjoining states, Thompson returned to Austin, where, after an initial defeat in 1879, he was elected marshal. He kept order fairly well, but more because he was feared as a gunman than because of any work he did. He was well behaved while sober but overbearing when intoxicated. He spent much of his time in gambling, drinking, and quarreling. On a trip to San Antonio, he killed Jack Harris, owner of the Vaudeville Theater and Gambling Saloon, a notorious night spot on the Main Plaza, and was placed in jail. That incident ended the career of Thompson as marshal of Austin, although his trial, in January, 1883, resulted in acquittal.

From that time on, Thompson became wilder than ever. He shot up parts of the town, broke up a cattlemen's banquet, and whipped a man in a courtroom while court was in session. On other occasions he emptied a theater during a performance by firing shots from a box seat and drove editors and printers from the *Statesman*'s office and pied all the type forms. On the night of March 11, 1884, he became involved in a gun fight in a variety theater in San Antonio and was killed.

As public opinion turned more strongly against crime, the work of local prosecutors became easier but often still required courage. At Uvalde young John N. Garner made life so rough for stock thieves that he started on a political path that led to Congress and the vice-presidency.

In many frontier counties the first court was held outdoors, under the trees. At Sherman in 1847, court met under a big pecan tree until the first Grayson County courthouse could be built, at a cost of $232.00. The Smith County courthouse, built at Tyler that year, was of pine logs, with a plank floor. Cooke County paid only $29.00 for its first courthouse, built at Gainesville in 1850. It was sixteen feet square and eight feet high. The logs were scotched down, inside and out. In the same year Ellis County acquired a courthouse of logs for $59.00. The contractor bought a vacant cabin that had been used as a church and school and moved it to Waxahachie.

In the 1870's the work of many Texas courts was hampered by the stealing of criminal records and the burning of courthouses to destroy such records. An incendiary burned the Parker County courthouse in March, 1874. Early the next month a roaring blaze consumed the Milam County courthouse and all the records it housed. Probers found a kerosene jug under the courtyard fence. A Negro arrested for setting this fire was believed to have been hired by an indicted white man who wanted to destroy the records in his case. The courthouse and records at Rockwall met a similar fate in March, 1875.

The wave of arson continued in Fort Worth, Denton, and other county seats. On an April night in 1877, four horsemen galloped into Castroville, poured coal oil on the records in the courthouse, and set the buildings ablaze. As they left, they fired sixteen shots at citizens who rushed out to try to stop the flames and save the records.

In spite of such burnings and the threats of blustering outlaws, Texas had its full share of courageous judges who tolerated no inter-

170

ference with their courts. One of the early heroes of the bench was a district judge in the republic period, Robert M. Williamson.

At Shelbyville in 1837, Judge Williamson, seated behind a dry-goods box, opened the first court in Shelby County. A few minutes later a tall ruffian strode in and told the judge that local citizens had decided that court should not be held. "What legal authority," Williamson asked, "can you give for such procedure?"

At that, the intruder drew a bowie knife from his belt and slammed it on the improvised bench. "This, sir," he snarled, "is the law of Shelby County!"

In a flash, the judge whipped out a long-barreled pistol and placed it beside the knife. "If that is the law of Shelby County," he thundered, "this is the constitution that overrides it! Mr. Sheriff, please call the grand jury."

Citizens of some frontier towns, when they were not out after desperadoes, found excitement in waging a county-seat war with a neighboring community. Often a town bidding for the county seat had little to offer. Of one three-way fight, a visitor noted that two towns each had a store, a hitching post, and a clothesline, while the third had only a buffalo skull. In one town, to make it appear that the site had enough water, settlers secretly hauled creek water at night to an otherwise dry well. In at least two cases, records were stolen from the courthouse of a rival town.

The Texas Legislature required that a new county must have at least 150 qualified voters to be organized. Some would-be counties failed in their first attempt to show the required number. When Deaf Smith County, on the west edge of the Panhandle, held its first election in 1885, in the shade of a haystack, the voting drew only "two Democrats, two Republicans, and one sheepman." The only way that some counties could qualify was to round up nesters and cowboys from adjoining counties. Such roped-in outsiders often were a factor in deciding county-seat wars.

In 1856 a purloined barrel of whisky helped Fort Worth in its contest with Birdville. In front of two Fort Worth stores were two barrels of free whisky, with new dippers and buckets of sugar for those who wanted to sweeten their drink. Birdville, too, had a barrel of whisky but had it hidden in an oak grove until the polls opened. From there, enemy scouts stole it and put it to use at Fort Worth.

Even then the outcome was in doubt. But in the nick of time a former Fort Worth resident, Sam Woody, rode in from his new ranch in Wise County, bringing fourteen cowboys. After all had voted, the tide turned in favor of Fort Worth. That night the winning town celebrated with bonfires, oratory, and more whisky. Torch-bearing merrymakers drove a wagon to Birdville, loaded it with the county law books, desks, and cane-bottom chairs, and returned in triumph to Fort Worth. A charge of fraud, however, allowed Birdville to remain the county seat until another election four years later.

In 1874, Graham won over old Fort Belknap to become the seat of Young County. Graham had appealed to the frontier cowmen by laying out one of the biggest courthouse squares in all Texas. In the following year, San Angelo and Ben Ficklin waged a hot contest for the seat of Tom Green County. San Angelo, the larger town, was confident of success; but Ben Ficklin, by naturalizing sixty-five Mexicans in a hurry and voting them en masse, was the winner. After a flood destroyed Ben Ficklin in 1882, San Angelo took over the honor without a fight.

Often the route of a railroad influenced the choice of a county seat. In 1877, Belle Plain nosed out Callahan City as the seat of Callahan County. Then in 1883, three years after the Texas and Pacific had built through the county, the new railroad town of Baird won over the stranded Belle Plain. Likewise, Buffalo Gap, which had defeated Taylor City in 1878 to become the seat of Taylor County, lost out in 1883 to Abilene, a mushroom town of tents and hastily assembled houses on the railroad.

Sweetwater used roughshod methods in seeking to become the seat of Nolan County early in 1881. The vote, held during a snowstorm, had favored a site about three miles west of Sweetwater. But the Commissioners Court reversed the outcome by throwing out the votes of residents of the southwestern part of the county, polled in a dugout because of the storm. When the commissioners met in a twelve-by-fourteen shack in Sweetwater to canvass the returns, they refused a hearing to a Fort Worth lawyer hired to represent the rival settlement.

Sometimes a county-seat war became a conflict between ranchmen and nesters. That was true in Fisher County in the spring of 1886. There the stockmen and cowboys supported Roby, while the farmers favored Fisher, four miles away. The promoters of each town virtually gave away building lots to prospective residents—and voters. In the end, Roby won by a vote of sixty-seven to fifty-two.

In rolling Runnels County, the cow town of Runnels City rested in its saddle after winning the county seat, by a vote of thirty to twenty-nine, over the rival village of Maverick in 1880. The winner held court in a rented room over a saloon, expecting to build a courthouse after more taxes were collected. In 1886, when the Santa Fe Railroad built through the county, it missed Runnels City. On the rail line the new town of Ballinger was laid out in a cow pasture. In a month it acquired one thousand residents, compared with seven hundred in Runnels City. The latter held on to the county seat in an election in the fall of 1886 but lost it to Ballinger in a vote taken in the following year.

In the western Panhandle, the wild town of Tascosa fought to remain the seat of Oldham County. In an election in 1911 it beat down the challenges of Adrian and Vega. But farmers were coming in fast, and town sites on the Rock Island Railroad had a big advantage. In 1915, Vega—after giving 160 lots to cowboys, nesters, and other voters—won. The next day, Vega men loaded the county records in a wagon and hauled them across the Canadian River and over a dim trail to the new seat.

A BLAST FROM THE HORN of a stagecoach driver quickly brought a crowd to the hotel of a frontier Texas town. Some were looking for mail or packages, and everyone wanted to see the new arrivals, who might be visitors, drummers, or new settlers.

By 1860, Texas was criss-crossed by at least thirty-one stage lines, with most of the coaches drawn by two or three spans of horses or mules. Although fresh teams were provided at intermediate stations, coaches averaged only five to eight miles an hour. Often the passengers, who had paid a fare of ten cents a mile, had to get out and help push the coach out of a mudhole. At least a fortnight was required to travel from Dallas to St. Louis and back.

Even slower were the ox wagons used in freighting. Twenty cents per ton mile was charged for the wagons that hauled grain to market. This price was prohibitive for cotton that had to be carried long distances, and it delayed cotton growing in much of Texas until railroads were available. An exception was the Civil War period, when the high prices paid by blockade runners at Brownsville made it profitable to send bales there even from the distant Dallas area.

North Texas towns had to haul building materials, dry goods, and staple groceries for long distances, usually from Jefferson, which unloaded river cargoes from New Orleans. When Dallas' frontier hotel, the Crutchfield House, was destroyed by fire in 1860, the owner had to wait six months for lumber for the new building to be brought by oxen from Buffalo Bayou.

A stage line of 1,476 miles from San Antonio to San Diego, with a mail contract, was opened in July, 1857. It had twenty-five four-horse Concord coaches. Because pack mules were used to carry

174

the first mail across the 180-mile stretch from Fort Yuma to San Diego, some called the new line the Jackass Mail.

In Limpia Canyon, a band of Apaches ambushed one of the coaches, killed the driver, and took out the mail bags. Opening one sack, the Indians discovered several illustrated papers. While they were absorbed in looking at the pictures, a squad of cavalrymen dashed into their camp, killing fourteen Indians and routing the others.

Texas' most exciting stagecoach line was the short-lived one of the famous Butterfield Overland Mail. The Texas part of this trail led from Sherman through the wilderness buffalo country to El Paso. The coaches stopped at Gainesville and Jacksboro and passed near the future sites of Albany and San Angelo. Later a change in the route took them through Denton, Decatur, and Bridgeport.

The Texas sector was part of a route that extended 2,650 miles from St. Louis to San Francisco. This was the longest mail route in the country that depended on vehicles drawn by horses or mules. An eastern branch from Memphis joined the main line at Fort Smith. The stages entered Texas by crossing the Red River at Colbert's Ferry, below Preston. After stopping at Sherman, where the Butterfield barn was the biggest building in town, they headed southwest.

Possible attacks by Comanches and other hostile Indians were among the many hazards faced by this frontier stage line. The drivers had to ferry across or ford flooded streams, make repairs in desert country, and be prepared for highwaymen and horse thieves. But John Butterfield had told the drivers, "Remember, boys, nothing on God's earth must stop the United States mail!" And nothing did.

This mail and passenger line was authorized by an act of Congress that became effective March 3, 1857. The law provided for a mail contract for carrying letters, twice a week in each direction, by four-horse coaches or spring wagons suitable for carrying passengers. Each trip had to be completed within twenty-five days. The government would pay $60,000 a year for the transport of mail and let the contractor have whatever extra he could obtain by hauling passengers.

This contract was awarded to John Butterfield and his asso-

175

ciates. Butterfield, born in a mountainous section of New York in 1801, was an old hand at operating stage lines. After starting his career at the age of nineteen as a stagecoach driver, he had become the operator of a livery stable and several stage lines. Later he had become a large holder of real estate, mayor of Utica, and one of the organizers of the American Express Company and a telegraph company.

The company first had to survey the long route and make a passable road. It improved old sections of the trail and made new ones, picked sites for fords or ferries, built stations for changing horses, and dug wells. It bought more than 1,800 horses and mules and spotted them at stations along the route. Mules were preferred in the dangerous Comanche and Apache country, since the warriors were less likely to steal them. Finally, the company had to make test runs and figure out two-way schedules.

To carry the mail and passengers, the company bought 250 or more stagecoaches, besides mail wagons, freight wagons, and tank wagons. It also obtained a vast quantity of harness. In addition to hiring trained drivers, it engaged conductors, station-keepers, blacksmiths, helpers, and men to look after the horses and mules. Everyone on the route needed to be an expert marksman.

The coaches were built by three firms—one in Concord, New Hampshire, and the others in Albany and Troy, New York. Some coaches were of the regular type, later known as Southern. A coach of this kind could carry nine passengers inside and others outside. The other coaches were a lighter and faster type designed by Butterfield for use on the rougher sections of the route. This "celerity wagon" had smaller wheels, and its frame was covered with heavy duck. It could carry nine passengers inside but none outside. The inside seats could be adjusted into a bed.

The postage rate for letters was ten cents a half-ounce, and the passenger fare for the whole route averaged $200 one way. At the start of operation, the line had 143 stations, averaging about twenty miles apart. At each station several armed men looked after the horses and had relays ready for quick changes. Some of the stations served meals for passengers at forty cents to one dollar. The fare varied but often included jerked beef or wild game, mesquite beans, corncake, and coffee.

The first coaches left each end of the line in mid-September, 1858. Each arrived ahead of schedule, the westbound one setting a record for an overland journey. John Butterfield rode the first westbound coach as far as Fort Smith. With him was the first through passenger, twenty-three-year-old Waterman L. Ormsby, a corre-spondent of the New York *Herald.* Ormsby reported that Butterfield seemed to know every foot of the ground. He sometimes helped change the horses, and on one occasion he drove a few miles.

At the Red River, wrote Ormsby, B. F. Colbert had slaves at work on the bank, "cutting away the sand to make the ascent easy. His boat is a raft pushed across the shallow stream by poles in the hands of sturdy slaves." Ormsby found Sherman "a pleasant little village of about six hundred." From there, he noted, the course "lay across a fine, rolling prairie, covered with grass but with no trees and scarcely a shrub for eighteen miles."

At one isolated station the passengers sat on upturned pails and ate breakfast on a shipping box. "There were no plates and but four tin cups for the coffee, which was served without milk or sugar," said Ormsby. The only food was "a kind of shortcake, baked over the coals, each man breaking off his chunk and plastering on butter with his pocketknife—butter a rare luxury between the Red River and the Río Grande."

The Butterfield line increased its loads of mail until, in 1860, it carried more California letters than the ocean steamers. Soon, however, the approach of war began to hamper its operations. When federal protection no longer could be given to parts of the route in Confederate territory, the line was abandoned in the spring of 1861. Even so, it left a record of heroic achievement over hardship and almost unbelievable odds.

In the republic period and the period of early statehood, river steamers supplemented the work of ox wagons in carrying Texas cotton and other crops to coastal markets and bringing back dry goods, groceries, and occasionally a few passengers. The boats were operated on the Red River, the Sabine, the Neches, the Trinity, the

Brazos, and the Río Grande. Usually they could come only short distances up the rivers, and their schedules were made undependable by low water, snags, and sand bars.

• In the early and middle 1880's steamboat navigation flourished on the lower Red River, from the mouth to Shreveport or beyond in Louisiana and up a tributary, Big Cypress Creek, to Jefferson, Texas. But the boats came up the main stream to Texas landings only in infrequent periods of high water. George Brinlee sometimes shipped cattle downstream from the wharf on his plantation in Bowie County, and occasionally a steamer came up as far as Fannin County.

The main obstruction to navigation on the border stream was a great mass of trees and driftwood, called the Raft, above Shreveport. Between 1828 and 1841 the government spent nearly half a million dollars in trying to clear the river, but as soon as the channel was opened, more debris would drift down and block it. By the time the Raft finally was removed in 1874, railroads had taken over most of the freight hauling.

Steamers regularly navigated the lower part of the Trinity River before the Civil War. Occasionally some of them penetrated to Magnolia, about ten miles west of Palestine. They brought up groceries and dry goods and took down cotton and other farm crops. Occasionally they carried a few passengers.

Traffic on the Trinity began at least as early as 1836. In that year Mrs. Mary Austin Holley said the river was navigable for about two hundred miles from its mouth. One of the early boats was the *Correro,* which in the spring of 1839 made a round trip from Galveston up as far as Carolina landing.

Other boats ascended as far as New Cincinnati and Osceola. In the spring of 1840, one called the *Trinity* went up about five hundred miles to Alabama landing. But in June, when it ventured further upstream, it was caught in a shoal, where it was stuck for several months.

One of the more pretentious Trinity steamers was the *Scioto Belle,* believed built on the Scioto River in Ohio. She arrived in Galveston from New Orleans in May, 1844. "She is a substantial, well built boat," said a Houston newspaper, "nearly new, well adapted for

178

carrying freight, and has excellent accommodations for passengers."

In the spring of 1843, Colonel Jacob Elliott and two other men had gone up the river to Dallas and back in a canoe hollowed from a cottonwood log. They reported that, at small expense, the stream could be made navigable for steamboats. In June of that year, John Neely Bryan and John Beeman of Dallas burned a pile of tree trunks that had clogged the channel.

In 1868, Captain James Garvey tied up in Dallas his sixty-foot stern-wheeler, the first steamer to ascend the river that far. He had taken one year and four days for the trip, with much time out for removing logs and snags and cutting overhanging branches.

A large steamer, the 113-foot *H. A. Harvey, Jr.*, arrived in Dallas in May, 1893, only two months and two days out of Galveston. The *Harvey* and its crew were given a tumultuous welcome, with the salute of a battery of guns, a gigantic parade, bursts of oratory, and a mammoth picnic.

The lower part of the Brazos River experienced sporadic navigation from 1830, when the *Columbia* steamed up to Washington and was wrecked on a sandbar. This traffic continued until the 140-foot, Ohio-built *Hiawatha,* with forty staterooms, called the fastest and most beautiful stern-wheeler ever brought to Texas, sank in 1895.

Early boats on the Brazos included the *Sabine,* which ran the Mexican blockade at Velasco in 1832, and the *Cayuga,* a side-wheeler that went into operation in 1835 and, the next spring, carried Texas officials to Columbia. Early in 1836 the *Yellow Stone,* of 130-foot keel, went up as far as Groce's landing, where it took on half a load of cotton. On the return trip downstream, it also carried some of General Sam Houston's soldiers. Later that year it brought the body of Stephen F. Austin from Columbia to Peach Point for burial. On other trips it went as far as Washington-on-the Brazos, paying three dollars a cord for firewood for its engine.

Other steamers on the Brazos in the 1840's included the *Mustang*, a large stern-wheeler that went up to Port Sullivan and Washington; the *Brazos,* which made many trips to Washington, hauling down cotton; the *Washington,* which once was stuck at Cuney's

179

Plantation for more than a year; the *Benjamin Milam,* which brought goods from a wrecked ocean vessel to Columbia; and the *Lady Byron,* which sank in the river.

Among the later boats on the river were the *Elite,* the *Galveston,* the *Camden,* the *Sam Williams,* the *Magnolia,* the *W. B. Travis,* the *J. H. Bell,* the *J. H. Whitelaw,* the *Kate Ross,* the *John Scott,* and the *Vicksburg.* The *Kate Ross,* named for a sister of Governor L. S. Ross, went up as far as Waco, where a dance was held on board.

The lower Río Grande, which had had some navigation even in the era of Spanish rule, became a busier channel after the Mexican War, with perhaps as many as ten boats carrying cotton and other goods. One of them was the *Colonel Cross,* which twenty-four-year-old Captain Richard King had bought in December, 1848. At a quartermaster's sale he acquired for $750 this steamer for which the government had paid $14,000 three years before and of which King recently had been captain.

In 1850, King went into partnership with a friend, Mifflin Kenedy, Charles Stillman, a shrewd and wealthy Brownsville trader, and Stillman's steamboat captain, James O'Donnell. The new company put better boats on the river, adopted improved methods, and soon had a monopoly of the river shipping.

After a few years, King left the river to establish what became a great cattle ranch, leaving the boats to the management of Kenedy. But when the Civil War brought an immense cotton boom to the river, both men were busy getting cotton to the Río Grande and carrying it on boats with Mexican flags to Matamoros, where it was exported under the noses of Union blockaders. After the war, the company ordered several new boats; but soon railroads made the river traffic unprofitable, and King and Kenedy gave their whole attention to ranching.

With the California gold rush pointing to the need for safer transportation across Texas and the states to the west, even camels were tried. Jefferson Davis, who foresaw national expansion and commercial growth, thought that camels might help to solve the transport problem until railroads could be built. As senator from Mississippi he promoted the camel idea in Washington. Later, as secre-

TEXAS RANGERS IN CAMP, 1892
The Texas Ranger "can ride like a Mexican, trail like an Indian, shoot like a Tennessean, and fight like a devil."

Texas State Library Archives

CROSSING THE PECOS

Pontoon bridges [as in this picture] and primitive ferries were often
employed for crossing streams.

Texas State Library Archives

EARLY HOUSTON AND TEXAS CENTRAL TRAIN
Railroad was a magic word—"One snort of the Iron Horse," wrote a farmer in 1866, "will wake to life the dormant energies of our rich and productive soil"

Southern Pacific Lines

BEAUMONT DURING THE SPINDLETOP OIL BOOM
The opening of the Spindletop field ushered in a new era: Every incoming
train was crowded . . . fifty thousand people descended on the town of
nine thousand.

American Petroleum Institute

KILGORE DURING THE EAST TEXAS OIL BOOM
Drilling continued at a rapid pace . . . nearly 30,000 wells in 1935, an
average of one well to every one and one-half acres.

Shell Oil Company

STOCK SHOW PARADE IN FORT WORTH

Cattle are still highly important to Texas, and the annual stock show
combines fun and serious business.

Fort Worth STAR-TELEGRAM

THE SAN ANTONIO RIVER
Flowing through the heart of the city, the river provides a charming
contrast to the bustling business district.

San Antonio Chamber of Commerce

TEXAS CAPITOL AT AUSTIN
This magnificent building was constructed in 1882, in exchange for
3,050,000 acres of land, the famous XIT Ranch.

Texas Highway Department

tary of war under President Franklin Pierce, he induced Congress to vote thirty thousand dollars for importing camels and dromedaries for military uses.

The first shipload of thirty-four camels from the Near East arrived at the Texas port of Indianola in May, 1856. Curious people came down to the wharf to watch the unloading of these strange beasts that wore red blankets and kneeled to receive their loads. Horses and mules were frightened by the humped animals. A driver had to be sent ahead to warn teamsters: "Get out of the road! The camels are coming!"

In San Antonio, near which the camels were stationed, residents soon became accustomed to seeing camels in the streets. When one of them was clipped, Mrs. Mary A. Shirkey carded and spun the hair and knit the yarn into a pair of socks which she sent to President Pierce.

In February, 1857, a second shipload brought the government camel herd in Texas to seventy head. The camels were matched against mules in several tests. Two wagons, each loaded with nearly two tons of freight and pulled by six mules, made a round trip from Green Valley to San Antonio in four days. Six camels with equal loads made the same journey in two and one-half days. In the Big Bend country, the camels proved themselves more sure-footed than the mules and superior in speed and endurance.

In the summer of 1857, the War Department sent an expedition with thirty-two camels from San Antonio to southern California. The journey was full of hazards. There were few watering places, and often the forage was scanty. The trails were without bridges, and some lacked tracks or markers to serve as guides. Much of the route was not even charted. Along some of the canyons savage Comanches and Apaches waited in ambush to rob and kill wayfarers. Lieutenant Edward F. Beale, in charge of the expedition, had almost every odd against him.

The outcome was highly favorable to the camels. The imported beasts of burden more than lived up to expectations. They adjusted themselves to their strange surroundings and survived the clumsiness of their amateur keepers. (The Turks, who knew best how to adjust

181

the animals' loads, had refused to leave San Antonio because the government, through a tangle of red tape, was seven months behind in their pay.)

The camels completed their arduous journey without mishap. By its end they were able to carry one thousand pounds each. One could carry a whole ton and, with a lighter burden, could travel sixteen miles an hour. The camels made much better time than the mules and horses of the caravan.

The Civil War put an end to the experiments with camels. In California some of the animals were used in freighting. At Camp Verde, Texas, the wives of cavalry officers occasionally rode camels to church services at Camp Ives, four miles away. An agricultural fair in Waco offered premiums for camels.

The Texas camels were neglected by the Confederates who captured them. During the war, loose camels on some Texas roads and trails were so common that children quit paying attention to them. Three wanderers captured by Union soldiers were sent to Iowa. Another was used to carry equipment for a Mississippi infantry company. One was bought by an Alabama planter who staged a contest which showed that, in a given time, a camel could plow more furrows than a mule. Later, Texas cowboys roped a few of the strays and sold them to zoos or circuses.

Some of the camels that went wild gave rise to folk tales. One story dealt with a great red beast believed to have carried for years the skeleton of a Mexican sheepherder. The victim, while still alive, was said to have been tied to the animal's back by Apaches. They then set the animal loose in the desert to become a specter that for decades haunted superstitious Mexicans.

For all who lived in the interior of Texas in the pioneer period, "railroad" was a magic word. Talk of proposed rail lines was on almost every tongue. Railways would extend the cotton kingdom inland, bring in new settlers, and give a start to booming cities. "One snort of the Iron Horse reverberating over our prairies," a farmer wrote in 1866, "will wake to life the dormant energies of our rich and productive soil."

The Republic of Texas, although it never heard a locomotive

182

whistle, saw the first efforts to build a railroad in the Southwest. The Texas Railroad, Navigation and Banking Company was chartered in the fall of 1836, but succumbed in the financial panic of the next year. Several other companies were chartered in 1840. One of them, using slave labor, began construction of a line that later became part of the Southern Pacific. In 1853 it completed its first twenty miles of track and bought its first locomotive, named for one of its financial backers, General Sidney Sherman.

Of greater interest to northern Texas was the Galveston and Red River Railway, later the Houston and Texas Central and still later a part of the Southern Pacific. Beginning construction in 1853, it crept north from Houston in slow stages. It used plows and barrows for grading and laid English-made rails weighing fifty-four pounds to the yard. The gauge was five and one-half feet. Much of the construction was done by prisoners in striped suits.

Strong rivalry to be on the railroad arose among the towns along or near the proposed route. Waxahachie people shunned it for fear it would bring a rough element into their town. A few Dallas men wanted to keep it out because it would wreck the business of a number of stagecoach and wagon-freighting lines; but Dallas, with only nine hundred residents, joined the other towns in a mad scramble for the road. By offering five thousand dollars in cash and 115 acres of land, Dallas induced the rail officials to have their track skirt the eastern edge of the town.

The arrival of the first train, on July 16, 1872, was a gala day in Dallas. As the puffing locomotive drew the first cars in from the south, frightened horses reared and bolted for home. The cheering townspeople celebrated with music, oratory, and a big feast of barbecued buffalo meat.

A little later, in bringing to Dallas the first east-west rail line, the Texas and Pacific, local leaders used a bit of strategy. In the legislature, John W. Lane of Dallas sponsored a bill requiring the new road to cross the Houston and Texas Central "within one mile of Browder's Springs." Rail officials discovered later that Browder's Springs was in Dallas.

The Texas and Pacific reached Dallas in the summer of 1873,

but the panic of that year stopped construction six miles beyond, at Eagle Ford. The result was that Fort Worth did not have a railroad until July, 1876. Even after that, although Fort Worth, Dallas, and Denison shipped many cattle by rail, most of the Longhorns continued to be trailed north for several years. It was cheaper to send them afoot than by rail.

Most of the early tracks and bridges were frail structures. Such was the narrow-gauge Dallas, Cleburne and Río Grande, later a part of the Santa Fe. On its completion to Cleburne, Dallas people arranged an excursion. With no passenger cars yet available, they placed benches on flatcars and draped them with bunting. After the little locomotive with a coffeepot smokestack had pulled its load into the hilly country to the southwest, a downpour of rain drenched the passengers and a chilly wind struck them.

As the excursion train progressed, the flimsy track sank deeper and deeper into the mud. "The engine panted harder than ever," a reporter noted, "but its task was too great. With a final groan," the locomotive left the rails and turned over.

"While in Cleburne a brass band waited vainly to welcome them, the bedraggled excursionists were stranded in the country. As best they could, they made their way to Midlothian and Alvardo, where they engaged every available horse and commandeered additional steeds from nearby farms. Finally they succeeded in reaching another train, which had been stalled near Midlothian. On it they arrived back in Dallas about noon the next day."

Schedules meant little on some of the early railroads. On the Orient line in western Texas, trainmen carried guns and often shot at game from the locomotive or the caboose. When they hit an animal, they would stop the train to retrieve it. They paid little attention to telegrams telling them where to pass other trains. If two trains approached head-on on a single track, they would stop, and the one closest to a siding would start backing.

Some towns missed by the railroads died completely. Many of those which did obtain a rail line began asking for more sidings and often for roundhouses and car shops. In 1885 the New York railroad financier, Jay Gould, explained why he skipped a trip through Texas:

"I could stand two miles of ground track," he said, "but I heard that there were sixteen miles of memorials setting out the advantages of building side tracks at certain points and twenty-two miles of petitions asking me to build car shops. I would expose a pair of weak lungs to the intemperance of Kansas weather before I would stand it."

The new railroads quickly extended the cotton country inland, but soon some of the farmers became disgruntled over the freight rates they had to pay. Many tried to revive interest in river navigation. A few even applauded Sam Bass and his brigand band when they held up and robbed four Texas passenger trains in the spring of 1878.

Farmers also stuck the railroads heavily for every horse, cow, and dog killed by a train, upping the value as much as they dared. "I don't think a train made a trip without killing somebody's cow," said C. A. Keating of the Texas Trunk. "The country was unfenced and was full of Longhorn cattle that were just being discarded for graded stock. Nobody ever claimed that the railroad killed his Longhorns. It was always high-grade stock that got in front of the engine."

Yet the railroads often came to the rescue of farmers and ranchmen in time of drouth, hauling in feed and even water. As late as 1953, after the rails had lost much of their business to trucks, buses, and airplanes, Texas railroads began helping sufferers from drouth by cutting in half the freight rate on emergency hay. This aid saved farmers and stockmen an estimated twenty-five million dollars and kept some of them from being pushed to the wall. In Dublin, ranchmen and dairymen showed their appreciation at a banquet at which rail officials were honored guests.

T HE FRONTIERSMAN IN BUCKSKIN, with his ax, his sod-breaker plow, and his Kentucky rifle, was followed by other pioneers who saw farming possibilities in parts of Texas that most earlier visitors had dismissed as desert. This later wave of settlers followed the ranchmen and the railroad builders into remote and arid sections, using dry farming, artesian wells, or water pumped from rivers.

A striking case was the lower valley of the Río Grande, in which explorers had had to make their way through prickly-pear cactus and thick growths of various thorny bushes. Even the cows later set loose in the region wore themselves thin trying to find enough grass to keep them alive. Yet the lower valley had deep and fertile soil; it lacked only moisture.

As early as 1749, Spanish colonists had diverted river water to irrigate crops, but they were not successful. In 1834, followers of an English colonist, Dr. John Charles Beales, settled near the Río Grande but soon abandoned their land because of drouths and danger from Indians.

Yet some saw the opportunities there. In 1869, Edward Dougherty of Brownsville wrote that valley land, which could be bought at one dollar an acre, was "unsurpassed in fertility." He pointed out that it was well suited for pastures and for growing such crops as cotton, sugarcane, vegetables, melons, and citrus fruits.

Successful farms began to appear there about a decade later. Celestina Jagou bought 640 acres on the river six miles east of Brownsville and grew cork, almonds, vegetables, grapes, and other fruits. In 1890 he sold 4,500 bunches of bananas. In 1870, George Brulay bought a 1,000-acre farm on the Río Grande nine miles

186

below Brownsville. After digging irrigation canals, he planted cotton and sugarcane. In 1876 he built a sugar mill, and by 1890 he was refining 1,500 barrels of sugar a year, averaging 350 pounds each. On another farm, near Santa Maria, a mechanical pump for irrigation was put into use in 1884. In 1897 the Santa Maria Canal Company began digging irrigation ditches that encouraged the growing of cotton, alfalfa, and other crops.

One of the most influential farming pioneers in what later came to be known as the "Magic Valley" was John Closner, a Wisconsin man who had gone to Mexico to work on a railroad-building project that failed. In 1883 he arrived in Río Grande City with his family and only fifteen dollars. After driving a stagecoach for a time, he served in turn as deputy sheriff, sheriff, and tax collector of Hidalgo County. All this time he was buying land at twenty-five cents to one dollar an acre until, by the time the railroad reached Brownsville in 1904, he had a plantation of 45,000 acres.

Closner put five hundred acres into alfalfa, from which he made several cuttings a year. His other crops included bananas, beans, cabbage, corn, cotton, melons, figs, onions, potatoes, squash, sorghum, tobacco, tomatoes, pecans, and walnuts. In 1895 he dug canals and ordered a pump big enough to irrigate two hundred acres. In that year he began growing sugarcane, and was so successful that, in 1904, his display at the Louisiana Purchase Exposition in St. Louis won the gold medal, besting even the entries of Cuba and Hawaii. In 1908 Closner and two other men formed an irrigation company to build reservoirs to store floodwaters, but this project did not materialize.

Many other irrigation projects followed, some of them started by land developers. Some were successful, while others succumbed to poor planning or to floods. Later, most of the irrigation came to be handled by groups of farmers who formed irrigation districts. The districts were empowered to issue bonds and to buy facilities from private developers.

The railroad and the irrigation projects soon began to call national attention to the Magic Valley and to interest land promoters. Fast-talking real-estate salesmen brought Middle Western farmers and snow-dodgers to the valley by the Pullman load and later by the trainload. Much of the land was sold on a boom basis, at inflated prices. Those who bought land in the boom included two who failed for every one who succeeded. Many who paid more than the land was worth were inexperienced in irrigation farming. They suffered from crop freezes and, in the case of growing citrus fruits, lacked the capital or financing to wait for their trees to mature.

The promoters who, over several decades, helped to populate the lower valley not only used the standard tricks of their profession but had to think up new ones because the not-yet-irrigated land they were trying to sell had little to recommend it but cactus, thorny bushes, brown grass, and rattlesnakes. On one trip a farm editor took along a potted yucca to embellish the photographs he made. The land salesman in the party had a truckload of palms in tubs, which were placed on each site before the party arrived, to be taken up after the group left and rushed to the next location.

On one auto ride through the monotonous brush country, a real-estate salesman had with him a Middle Western farmer whose foreboding silence was broken when a roadrunner or chaparral bird sprinted across the highway. "What kind of fowl is that?" he asked.

The promoter, with more salesmanship than accuracy, replied, "That's what we call a bird of paradise." But he received no encouragement when the farmer commented, "Mighty long way from home, ain't he?"

George Sessions Perry told of one quick-witted man who, while herding a group of prospects through the valley on an excursion train, noticed that the train was approaching an area which, in contrast to its surroundings, was flooded with the muddy overflow of a rampaging creek. To keep this disheartening sight from his charges, he called on them to kneel in the aisle and give thanks to Providence for the great opportunity they had before them. His prayer, one may be sure, lasted from dry land to dry land.

In later decades, residents of the blossoming valley could laugh at they told such stories, knowing that the promised productiveness had come about in spite of the original appearance of the land. They knew, too, that irrigation from the Río Grande had been mainly responsible. Any stranger who might question the area's dependence on water needed only to notice the occasional unirrigated patches between the lush farms and orchards or contrast the brown grass in many a front yard with the green trees or field crops in back or at the sides of the house.

By 1948, a century after the close of the Mexican War, the Magic Valley, which made up only two-tenths of 1 per cent of the nation's cultivated land, was producing 2 per cent of its cotton, 12.5 per cent of its winter carrots, nearly 15 per cent of its cabbage, 15.5 per cent of its citrus fruit, and large quantities of other fruit and vegetables. Its grapefruit and oranges had the highest juice and sugar content of any grown in the United States.

The productiveness of the Magic Valley was enhanced by the building of the sixty-million-dollar Falcon Dam, dedicated by President Dwight D. Eisenhower and President Adolfo Ruiz Cortines late in 1953. The success of this irrigation, flood-control, and power project led to the building of the Amistad Dam to form a still larger reservoir farther up the river.

The Magic Valley was not the only part of Texas hit by later waves of farm settlement spurred by active promotion. Some sections were on the coastal plains; and one was the Winter Garden area around Crystal City and Carrizo Springs, between San Antonio and the Río Grande. Using water from wells, streams, and a lake, the Winter Garden began growing vast quantities of spinach and other vegetables. Its people erected a statue of Popeye, a spinach-eating character from the newspaper comic page.

Another such area was the Post settlement at the edge of the Caprock in western Texas. In 1907, C. W. Post, the breakfast-cereal king, bought the 200,000-acre Curry Comb Ranch, partly on the High Plains and partly in the breaks and on the rolling prairies below. On a shelf in the breaks he built the town of Post City, later shortened to Post. He improved the former grasslands for farming and experimented with various crops, finding that grain sorghum did well there. Although his efforts to bombard rain out of the skies were a flop, there was strong demand for his farms.

The most widespread farm boom of this later period was that

189

of the High Plains, which was on at the time of the Post colonizing. While western Texas was still ranch country, some nesters had wandered in, often to return in disappointment after grasshopper plagues and severe drouths. "Wagons with white tops, rope-bottomed chairs, towheads, brindle cows, yellow dogs, and a pervading air of restlessness have poured through," reported the Tascosa *Pioneer*. Sometimes a wagon had a moldboard plow tied to the coupling pole, along with a well-sharpened ax.

The ax led some old-timers to laugh. "A grass sickle," they said, "will chop down all the trees where you're going."

Although there was a sprinkling of farms in the Panhandle and South Plains, general farm settlement had to wait until there were more railroads and until some of the vast ranches were broken up and sold in small parcels. Although the average cowboy looked down on the "fool hoe man" almost as much as he did on the sheepman, the owners of the big ranches looked forward to selling their grasslands to farmers. "I'll live to see the day," predicted one of the XIT men, "when the plow will push the cattle off this range and grain crops will be fed to dairy cows."

The big land boom on the High Plains of Texas began in 1906 when W. P. Soash, a real-estate promoter from Race, Iowa, visited the XIT Ranch. He signed a contract to buy several hundred thousand acres and hurried back to Iowa to look for customers. "Special Train Going to the Texas Plains With Soash, the Man of the Hour!" he advertised. He and his agents over the Middle West offered a free trip to Texas, with no obligation.

Soon the first Soash Special, an all-sleeping-car train, was ready to roll. With fine food and top service, the passengers were in a good humor when they reached Dalhart and climbed into buggies and buckboards. The drivers, who were supersalesmen, went past prosperous-looking farms and kept up a patter about deep topsoil and bumper crops of wheat, corn, and alfalfa.

Back in Dalhart, many of the pleased visitors signed contracts, and Soash began making plans for his next special train. He spent several thousand dollars a month in advertising, issued his own magazine, and employed a big staff of salesmen. He ran eighty-seven trains to Texas, with 75 to 250 passengers each, built two hotels on the prairies to house them, and started two towns.

Many of the buyers aided the Soash campaign, as did the newspaper writers he sometimes took along. "The last opportunity to acquire good land has not gone by," wrote one in the Waterloo (Iowa) *Tribune.* "Do you want to see the prettiest land ever God's sun looked upon? Would you like a trip to one of the richest and most promising portions of this earth? Then come with me to the great plains of Texas, that great undeveloped empire of the Southwest. Here at last is the land of promise."

The biggest and most expert colonizers were the railroads. Some had received large grants of land which they wanted to sell advantageously. All wanted settlers along their lines who would ship out crops and livestock and order farm equipment and household goods. They even sent agents to Europe to scour the countrysides for settlers. Six of the western roads joined in forming the Southwestern Colonizing Bureau, which spent vast sums in advertising aimed to attract farmers.

With the early dugouts and sod houses giving way to sturdy homes, the plains looked better than they had two or three decades earlier. Newspaper and magazine articles emphasized the healthful climate and rich soil, saying nothing about drouths and blizzards. Mentioning "waving fields of wheat, corn, oats, cotton, and alfalfa," the Wellington *Leader* was convinced in 1909 that "there is a big future for the country. One man can cultivate from seventy-five to a hundred acres. Melons, vegetables, and fruits flourish and are noted for their excellent flavor."

More and more trains, some of them with as many as eight sections, kept bringing in prospects; and about half of them bought land. In the South Plains the population increased nearly 350 per cent between 1900 and 1910, wheat acreage leaped nearly 350 per cent, and corn acreage almost 400 per cent. Hardly anyone read the report of the experiment station at Cheyenne Hills in 1909: "Dry-land farming is a continual fight against relentless, unfavorable conditions. Exclusive grain growing has been a failure wherever tried in the last thirty years. A dry-land country is always a land with much wind, and the drier the season the steadier and harder the wind blows."

Opening vast sections of grasslands to the plow led to the rapid spread of cotton and wheat farming in western Texas, mainly cotton in the South Plains and wheat in the Panhandle. Cotton growing, once confined mainly to the lower valleys of the rivers of eastern Texas, spread west until the lint was produced in nearly 200 of the 254 Texas counties. In 1959, 40 per cent of Texas cotton was raised in the South Plains.

Texas cotton growing, while shifting geographically, was making other changes. Tenancy, mainly share-cropping, was in effect on 37 per cent of the Texas farms in 1880. This figure rose to 49 per cent in 1900 and to more than 60 per cent in 1930. But after that it began to decline—to 57 per cent in 1935 and 49 per cent in 1940. The reason? Many of the former tenants could do better for themselves in the towns and cities. Without them, the landowners had to combine small farms into larger ones and adopt mechanical cultivation and harvesters.

On the South Plains farms around Lubbock, the use of machines cut by two-thirds the human labor needed to grow and harvest a crop of cotton. Work that formerly averaged twenty-two hours to the acre was cut to seven hours. Instead of having a man, woman, or child take several days to pick a bale of cotton by hand, the grower used a mechanical stripper to bring in one in an hour. The cost of harvesting by stripper was only about one-eighth that of hand labor.

The mechanical cotton harvesters that came into use on the High Plains were not complex, expensive machines. They were developed from crude, homemade sleds and were suitable only for flat country and for plants that do not grow high and that produce their bolls within a short period of time.

The cotton sled, named from the appearance and operation of the earlier and simpler types, dated from 1914. In that year, cotton growers in the High Plains had a big crop but could not get much for it. Several farmers took sections of a picket fence and converted them into combs. They dragged these contraptions back and forth

192

through their fields. The sleds pulled off loose cotton—bolls in various stages of opening, and leaves, stems, and burs as well.

Gradually the crude, homemade sled was refined into a factory-built stripper that could be drawn by either horses or a tractor. It did not pick the cotton but denuded the plant of both lint and leaves, either uprooting it or making it incapable of further output. Its big disadvantage was in giving the ginner the problem of getting rid of leaves, burs, and stems.

Meanwhile, the true mechanical cotton picker, which sought to duplicate the hand process and did not take off leaves or stems or harm the plant, made some progress in other sections of Texas. Its main disadvantage was its much higher price. But in 1963 about 80 per cent of Texas cotton was mechanically harvested, mainly by stripper. This was a higher percentage than for the Old South but lower than for New Mexico, Arizona, and California. The increased use of this equipment reflected improvements in machines, better cleaning processes in the gins, and increased difficulty in obtaining Mexican seasonal workers, called *braceros,* for hand picking.

In spite of the spread of cotton growing and the increased efficiency in cultivation and harvesting, expansion in total cotton acreage was checked by competition from foreign lint and from synthetic fibers. Texas land devoted to cotton declined from sixteen million acres in 1930 to six million in 1959, but the number of bales harvested increased slightly during that time as a result of more scientific cultivation. Land retired from cotton was used for grain sorghums or returned to grazing.

The sale of Panhandle lands greatly increased the raising of wheat in that area, and the wheat demands of World War I gave an added stimulus. The flat plains were well adapted to the use of combine harvesters. Texas wheat production leaped from 2,500,000 bushels in 1910 to 36,400,000 in 1920 and 44,000,000 in 1930. The plowing of so much former grassland on the High Plains was blamed for making worse the serious dust storms of the 1930's, and efforts were made to return some of the land to pasture and to plant strips of trees to check wind erosion.

193

The call for wheat in World War II, however, brought more plowing and bigger Texas wheat crops, that reached 100,000,000 bushels in 1949. This deluge brought such a surplus that there were not enough freight cars or trucks to carry it, and vast quantities had to be piled on the ground to await shipment. With the grain overflowing the elevators, the government acquired most of the surplus, storing some in idled transport ships and sending much abroad either as gifts or for sale at nominal prices. In the following decade, Texas wheat acreage was cut in half and the output reduced to 59,800,000 bushels.

Latter-day farmers profited from the development of new crops and methods by the Agricultural and Mechanical University of Texas and by such privately supported agencies as the Texas Research Foundation. The latter, with more than five hundred acres and a score of laboratories just north of Dallas, was set up to revitalize the worn-out soils of the state. It worked out a program of using grass to restore depleted soil. It also developed a white corn hybrid of high quality and large yield and adapted oil-seed crops, such as sesame, for land retired from cotton.

T

EXAS FRONTIERSMEN regarded as nuisances the dark, smelly seeps and springs that a few found on their farms. Only their grandchildren would know how near they had come to striking oil. Earlier generations of Indians had come to the springs, wallowing in the "sour dirt" to drive away rheumatic pains and rubbing the oil on burns, cuts, and sores. A few drank some of the ill-tasting fluid, hoping to end "internal agonies."

In a July storm of 1543, Spanish ships carrying survivors of the expedition of Hernando de Soto sought shelter in a protected bay on the Gulf Coast near what later was called Sabine Pass. On the water the sailors found a dark scum that looked like the pitch they had used in Spain to calk their wooden vessels. So, before going on, they used some of it to paint the bottoms of their ships.

As early as 1790, Spanish drivers of wagons and carts made a practice of stopping at an oil spring in Nacogdoches County to grease axles and wheels.

Later, in 1859, Jack Graham dug a well at an oil seep on his farm in Angelina County; but he found only a little oil. Soon afterward, Lynis T. Barrett began drilling in another seep, in the Nacogdoches area, but quit to enlist in the Confederate Army. After the war, he and three associates renewed his lease and began boring. At 106 feet they found a small reservoir of oil, which they sold by the bucketful for lubrication.

Barrett next went to Pennsylvania with samples of the oil and interested a drilling company in sending equipment to Texas. But early in 1867, before the Texas well could be tested, the drillers were recalled because of the low price of oil and the unsettled political conditions in Texas.

The next year two men dug pits near Oil Springs, southeast of Nacogdoches, and found a little oil. They had it tested for softening leather but apparently did no more about it. In 1887, B. F. Hitchcock formed a company that drilled a well near Oil Springs. At about seventy feet the well blew in, becoming the first Texas gusher. By 1890 this and other companies had drilled approximately ninety wells, and a three-inch pipeline was carrying oil fourteen and one-half miles to a shipping tank.

Meanwhile a little oil and some natural gas were being found in other parts of the state. In 1886, while drilling for water on his ranch near San Antonio, George Dullnig struck oil at 235 feet. Soon afterward he drilled three other wells, with all the work done by ranch hands. In 1889 his wells produced forty-eight barrels of oil, which he retailed at twenty cents a gallon, and $1,728 worth of natural gas, which was used for fuel on the ranch.

In 1894, Texas interest in oil shifted to Corsicana, where city officials had engaged a company to drill three water wells. On June 9 of that year, at a depth of 1,027 feet, the drillers struck oil. Annoyed, they drilled on down to 2,470 feet for the artesian water they had been hired to find, but they could not keep the black crude oil from coming up through the pipe and soaking the ground about the well.

The oil stirred excitement, and many people came to see the well. Some local businessmen were willing to invest in oil drilling, even though three derricks over the first well were burned by careless spectators. Several men formed the Corsicana Oil Development Company and began to lease land. They gave half their holdings to two experienced Pennsylvanians, who agreed to bore and equip five oil wells for them.

The five wells, completed in 1896, had only small production but attracted new drillers. As the oil craze hit the town in 1897, derricks sprang up over the east side. Many were in front or back yards of homes, and some were only a few feet from other wells. Visitors from Pennsylvania and other oil states crowded into town and overtaxed the hotels and boardinghouses, rocketing rents and other prices. In 1897, fifty-seven wells were completed, of which fifty were producers. By the close of 1898, Corsicana had 316 wells, 287 of them producers, and a daily output of 2,300 barrels of oil a day. A small refinery was completed on the outskirts of town early in 1899.

The Corsicana boom was the curtain-raiser for more extensive exploring for oil to the southeast. It began with Patillo Higgins, a Beaumont dealer in real estate and a teacher in the Baptist Sunday school. Higgins, who had bought several hundred acres of land, noticed that some of it contained good brick clay. To learn more about brick-making, he went on a tour north and east. He noted that most of the brick plants he saw used fuel oil or natural gas.

The Beaumont brick venture did not come to life, but Higgins began studying a government book on geology. From it and the oil indications near Beaumont, he was convinced that oil lay under a nearby hill which some called Sour Spring Mound because of oil seeps. In 1892 he persuaded three other men to join him in forming an oil company. The next year a test well was drilled to 418 feet but was abandoned because of quicksand. Two others were drilled in the next two years but failed for the same reason.

Before the third well was drilled, Higgins was out of the oil company and back in real estate; but he retained his faith in Sour Spring Mound, even after a visiting geologist declared that no oil would be found there. In 1899 the company, through Higgins, advertised for someone to take a lease and option-sale contract. The taker was Captain Anthony F. Lucas, an able mining engineer of Austrian birth. His experience with salt domes in Louisiana led him to agree with Higgins on the prospects at Sour Spring Mound.

Lucas drilled a test well in 1900, but at 575 feet he ran out of money and had to quit. For financing, he went to Pittsburgh and obtained backing from the two men who had underwritten the drilling at Corsicana. With a rotary outfit from Corsicana, Lucas began drilling in December.

On the morning of January 10, 1901, after the well had reached 1,020 feet, mud and water began to flow out with force. A man on

197

the rig was drenched. Then the drill pipe shot up through the derrick, knocking off the crown and heading skyward. After the water, mud, and pipe were blown out, gas flowed for a few minutes. Then the well quieted down.

After their scramble for safety, the men ventured back to find six inches of mud on the derrick floor. As they began shoveling, the well started spouting mud again. With a boom like that of a cannon, heavy mud shot up through the top of the derrick. It was followed by more gas, and then by dark-green oil. In a few minutes, tons of oil and rocks were heing shot hundreds of feet into the air. One of the mud-soaked men ran to tell Captain Lucas, who came dashing over the hill in a buggy. Higgins, who was out of town, arrived in the afternoon.

Within a few hours, the black geyser attracted hundreds of awed spectators. The gusher was flowing at the rate of 70,000 to 100,000 barrels a day. Every pond and gully was filled with oil. It took fifty men by day and forty by night to keep the spectators back. Other men, with four-horse teams, built a dike to catch the oil. After nine days, the drillers succeeded in capping the well, which the world soon would call Spindletop.

Every incoming train was crowded with visitors, some of them from distant cities. As fifty thousand people descended on the town of nine thousand, ham and eggs went up to one dollar a plate. A cot cost five dollars a night, and visitors even slept on pool tables. Tents and shacks appeared overnight. A hack driver charged eighteen to twenty dollars to take excursionists from the depot to the gusher, four miles away.

Land prices soared. A woman who had been collecting garbage sold her pig pasture for $35,000. Land close to the well, which had gone begging at eight to ten dollars an acre, sold at $200,000 to $900,000 an acre. Tracts farther away brought $35,000 to $40,000 an acre. New oil companies were formed almost every day. On March 3, sparks from a locomotive set fire to the great lake of oil, but the well was saved.

Within a year the population of Beaumont had grown to thirty thousand, and Spindletop oil was burned as far away as England

and Germany. Derricks were so close together that plank runways were built from one to another. Shipments of crude oil from the new field totaled 1,750,000 barrels during 1901. The discovery well had a flow sixteen times as great as that of any earlier well.

The opening of the Spindletop field ushered in a new era of petroleum use. Previously this oil had been used mainly for lighting and lubrication. The fuel-oil era began with Spindletop and the gasoline age a decade later. Spindletop also gave rise to many flourishing oil companies and made the Beaumont area a great refining center.

Although Spindletop overshadowed other Texas oil booms for years, many other discoveries were made in the next decade. Tom Waggoner, a big cattle raiser in northwestern Texas, had several water wells drilled on his ranch; but each brought only salt water with traces of oil. In disgust, he abandoned the wells. "What do I want with oil?" he asked. "I'm looking for water. That's what the cattle need."

Later Waggoner relented enough to let oil scouts and drillers through his pasture gates, and in 1911 a discovery well blew in and set off a boom. The cowman named the new field Electra, for his daughter, and made a fortune from its 8,500 wells.

When a gusher blew in to open the Burkburnett field in 1918, it started one of the wildest, if short-lived booms, with fifty-six rigs set up inside the town. Among the most colorful Texas booms were those of the neighboring fields of Ranger, Desdemona, and Breckenridge, in western Texas. The Ranger gusher spouted late in 1917, and those of the other fields in the following year. In Ranger, where the population leaped from one thousand to thirty thousand within a year, men paid two dollars to sleep in a barber chair for a night. Water was so scarce that motorists drained their radiators at night, keeping the water in their hotel rooms to avoid theft. The Ranger *Daily Times* was called the *"Daily Crimes."* Conditions were similar in Desdemona and Breckenridge. The latter had more than two hundred rigs in the town and more than two thousand close around.

A favorable rock structure which an Oklahoma geologist, Charles N. Gould, had found in 1905 led to the discovery in the

Texas Panhandle, late in 1918, of what turned out to be the world's largest single producing gas field. Oil was discovered in the Panhandle in 1920, and in 1927 that area's oil production exceeded forty million barrels.

The Mexia boom began in 1921 when two big gushers blew in on the same day. Quickly the town filled not only with oil men but with bootleggers, dope peddlers, gamblers, hijackers, and ladies of easy virtue. Popular places of entertainment included the Chicken Farm and the Winter Garden, both heavily guarded outside and in, with checkrooms for the six-shooters of patrons. Crime became so rampant that the governor declared martial law and sent Texas Rangers to restore order.

Other discoveries, including that at Luling in 1922 and those in the Permian Basin, continued. In the latter area, the Santa Rita gusher in 1923, on land owned by the University of Texas, brought in the Big Lake field. This not only provided new wealth for a section of West Texas but made the university one of the wealthiest in the nation.

Wildcatting went on until 198 of the 252 Texas counties were producing oil. Texas, the leading state in output of both petroleum and natural gas, produced 23 per cent of the world's oil in 1940; but by 1963, increases in foreign production had reduced this proportion to 10 per cent.

While fabulous oil booms spotted other parts of the state, upper East Texas had a shoestring wildcatter who persisted in drilling where orthodox geologists had said there was no oil. He was Columbus M. (Dad) Joiner, a native of Alabama and a former lawyer and legislator in Tennessee. He had gone to Oklahoma in 1897 and had made and lost two fortunes in oil before coming to Texas in 1926.

In spite of seventeen dry holes and the scorn of experts, Joiner believed there was oil under the soil of Rusk County. People there had almost given up hope. In that land of rolling woods, pastures, and cotton patches, geologists of the major companies had made tests and shaken their heads. Only Humble and Mid-Kansas had been interested enough to do any leasing even as a protective measure.

In Fort Worth, Joiner found a geologist, A. D. Lloyd, who

agreed with him. On the five to six thousand acres that Joiner had leased, Lloyd mapped the underground structure and chose a site for the initial well. This was on the farm of Mrs. Daisy M. Bradford, between Arp and Henderson and a few miles south of Overton. Hiring Ed C. Laster as head driller, Joiner put together a crew and collected equipment, most of it second-hand.

Drilling began in August, 1927, with a flimsy pine rig and battered tools. The drill pipe, old and unreliable, often stuck in the hole or twisted off and had to be fished out with much loss of time. Mechanical and financial difficulties slowed the work, and Joiner had to sell some of his holdings to keep going. Finally, when a drill pipe stuck in the well and could not be loosened, the well was abandoned in February, 1928, at 1,098 feet. Later, after selling more of his leases, Joiner drilled another and deeper well but without finding oil. By this time he was almost at the end of his financial rope.

But, in 1930, at seventy, financially broke and in poor health, Joiner sold more leases and managed to start a third well. This hole, which he called Daisy Bradford Test No. 3, was almost two miles southeast of the first well and was on the same farm. It was seven miles west of Henderson and six miles southeast of Overton. There, about the first of September, Laster found traces of oil and sent to Dallas for the ailing Joiner.

One of the scouts of a major oil company heard the report and went to see the well but since he thought it had been salted, his and other companies took no action. Yet Joiner was confident as the drill went deeper into the Woodbine sands and came up greasier. Hundreds of Rusk County people flocked to the well to see what might happen.

About eight-thirty on the evening of Friday, September 5, when the well had reached a depth of 3,592 feet, a great stream of black oil shot out, spurting above the top of the 118-foot derrick. Approximately one thousand people watched this exciting blowout. After a few minutes, the men were able to close the valves and mud-in the well. Immediately news of the discovery spread across Texas and into other states.

With a report of the gusher on the front page of the Dallas *News* the next morning, crowds of oilmen began surging into Henderson. Leases that had gone begging at ten dollars an acre began bringing five hundred to fifteen hundred dollars. As more men arrived by car and airplane, hotels and rooming houses overflowed. The highway to the well was almost blocked by traffic. America's biggest oil boom had started.

Joiner opened an office in Overton, whose streets, like those of Henderson, became almost impassable from the inflow of visitors. As the frenzy of leasing spread, cotton picking was neglected, and almost everyone carried an oil map. Roads to the Joiner well were so jammed that cars could move only six to eight miles an hour. Joiner sold part of his remaining holdings to H. L. Hunt for $40,000 cash, $35,000 in notes, and $1,200,000 in oil.

Continued exploratory drilling showed that the Joiner well was in the southern part of a great field that spread through several counties. It was forty-three miles long, north to south, and an average of five miles wide. In its heart were the towns of Kilgore and Longview, which quickly started booming. In a few months the population of Kilgore leaped from 1,000 to 8,000 or more. In a single month, Longview jumped from 5,025 to more than 10,000.

By the end of 1931, less than sixteen months after Dad Joiner's discovery, the new East Texas field had 3,612 producing wells, and 109,000,000 barrels of oil had been taken out. Humble and a number of other companies had opened offices in Longview and had built storage tanks and pipelines to handle the deluge of oil. In the boom towns, bootleggers peddled corn whisky in fruit jars at fancy prices and gamblers operated openly. At night the barrel houses with their tinny pianos and shrieking gals offered entertainment to those men who could take their minds off leases.

Yet oil did not bring quick riches to all the producers. When the Joiner well spouted oil in September, 1930, the price of crude was $1.10 a barrel. Early in 1931 the flow of oil from the new field was so great that the price tumbled to ten cents a barrel, and some had difficulty in selling it even at that. In the summer, oil sold as low as five cents. Some producers favored a shutdown, but others were opposed. In April, acting under a 1929 conservation law, the

Texas Railroad Commission ordered the field's daily output of 140,000 barrels cut in half in May. Some operators observed this drastic ruling, but others ignored it, and forty started injunction suits.

A later order raised the allowable output to 90,000 barrels a day, but the field then was producing 300,000 barrels. A third order allowed 160,000 barrels, but by that time the field was turning out 360,000 barrels. Then, on August 16, after the East Texas field had hit a production peak of 848,398 barrels a day in violation of the commission's orders, Governor Ross S. Sterling, a former president of Humble, ordered the field closed down, declared martial law, and sent National Guard cavalrymen to enforce his proclamation. When production was resumed early in September, under proration and stiffer penalties for violation, higher oil prices led many to support the limit on output. But so many flouted it surreptitiously to produce and sell what came to be called "hot oil" that enforcement continued to be a serious problem, even after federal laws supplemented those of the state.

Drilling continued at a rapid pace and in a wasteful manner. The field had 15,271 wells early in 1935, and eventually nearly 30,000, an average of one well to every four and one-half acres. Four thousand wells, properly spaced, would have drained the underground reservoir as easily and at only a fraction of the cost.

Some producers of hot oil hired gunmen to try to keep out state and federal inspectors. Others tried bribery. More resorted to trickery of various kinds. Some pretended to drill three or four other wells beside one real one, supplying the dummies from pipes from the original well and thus multiplying the production allowance. Others tapped underground pipes or reservoirs, loading trucks by starlight or piping oil to moonshine refineries. Much of the illegal oil was sold to big companies that would not take chances by producing it themselves.

One defiant producer kept a lookout at the top of a derrick to shut off the illegal flow whenever he saw investigators approaching. Another built a concrete blockhouse over the controls of his well. A third laid a bypass pipeline with the controlling valve behind the bathtub in his home. Some operators used "left-hand" valves,

valves that worked in the opposite way from normal ones. Thus an inspector might seal a well or a pipeline wide open.

Some of the mushroom refineries were only dummies. The crude oil piped to them through scores of hidden lines was not refined but was shipped out by the trainload, mislabeled as gasoline or fuel oil. New tricks kept popping up. In one instance, giant moving vans rumbled out of the pine woods and followed a wide concrete road across the horizon. So many came over the highway that agents became suspicious enough to investigate. They found that every van was a camouflaged oil truck carrying bootleg gasoline to a distant market.

Even stiff fines did not always deter the runners of hot oil. An operator who took out $8,000 worth of oil a day could pay a fine of $1,000 every day, retaining the oil, and still fatten his bank account.

The job of the fifty state oil inspectors in the field, who received $150 a month, was hard and dangerous. One of them, Otis Ramsey, was peppered with birdshot one night in 1932 when he and a guardsman approached an oil tank near Henderson. All the men had to cope with offers of bribes. One, who had spurned a $100 bill to let a hidden bypass go unnoticed, later succumbed to other offers and was caught. "My income was never less than $500 a month," he admitted. "One month I made nearly $2,000."

The flow of hot oil was estimated at 55,000 barrels a day by the Railroad Commission and at 90,000 to 150,000 barrels by some oilmen and federal officials. This excess oil on the market brought on sporadic price wars and threatened to wreck the quota production control. As the flow reached its peak in late 1934 and early 1935, a Congressional committee probed the situation.

Enforcement of proration limits was achieved gradually after an interstate compact, drawn up in Dallas in February, 1935, was ratified by the legislatures of the oil states. Further help came from Congress. In 1935 it passed the Connally Hot Oil Act, reimposing federal control of interstate oil shipments. Such control had been set up two years earlier by a provision of the national Industrial

Recovery Act, but the Supreme Court had thrown out that provision as an unwarranted delegation of power.

After that, Texas soon stabilized its production of oil but continued to be the leading state in this field. By the close of 1963, it had produced 26,700,000,000 barrels of oil, or 36.3 per cent of the nation's total output. In that year it had 47.1 per cent of the country's oil reserves, and Texas oil and gas provided 27 per cent of the fuel energy produced in the United States.

SINCE THE DAYS of their first dugouts, log cabins, and adobe huts, Texans have been a singing people. Perhaps only pioneers with a song in their hearts would have had the courage to tackle and tame the wilderness they faced. Even in combat, early Texans went forward singing and shouting. The Battle of San Jacinto was won to the tune of "Come to the Bower."

Texas politics, too, had its songs. W. Lee (Pappy) O'Daniel and his hillbilly band were only an outcropping of long tradition in campaign music. Charlie Siringo, who was a boy in Matagorda County during the Civil War, remembered a song with the lines:

> *Jeff Davis rides a big gray horse,*
> *While Lincoln rides a mule.*

Years later, Siringo saw Davis and realized that he had been misled about his appearance. He had expected to see a portly man on a gray stallion.

Southwestern Texas had lilting songs in Spanish about El Rancho Grande and smiling *señoritas*. The woodlands and farms to the east resounded to rhythmic cotton-chopping songs, spirituals, sinful songs, reels, and blues. In 1845, while Texas was still a republic, German settlers formed a singing society under a live oak on a bank of the Comal River. Other choral groups followed; and in 1853 the first Texas *Saengerfest* was held in New Braunfels, with people from Austin and San Antonio taking part. Although floods carried away their baggage and their music books, the visitors finally arrived by wagon and made the song festival a success. The twenty-fifth *Saengerfest* was held in Dallas in 1904, with Madame Marcella Sembrich and the Chicago Symphony Orchestra taking part.

Yet the songs for which Texas became best known were the cowboy ballads. These songs sprang from the grass roots and originally served a practical purpose. At night they helped to keep the bedded cattle quiet and the singers awake. In 1857, when several cowmen gathered 1,200 mossy-horned steers in southern Texas and pointed them toward Chicago, one of the hands they took along was a Negro called Big-Mouth Henry. He had gained his name because he was a great singer and could almost charm a bunch of Longhorns.

Even the cowboy who "couldn't carry a tune in a corked jug" hummed or crooned to soothe the cattle. In threatening weather, when the steers began to drift and showed signs of stampeding, a hymn or a ballad might quiet them. "The confidence a steer's got in the dark," observed Charlie Russell, "is mighty frail." Songs were the best antidote for rumblings in the sky or the howl of a lobo on a distant hill.

In the era of the Longhorn, the cowpuncher who could sing better than the average had a big advantage. In his long days in the saddle, songs of the range and the trail helped to speed the hours and to keep him from growing lonesome. In the evenings around the campfire, they gave a bit of diversion before the tired men hit their bedrolls.

Some trail bosses didn't like to hire a fellow who couldn't sing, said J. M. Grigsby of Fort Worth. "We boys would consider it a dull day's drive if we didn't add at least one verse. On bad, dark nights the cowboy who could keep up the most racket was the pet of the bunch. We called him the bellwether, and he always brought up his side of the herd." One Texas cowman used to put a few mouth organs in his wagon when he sent a herd up the trail.

Most of the cowboys who gargled their throats, as some called it, were a long way from being polished singers. They were without training and sang by ear. Jack Thorp, who made a collection of western songs that came out in 1908, wrote afterward that he never knew a cowboy with a good voice. "If he had one to start with, he lost it bawling at cattle, sleeping in the open, or telling the judge he didn't steal that horse."

Those who sang on horseback in the era of the open range had a sense of rhythm—a rhythm that often was set by a pony's gait. Happily, they were unaware of their musical shortcomings. They had a sense of the appropriate, choosing loud, lusty songs when trailing the Longhorns and crooning soft ones after the herd had been bedded down for the night. Many, without being aware of it, became folk composers as they added fresh stanzas to the songs they had heard.

Many of the trail hands liked to sing about horses. They had a ballad about "The White Steed of the Prairies." Some sang of trying to ride wild or outlaw horses. Others recalled affectionately "Old Paint" or some other favorite mount. Songs that turned up in the 1870's included "The Buffalo Skinners," a narrative of the hunting range, and "Sam Bass," which told the story of a cowboy who went wrong and paid with his life.

One of the most popular songs, which eventually had several hundred stanzas, was "The Old Chisholm Trail." It was not a lullaby but a rousing ballad that recounted many troubles with the Longhorns. It rated high with Bill Walker. "It could put life into a footsore cow herd and a saddle-sore puncher," he recalled. "It has been known to throw several kinds of panic into a bunch of Mexican cow thieves and into Indians on the warpath."

Often what the cowboy sang was a parody of an earlier song or at least used an old tune. The popular "Whoopee Ti Yi Yo, Git Along Little Dogies" had its origin in an English song. The doleful "Oh, Bury Me Not on the Lone Prairie" was suggested by a sailor ballad, "The Ocean Burial," which began, "Oh bury me not in the deep, deep sea." "Red River Valley" was an adaptation of "The Bright Sherman Valley," which in turn was derived from an upstate New York song, "The Bright Mohawk Valley." That favorite, "A Home on the Range," which the trail hands brought back from Kansas, had a tune similar to "Home of the Soul."

Much of the best Texas folk music might have been lost forever except for the long efforts of a patient collector, John A. Lomax, (1867–1948). For many years, Lomax, sometimes with his son

Alan along, went about the country, even into prison cells, with a pencil and a recording machine, taking down songs that had come from the hearts of the people. Credit should go also to two Texas composers, Oscar J. Fox of San Antonio and David Guion of Dallas, for their arrangements of cowboy songs and other folk music. Fox, who died in 1961, was known also for his popular song, "The Hills of Home."

Texans who composed more serious music included Paul Van Katwijk and Jack F. Kilpatrick of Dallas, Carl Venth and John William Marsh of Fort Worth, and John M. Steinfeldt and Harold Morris of San Antonio. Olga Samaroff from San Antonio and Van Cliburn from Kilgore gained international repute as pianists.

Since the days of the republic, Texans have shown appreciation for fine music. A French opera company from New Orleans performed in Galveston in the 1870's, and Adelina Patti sang there in the following decade. Texas was visited by several opera companies in that period and gave the Cincinnati Grand Orchestra a large patronage in 1892. When Ignace Jan Paderewski played in Houston in 1896, a special train brought patrons from Dallas for his concert. Since then, almost every musician of note has found attentive listeners in Texas. The larger Texas cities formed civic music associations and sponsored symphony orchestras, with some of the orchestras making annual tours outside the state. Several cities started opera companies, that of Dallas receiving national and international attention.

Aside from Indian festivals, Texas theatrical history probably began with a Spanish play presented near the present city of El Paso in 1598. It celebrated the arrival of Don Juan de Oñate and his conquistadors at the Río Grande. The Spanish influence continued, especially in nativity plays in cities toward the Mexican border. Traveling dramatic companies began coming to Texas soon after Houston opened a theater in 1838.

Opera houses that were opened in Galveston in 1871, Dallas in 1873, and other cities soon afterward attracted touring Shakespearean and contemporary dramas with such actors as Edwin Booth, Lawrence Barrett, James O'Neill, Joseph Jefferson, Frederick Warde,

209

and Lillie Langtry. Sarah Bernhardt made triumphal tours of Texas in 1892 and 1906.

After Stark Young formed the Curtain Club at the University of Texas in 1909, similar acting groups blossomed in other universities and colleges and in more than thirty Texas cities. The Dallas Little Theater, opened in 1920, won for three successive years, 1924–26, the Belasco Cup offered in a national competition in New York. The Dallas Theater Center, housed in a building designed by Frank Lloyd Wright, opened late in 1959. In 1963, Houston's Alley Theater, started a decade earlier and directed by Mrs. Nina Vance, was granted $2,100,000 by the Ford Foundation to apply on a new building and an operating subsidy for ten years. Meanwhile, national recognition was given to the University of Texas annual Shakespeare production, directed by B. Iden Payne.

Texas painting, which began with the pictographs that Indians made on rock surfaces, was subject to many influences, including those of Spain and Mexico, yet much of it retained a distinctive cast. Among the state's early artists of note were two political refugees from Germany who settled near Fredericksburg about 1850. These men, who had to make their own paints, were Herman Lungkwitz, who painted landscapes, and his brother-in-law, Richard Petri, who made portraits of settlers and Indians.

H. A. McArdle, an orphan youth from Ireland, settled in Texas in 1868 and became known for his historical pictures, some of which were hung in the Capitol. Also placed in the Capitol were several paintings by William H. Huddle, who came from Virginia and settled in Paris, Texas. Robert J. Onderdonk, from Maryland, spent most of his adult life in San Antonio and Dallas and became known for his portraits, landscapes, and historical paintings. His son, Julian Onderdonk, became one of the best-known Texas artists.

Frank Reaugh, often called the dean of Texas artists, became especially noted for his paintings of cattle. He immortalized the Longhorn as Charles M. Russell did the buffalo. Born in Illinois late in 1860, Reaugh lived close to cattle through his eighty-four years. As a youngster he showed strong interest in animals and in drawing. Sketching and painting animals became his chief hobby.

210

In 1876, before Frank was sixteen, the family moved to Texas and settled on a farm four miles northwest of Terrell, in Kaufman County, and one mile east of Brushy Creek. Soon the picturesque Longhorns became the favorite subject of the young artist, and he set up his easel in a pasture.

Reaugh was encouraged by his mother and by two cattlemen, Frank and Romeo Houston. In 1884–85 he attended the School of Fine Arts in St. Louis. Later he went to Europe, studying under Lucien Doucet and Benjamin Constant at the Julien *Académie* in Paris and under Anton Mauve in Holland. While developing his technique in distant schools, Reaugh did not lose his interest in the Longhorns. They were shown in most of the paintings he began exhibiting in Texas and in the art museums of Chicago, Pittsburgh, Philadelphia, and New York.

Canvases by Reaugh were among those chosen for exhibit at the Columbian Exposition in Chicago in 1893 and the Louisiana Purchase Exposition in St. Louis in 1904. Of forty-four paintings sold at the Chicago fair's exhibit, two were his. They were "February in Texas" and "Springtime."

Reaugh moved to Dallas in 1890 and established a studio in Oak Cliff. Although he taught for a time in Baylor University, he did most of his painting and teaching at his home studio and on trips with students to western Texas. A bearded six-footer, he was a striking figure. He never married. He lived to see the work of two of his pupils, Edward G. Eisenlohr and Reveau Bassett, accepted by the National Academy in New York.

Five years after the death of Reaugh in 1945, a collection of his paintings was placed on permanent display in a special room at the University of Texas. Others were on view in Dallas, including two in the Museum of Fine Arts and one in the Public Library.

Seymour Thomas, born in San Augustine and schooled in Dallas, received many awards and became well known for his equestrian portrait of Sam Houston. Dawson Dawson-Watson, of London birth, settled in San Antonio and won a $5,000 first prize with his painting of a group of cacti, "Glory in the Morning." J. O. Mahoney, Jr., of Dallas, won the 1932 *Prix de Rome,* offered by the American Academy, an $8,000 prize that made it possible for him to study in Rome for three years.

Other Texas artists of the middle twentieth century included Harold D. Bugbee of Clarendon (1900–63), and Tom Lea of El Paso. Both were noted as book illustrators and as painters of western scenes. Another was bowlegged H. O. (Cowboy) Kelly of Blanket (1884–1955), whose neoprimitive paintings were in strong demand.

In another field, Texas gave the nation its outstanding photographer of western cowboy life, Erwin E. Smith (1886–1947). Smith, born in Honey Grove, worked from one cow outfit to another, following the roundups and living with the chuck wagons. Although he was too late to record the Longhorns, he depicted the cowboy at work and at play in an era during which frontier conditions and practices still held.

The earliest Texas sculptor of note was Elizabet Ney, of German birth, who had achieved fame in Europe before coming to Texas in 1870. Opening a studio in Austin in 1892, she was commissioned by the state to make statues of Stephen F. Austin and Sam Houston for exhibit at the Columbian Exposition in Chicago. Only the first was done in time for the Chicago fair, but later these statues were placed in the Capitol in Austin and represented Texas in the Capitol in Washington. Many considered her best work to be the recumbent statue of General Albert Sidney Johnston in the State Cemetery in Austin.

Pompeo Coppini, from Italy, lived in San Antonio from 1901 to 1916 and left many statues and monuments in Texas cities. They included a statue of Stephen F. Austin in Austin, the equestrian statue of Terry's Ranger in Austin, the John H. Reagan monument in Palestine, the Sam Houston memorial at Huntsville, the Confederate memorial at Victoria, the cowboy equestrian group at Ballinger, and the Littlefield memorial fountain and arch at the University of Texas.

Enrico F. Cerracchio, also of Italian birth, lived in Houston for a number of years. He became best known in Texas for his equestrian statue of Sam Houston and his World War I memorial, both in Houston, and his General John A. Wharton monument at the Capitol in

Austin. Allie V. Tennant, born in St. Louis, spent most of her life in Dallas and won several prizes for her portrait sculpture. Her statue of an Indian warrior was placed in the front of the Hall of State in Dallas.

In home architecture, Texas owes much to David R. Williams (1890–1962), who developed an indigenous type of house. Williams, born on a ranch near Childress, studied architecture in the University of Texas and in France and Italy. Back in Texas, he examined early homes designed, without conscious style, to serve local needs. In the German towns of Fredericksburg and New Braunfels and the Alsatian settlement of Castroville he studied old houses that seemed to blend with the landscape. He noted solid homes built by skilled stone masons like Whisky Jack Green of Salado. From all of them he designed a functional two-story home that faced the Gulf of Mexico, had a narrow balcony on the south side, and was arranged to catch the sea breeze. The Williams home, commonly but inexactly called the Texas ranch house, was widely imitated and had a widespread influence on residential architecture.

Art activity and art appreciation were fostered by the formation of the Texas Fine Arts Association in 1911 and by the establishment of art museums and art competitions in the principal Texas cities. In addition to the regular museums, Fort Worth opened in 1961 the Amon Carter Museum of Western Art.

Stephen F. Austin, who had shelves of good books in his frontier home, was an exception. Most of the covered wagons that brought pioneer settlers to Texas carried few books beyond a Bible and a handful of classics and school texts. But whatever books found their way into the log cabins were read carefully, even by candlelight, and new ones were acquired when they became available and there was money to buy them.

Aside from a few reports by Spanish explorers, which were not obtainable in Texas until generations later, and a novel published anonymously in Paris in 1819, little was written about Texas until after the Revolution. One of the early books was a historical romance, *Texas Vs. Mexico,* by Anthony Ganilk, issued in Philadelphia in 1838. The memoirs of David Crockett and Peter Ellis

213

Bean also proved popular. A two-volume work, *Narrative of the Texan Santa Fe Expedition,* by George Wilkins Kendall, a participant, was issued in 1844 and found many interested readers. *Mustang Gray,* by Jeremiah Clemens, 1858, was widely read for many years.

A travel book by a visitor from New York, *A Journey Through Texas,* by Frederick Law Olmsted, published in 1857, went through several editions. John P. Sjolander, born in Sweden in 1851, came to Texas at twenty and became a widely known poet.

Cowboy life on the Texas ranges and the long trails was described by many writers. Notable among them were Andy Adams, whose best-known novel, *The Log of a Cowboy,* appeared in 1903, and Charles A. Siringo, whose memoirs, with several revisions and various titles, began coming out in 1912.

Perhaps the most widely known author to live in Texas was William Sidney Porter, familiar to readers through his pen name, O. Henry. Born in North Carolina in 1862, Porter came to Texas twenty years later and at first worked on a ranch. In 1885 he moved to Austin, where he was a clerk and bookkeeper for the next two years. In 1887, he became a draftsman for the General Land Office, and in 1891 a teller in a bank. In 1894 he quit the bank to edit a humorous weekly. When that failed the next year, he moved to Houston and wrote for the *Post* for a year. Many of the short stories that he wrote later had Texas settings.

Historical works rank high among Texas writings. Herbert E. Bolton, once of the University of Texas and later of the University of California, became known for many narratives, especially for *The Spanish Borderlands,* 1921, and a scholarly biography of Coronado, 1949. Eugene C. Barker of the University of Texas wrote the definitive life of Stephen F. Austin, 1925, and edited the Austin and Houston papers. Walter P. Webb (1888–1963), of the same university, became widely known for *The Great Plains,* 1931, and *The Texas Rangers,* 1935.

Prominent among histories of Texas ranches and biographies of ranchmen were *The XIT Ranch of Texas,* 1929, and *Charles Goodnight: Cowman and Plainsman,* 1936, both by J. Evetts Haley of Canyon. Others included *Shanghai Pierce: A Fair Likeness,* 1953, by Chris Emmett, then of San Antonio, and *The King Ranch*, 1957, by Tom Lea of El Paso.

J. Frank Dobie of Austin, who died in 1964, became nationally known as a folklorist, but some of his books went beyond that range. Among the most popular were *A Vaquero of the Brush Country*, 1929; *Coronado's Children*, 1930; *The Longhorns*, 1941; and *The Mustangs*, 1952.

From the Texas centennial year of 1936 onward, novels by Texas authors began appearing in much greater numbers, some of them of high quality. Among those receiving unusual praise were *Hold Autumn in Your Hand*, by George Sessions Perry, 1941; *Hound-Dog Man*, by Fred Gipson, 1947; *The Brave Bulls*, by Tom Lea, 1949; and *Soronia, Texas*, by Madison Cooper, 1952.

Novels such as these were further evidence that the rawhide era had ended and that Texas had come of age.

Manuscripts

Baker, J. H. Diary, 1858–1918. Transcripts in the University of Texas Library, Austin.

Batchler, Henry T., Dallas. Letter to Will Williams, Denton, July 12, 1922. The race match between Steel Dust and Shiloh.

Bryan, Frank, Groesbeck. Letters to the author, 1955, 1957. Blizzards and bear hunting.

Mooar, Josiah Wright. Interviews. Transcripts in the University of Texas Library. Buffalo hunting.

Stewart, Walter P. Diary. Transcript in the University of Texas Library. The drouth of 1886.

Williams, Will, Denton. Letter to the author, April 22, 1949. Grasshoppers that darkened the sky and covered the earth.

Wilson, Francis A. Autobiography. University of Texas Library. Frontier preaching and camp meetings.

Withers, Mark A. Reminiscences. J. Frank Dobie, Austin.

Public Records

Shackleford County. Minutes of the Commissioners Court, 1876–77, I.

Texas Rangers. Reports and correspondence, Adjutant General's Papers, Texas State Library, Austin.

Newspapers

Albany *Echo*, August 18, December 15, 1883, fence cutting; August 25, 1883, raid by cattlemen against sheepmen.

Albany *Star*, August 24, 1883, defiance of a sheriff by a Vernon editor; December 12, 1883, fence cutting.

Austin *Intelligencer-Echo*, March 29, 1875, justice court at Callisburg.

Austin *Republican*, February 24, September 15, 1869, feud of Houston editors.

Clarksville *Standard*, January 1, 1859, Pecan Point Plantation; January 22, 29, February 5, 12, March 5, 26, July 9, September 24, 1859, Red River navigation.

Dallas *Herald*, April 4, 1868, September 26, 1876, grasshoppers; April 9, 1876, duel by editors at Jefferson.

Dallas *Morning News*, 1885–1964.

Denton *Monitor*, May 21, 1870, editor's low opinion of a San Antonio editor.

Fort Worth *Democrat,* 1875–79, cattle drives; 1883, fence cutting.

Frontier Echo, Jacksboro, October 16, 1875, August 17, 1876, acceptance of cord wood and wheat for subscriptions; March 24, 31, 1876, wild pigeons.

Galveston *News*, December 20, 1858, loading of camels; February 22, December 5, 12, 19, 1860, Indian raids; April 28, May 5, June 10, 1869, May 1, 1877, June 26, 1878, hanging of horse thieves and cattle rustlers by vigilantes; December 25, 1879, January 31, 1880, January 15, 1884, raids by cattlemen against sheepmen; 1883, fence cutting.

Houston *Post,* October 10, 1963, Alley Theater.

San Antonio *Express*, February 27, 1873, horse thieves; July 1, 1906, scalping of Indians by whites.

Waco *Daily Telephone*, November 19, 1897, extra, street battle.

Waco *Examiner*, August 26, 1883, raids by cattlemen against sheepmen.

PERIODICALS

Berger, Max. "Education in Texas During the Spanish and Mexican Periods," *Southwestern Historical Quarterly,* Vol. LI, No. 1 (July, 1947), 41–53.

————. "Stephen F. Austin and Education in Early Texas," *Southwestern Historical Quarterly*, Vol. XLVIII, No. 3 (January, 1945), 387–94.

Carpenter, Mrs. Laura J. Clark. Letter, *Southwestern Historical Quarterly*, Vol. LVII, No. 4 (April, 1954), 516. Plantation school.

Collinson, Frank, "Prairie Fires," *Ranch Romances*, Vol. CII, No. 4, (October, 1941), 110–11.

Gard, Wayne. "Hot Oil From Texas," *American Mercury*, Vol. XXXV, No. 137 (May, 1935), 71–76.

————. "How They Killed the Buffalo," *American Heritage*, Vol. VII, No. 5 (August, 1956), 34–39.

Harris, Mrs. Dilue, "The Reminiscences of Mrs. Dilue Harris," *Quarterly of the Texas State Historical Association*, Vol. IV, No. 2 (October, 1900), 85–127; No. 3 (January, 1901), 155–89.

Havins, T. R., "Sheepmen-Cattlemen Antagonisms on the Texas Frontier," *West Texas Historical Association Year Book*, Vol. XVIII (October, 1942), 10–23.

Holt, Roy, "The Old Horsehead Crossing on the Pecos," *Sheep and Goat Raiser*, Vol. XXXIII, No. 2 (November, 1952), 34–37, 44–45.

————. "The Woes of a Pioneer Sheepman," *Sheep and Goat Raiser*, Vol. XXI, No. 3 (December, 1940).

————. "Texas Had Hot County Elections," *West Texas Historical Association Year Book*, Vol. XXIV (October, 1948), 3–26.

Kenney, M. M., "Recollections of Early Schools," *Quarterly of the Texas State Historical Association*, Vol. I, No. 4 (April, 1898), 285–96.

Ledbetter, Roy C. "Frank Reaugh—Painter of Longhorn Cattle," *Southwestern Historical Quarterly*, Vol. LIV., No. 1 (July, 1950), 13–26.

Smith, Joe Heflin. "Mercy in Saddle Bags," *Cattleman*, Vol. XXXVII, No. 8 (January, 1951), 26, 100–106.

PAMPHLETS

Plummer, Rachel. *The Rachel Plummer Narrative.* N.p., privately published reprint of an early account.

Catalogs of early Texas academies, military schools, and colleges. Texas Collection, University of Texas Library, Austin.

BOOKS

Allen, J. Taylor. *Early Pioneer Days in Texas.* Dallas, Wilkinson Printing Company, 1918.

Allred, B. W., and J. C. Dykes, editors. *Flat Top Ranch.* Norman, University of Oklahoma Press, 1957.

Boatright, Mody C., Wilson M. Hudson, and Allen Maxwell, editors. *Madstones and Twisters.* Vol. XXVIII of *Publications* of the Texas Folklore Society. Dallas, Southern Methodist University Press, 1958. Includes a chapter on "Madstones and Hydrophobia Skunks," by J. Frank Dobie, and one on "Twister Tales," by Howard C. Key.

Bollaert, William. *William Bollaert's Texas.* Edited by W. Eugene Hollon and Ruth Lapham Butler. Norman, University of Oklahoma Press, 1956.

Bosworth, Allan R. *Ozona Country.* New York, Harper and Row, 1964.

Carver, Charles. *Brann and the Iconoclast.* Austin, University of Texas Press, 1957.

Clark, James A., and Michel T. Halbouty. *Spindletop.* New York, Random House, 1952.

Conkling, Roscoe P., and Margaret B. Conkling. *The Butterfield Overland Mail, 1857–1869.* 3 vols. Glendale, The Arthur H. Clark Company, 1947.

Connor, Seymour V., editor. *A Biggers Chronicle.* Lubbock, Texas Technological College, 1961.

Cook, John R. *The Border and the Buffalo.* Topeka, Crane and Company, 1907. Experiences of a buffalo hunter.

Cox, Mary L. *History of Plainview, Texas.* Plainview, 1937.

Cranfill, James Britton. *Dr. J. B. Cranfill's Chronicle.* New York and Chicago, Fleming H. Revell Company, 1916.

Dewees, W. B. *Letters From an Early Settler of Texas.* Compiled by Cora Cardelle. Louisville, New Albany Tribune Plant, 1852.

Dobie, J. Frank. *The Longhorns.* Boston, Little, Brown and Company, 1941.

————. *The Mustangs.* Boston, Little, Brown and Company, 1952.

Dobie, J. Frank, editor. *Man, Bird, and Beast.* Volume VIII of *Publications* of the Texas Folklore Society. Austin, Texas Folklore Society, 1930. Chapter on "Ranch Remedies," by Frost Woodhall.

Eaves, Charles Dudley, and C. A. Hutchinson. *Post City, Texas.* Austin, Texas State Historical Association, 1952.

Emmett, Chris. *Shanghai Pierce: A Fair Likeness.* Norman, University of Oklahoma Press, 1953.

————. *Texas Camel Tales.* San Antonio, Naylor Printing Company, 1933.

Featherston, Edward Baxter. *A Pioneer Speaks.* Dallas, Cecil Baugh and Company, 1940.

Gard, Wayne. *Fabulous Quarter Horse: Steel Dust.* New York, Duell, Sloan and Pearce, 1958.

————. *Frontier Justice.* Norman, University of Oklahoma Press, 1949.

————. *Sam Bass.* Boston, Houghton Mifflin Company, 1936.

————. *The Chisholm Trail.* Norman, University of Oklahoma Press, 1954.

————. *The Great Buffalo Hunt.* New York, Alfred A. Knopf, 1959.

Graves, H. A. *Andrew Jackson Potter, the Fighting Parson of the Texas Frontier.* Nashville, Southern Methodist Publishing House, 1882.

Greer, James Kimmins. *Colonel Jack Hays.* New York, E. P. Dutton and Company, 1952.

Haley, J. Evetts. *Charles Goodnight, Cowman and Plainsman.* Boston, Houghton Mifflin Company, 1936. New edition, Norman, University of Oklahoma Press, 1949.

————. *F. Reaugh, Man and Artist.* El Paso, Shamrock Oil and Gas Corporation, 1960.

————. *The XIT Ranch of Texas.* Chicago, The Lakeside Press, 1929. Revised edition, Norman, University of Oklahoma Press, 1953.

Harter, Harry. *East Texas Oil Parade.* San Antonio, The Naylor Company, 1934.

Hendrix, John. *If I Can Do It on Horseback.* Austin, University of Texas Press, 1964.

Hogan, Jane and Bill, editors. *Tales From the Manchaca Hills.* New Orleans, Hauser Press, 1960. The memoirs of Mrs. Edna Turley Carpenter.

Hogan, William Ransom. *The Texas Republic.* Norman, University of Oklahoma Press, 1946.

Holden, William Curry. *Alkali Trails.* Dallas, Southwest Press, 1930.

Holmes, Floyd J. *Indian Fights on the Texas Frontier.* Fort Worth, Pioneer Publishing Company, 1927.

Hornby, Harry P. *Going Around.* Uvalde, Texas, Hornby Press, 1945. Country newspaper.

House, Boyce. *Oil Field Fury.* San Antonio, The Naylor Company, 1954.

————. *Roaring Ranger.* San Antonio, The Naylor Company, 1951.

————. *Were You in Ranger?* Dallas, Tardy Publishing Company, 1935.

Hoyt, Henry F. *A Frontier Doctor.* Boston, Houghton Mifflin Company, 1929.

Huckaby, Ida Lasater. *Ninety-Four Years in Jack County, 1854–1948.* Austin, The Steck Company, 1949.

Hunter, J. Marvin. *Peregrinations of a Pioneer Printer.* Grand Prairie, Texas, Frontier Times Publishing House, 1954.

Johnson, Vance. *Heaven's Tableland: The Dust Bowl Story.* New York, Farrar, Straus and Company, 1947.

Johnson, William Weber. *Kelly Blue.* New York, Doubleday and Company, 1960. H. O. (Cowboy) Kelly, painter.

Kupper, Winifred. *The Golden Hoof.* New York, Alfred A. Knopf, 1945. Sheep of the Southwest.

Langford, Gerald. *Alias O. Henry.* New York, The Macmillan Company, 1957.

Lea, Tom. *The King Ranch.* 2 vols. Boston, Little, Brown and Company, 1957.

Leach, Joseph. *The Typical Texan.* Dallas, Southern Methodist University Press, 1952.

Leslie, Lewis Burt. *Uncle Sam's Camels.* Cambridge, Harvard University Press, 1929.

Long, E. Hudson. *O Henry: The Man and His Work.* Philadelphia, University of Pennsylvania Press, 1949.

McConnell, Joseph Carroll. *The West Texas Frontier.* Palo Pinto, Texas Legal Blank and Book Company, 1939.

McDaniel, Ruel. *Some Ran Hot.* Dallas, Regional Press, 1939. Hot oil in East Texas.

Moore, Harry Estill. *Tornadoes Over Texas.* Austin, University of Texas Press, 1958.

Nix, John W. *A Tale of Two Schools and Springtown,* Parker County. Fort Worth, Thomason and Morrow, Printer, 1945.

Olmsted, Frederick Law. *A Journey Through Texas.* New York, Mason Brothers, 1857.

Ormsby, Waterman L. *The Butterfield Overland Mail.* San Marino, California, Huntington Library, 1955.

Pearce, W. M. *The Matador Land and Cattle Company.* Norman, University of Oklahoma Press, 1964.

Phares, Ross. *Bible in Pocket, Gun in Hand.* New York, Doubleday and Company, 1964. Frontier religion.

Phillips, Edward Hake. *The Texas Norther.* Houston, Rice Institute (now Rice University), 1955.

Richardson, Rupert Norval. *The Comanche Barrier to South Plains Settlement.* Glendale, The Arthur H. Clark Company, 1933.

———. *The Frontier of Northwest Texas, 1846 to 1876.* Glendale, The Arthur H. Clark Company, 1963.

Rister, Carl Coke. *Comanche Bondage.* Glendale, The Arthur H. Clark Company, 1955. Mrs. Horn's narrative.

———. *Oil! Titan of the Southwest.* Norman, University of Oklahoma Press, 1949.

Robinson, Duncan W. *Judge Robert McAlpin Williamson*. Austin, Texas State Historical Association, 1948.

Rye, Edgar. *The Quirt and the Spur*. Chicago, W. B. Conkey Company, 1909.

Sheffy, Lester Fields. *The Francklyn Land & Cattle Company*. Austin, University of Texas Press, 1963.

Siringo, Charles A. *A Texas Cow-boy*. Chicago, M. Umbdenstock and Company, 1885.

Smithwick, Noah. *The Evolution of a State, or Recollections of Old Texas Days*. Compiled by Nanna Smithwick Donaldson. Austin, Gammel Book Company, 1900. Facsimile reproduction, Austin, The Steck Company, 1935.

Smythe, H[enry]. *Historical Sketches of Parker County and Weatherford, Texas*. St. Louis, Louis C. Lavat, 1877.

Sonnichsen, C. L. *Roy Bean: Law West of the Pecos*. New York, The Macmillan Company, 1943.

Stambaugh, J. Lee, and Lillian J. Stambaugh. *The Lower Rio Grande Valley of Texas*. San Antonio, The Naylor Company, 1954.

Stanley, F. *Jim Courtright, Two Gun Marshal of Fort Worth*. Denver, World Press, 1957.

Streeter, Floyd Benjamin. *Ben Thompson: Man With a Gun*. New York, Frederick Fell, 1957.

Strobel, Abner J. *The Old Plantations and Their Owners of Brazoria County*. Houston, Union National Bank, 1930.

Sweet, Alexander E., and J. Armory Knox. *On a Mexican Mustang Through Texas*. Hartford, S. S. Scranton and Company, 1883.

————. *Sketches From Texas Siftings*. New York, 1882.

Taylor, Bride Neill. *Elizabet Ney, Sculptor*. Austin, Thomas F. Taylor, 1916.

Taylor, T. U. *Fifty Years on Forty Acres*. Austin, Alec Book Company, 1938.

Terrell, C[harles] V. *The Terrells*. Austin, C. V. Terrell, 1948. Tells of killing wild pigeons, hunting buffalo, and the use of a madstone.

Towne, Charles Wayland, and Edward Norris Wentworth. *Shep-*

herd's Empire. Norman, University of Oklahoma Press, 1945. Chapter V, "Under the Lone Star," on Texas sheep raising.

Wallace, Ernest, and E. Adamson Hoebel. *The Comanches: Lords of the South Plains*. Norman, University of Oklahoma Press, 1952.

Wallis, Jonnie Lockhart, editor. *Sixty Years on the Brazos: The Life and Letters of Dr. John Washington Lockhart*. Los Angeles, privately printed (Press of Dunn Brothers), 1930.

Walter, Ray A. *A History of Limestone County*. Austin, Von Boeckmann-Jones, 1959.

Walton, William M. *Life and Adventures of Ben Thompson, the Famous Texas*. Austin, the author, 1884. New edition, Houston, Frontier Press of Texas, 1954.

Warner, C. A. *Texas Oil and Gas Since 1543*. Houston, Gulf Publishing Company, 1939.

Webb, Walter Prescott. *The Great Plains*. Boston, Ginn and Company, 1931.

———. *The Texas Rangers*. Boston, Houghton Mifflin Company, 1935.

Weems, John Edward. *A Weekend in September*. New York, Henry Holt and Company, 1957. The Galveston storm of 1900.

Wentworth, Edward Norris. *America's Sheep Trails*. Ames, Iowa State College Press, 1948. Chapter 17, "The Rise of Texas."

Wilbarger, J. W. *Indian Depredations in Texas*. Austin, Hutchings Printing House, 1889. Facsimile reproduction, Austin, The Steck Company, 1935.

Winfrey, Dorman A. *A History of Rusk County, Texas*. Waco, Texian Press, 1961.

Woolworth, Laura Fowler. *Littleton Fowler, 1803–1846*. Shreveport, La., Mrs. Laura Fowler Woolworth, 1936.

(Place names, unless otherwise indicated, refer to Texas)

232